Passing on the truth

Passing on
the
truth

1 & 2 Timothy simply explained

Michael Bentley

EVANGELICAL PRESS

EVANGELICAL PRESS
12 Wooler Street, Darlington, Co. Durham, DL1 1RQ, England

First published 1997

British Library Cataloguing in Publication Data available

ISBN   0 85234 389 2

Other books by Michael Bentley in the Welwyn Commentary Series:
Balancing the Books — Micah and Nahum
Building for God's Glory — Haggai and Zechariah
Saving a Fallen World — Luke
Living for Christ in a Pagan World — 1 and 2 Peter

Printed and bound in Great Britain by The Bath Press, Bath

Dedicated to the memory of my very good friend,
spiritual companion, secretary and mother-in-law,
Elizabeth Clarkson,
who typed the notes for the original sermons
on which the book is based,
and was called on 20 March 1995
into the presence of the Lord she loved and served so well.

Contents

2 Timothy

Preface

If we were to watch a special ceremony taking place today in a Roman Catholic or Anglican cathedral, we would notice that while the opening hymn of the service was being sung a great procession of clergy would be walking slowly down the main aisle. They would be dressed in the finest of robes and they would be preceded by mace bearers and ceremonial crosses. As the culmination of this column came into view our eyes would be focused on one or more bishops, resplendent in rich copes and mitres, who were going to be the main participants in the service which was to follow.

However, if we hold that picture in our minds and turn to the New Testament letters we find a very different scene. The pomp and ceremony of the twentieth-century church are not there; instead we discover bishops who are ordinary men whose task it is to gently lead the people of God into the ways of the Lord (1 Tim. 3:1-7).

This was one of the problems our congregation had when we first looked at these Pastoral Epistles. It was especially difficult for the vast majority of our people, who have not been brought up in evangelical churches, to divorce in their minds the ritual of churchianity from New Testament simplicity. But as we looked at Paul's first and second letters to Timothy we saw much that was immediately applicable to our own church situation. Particularly we learned 'how people ought to conduct themselves in God's household, which is the church of the living God, the pillar and foundation of the truth' (1 Tim. 3:15).

This book was based on a series of sermons, the first of which was preached on the first Sunday morning in 1993 and the last on almost the final Sunday in that same year. I wish to put on record my gratitude to all those who have helped in the preparation of this book, especially the members of Great Hollands Free Church who sat so patiently through the expositions of 1 and 2 Timothy and made many helpful comments.

It is my desire that this book will be of some assistance in helping all those who labour in the Word (1 Tim. 5:17) to correctly handle the word of truth (2 Tim. 2:15). May all of us, whether preachers or not, be constantly endeavouring to preserve the truth of God's Word (2 Tim. 1:14) and passing it on to others (2 Tim. 2:2).

Michael Bentley
Bracknell
February 1997

Introduction

The book of the Acts of the Apostles is the story of the early church, but is it the whole story? When we look at the closing verses we see that Paul is living in his own rented house. However, he is not a free man. He is under guard, waiting to hear the result of his appeal to Cæsar.

During the two years that Paul was in this situation he was free to receive visitors, and many came to him. The book closes by saying that Paul 'boldly and without hindrance ... preached the kingdom of God and taught about the Lord Jesus Christ' (Acts 28:31) and we are told nothing further about the apostle.

If this was how Paul ended his days then it seems strange that we are not told of his death. If he was eventually released, he was hardly the sort of man who would have retired to a peaceful cottage by the sea and ended his days in obscurity. Many scholars believe that following his imprisonment at the end of Acts he was indeed set free and resumed his life of visiting and encouraging the churches in their faith.

Throughout the New Testament we are told about the apostle's preaching and the long discourses he had with the Jews and others, but the majority of what we know of Paul's teaching is what we glean from his thirteen letters which are preserved in the New Testament. These letters were written some time between A.D. 48 and A.D. 64 and they cover a variety of subjects and situations.

His final three letters (1 Timothy, Titus and 2 Timothy) were written towards the end of his life, some time after A.D. 62. They were not addressed to churches but to two of Paul's 'lieutenants'. These young men were among those who had been groomed by the apostle to share some of the load of leadership in the emerging Christian community. At the time when Paul wrote to them Timothy was at Ephesus and Titus in Crete, but neither of these men spent all of his time ministering in these places. All three of these letters are largely concerned with the welfare and conduct of the church. Because the major part of each letter is devoted to the duties of those who are called to lead the flock of God, they are often called 'the Pastoral Epistles'.

Down through the ages it had always been accepted that these were authentic letters of the apostle Paul but, with the advent of the movement known as Higher Criticism during the nineteenth century, modern scholars began to doubt this on the grounds that they differ in language and content from Paul's other (earlier) letters, and also that they counter heresies which were thought not to have arisen until the second century. This commentary, however, assumes that Paul is indeed the author of these letters and that they contain his final instructions to Timothy and Titus on how churches should be governed and cared for.

Those who wish to enquire more deeply into the questions of dates and authorship of these letters should consult books such as William Hendriksen's *Commentary on I and II Timothy and Titus*,[1] Geoffrey Wilson's, *The Pastoral Epistles*,[2] or Donald Guthrie's commentary, *The Pastoral Epistles*.[3]

1 Timothy

This letter was probably written from Macedonia to remind Timothy of those things which he had already learned from talking with Paul and hearing him preach during their many times of travelling together. Timothy was not one of the twelve apostles and he was probably not an overseer since he was given instructions about overseers (1 Tim. 3:1-7; 5:17-22). Instead he seems to have been Paul's representative who had been entrusted with keeping the church at Ephesus (and possibly those in the surrounding area) free from heresy.

The broad outline of the letter is as follows:

Chapter 1: Timothy is to remain at Ephesus to combat error and oppose those who claimed to be experts in the law, but were really false teachers.

Chapter 2: He is to ensure that public worship is conducted properly and that both men and women know how to behave.

Chapter 3: He is to see that those who are appointed as elders and deacons are properly qualified to hold these offices.

Chapter 4: He is given instructions on how to deal with those who have departed from the faith and exhorted to set an example to others.

Chapters 5-6: He is given directions with respect to certain groups and individuals in the church. He himself is to 'guard the deposit' entrusted to his care.

2 Timothy

Since the time when Paul wrote his first letter to Timothy he had been arrested. In between writing his first and second letters to Timothy the apostle had written to Titus. When he wrote to Timothy the second time he was in a dismal, cold cell. This prison was quite different from the comfortable rented house which he had in Rome (Acts 28). He had been deserted by almost all of his friends and he was convinced that he had little time left upon this earth.

This second letter bears the marks of being written by an old man who has been physically worn out by his punishing schedule of activity for the spread of the gospel. Throughout this letter he is concerned about sound doctrine. He is aware that there are many who are seeking to corrupt the truth of God's Word and he wants to ensure that it remains pure.

His one dying wish is that he might see his dear son in the faith Timothy once again and he writes this letter in the hope that his young friend might be able to leave the work at Ephesus in the hands of others and travel to see him before it is too late.

The broad outline of the letter may be summarized as follows:

Chapter 1: Timothy must hold on to the faith, which is a precious deposit.

Chapter 2: He is to teach the faith and see that faithful men learn it in such a way that they, too, can pass it on to others.

Chapter 3: He is to stand firm in the faith, rooted and grounded in the teaching of Scripture, which is God's inerrant Word, despite the grievous times which are coming in the future.

Chapter 4: He is to preach the faith at every opportunity, because the time is coming when men will not put up with sound doctrine. The letter ends on a more personal note, with the apostle expressing his sense of isolation and urging Timothy to come to him.

1 Timothy

1.
Meet Paul and Timothy

Please read 1 Timothy 1:1-2

The first and second letters to Timothy and that written to Titus are the last of Paul's epistles. The recipients, Timothy and Titus, were two of the great apostle's young 'lieutenants'; they were Paul's representatives at the churches of Ephesus and Crete respectively. Some would say they were the bishops of these churches. Paul wrote these letters to encourage Timothy and Titus in their onerous tasks of pastoring the people of God who were under their care.

These documents are often referred to as the 'Pastoral Epistles' because they contain much help and instruction on the administration and pastoral care of local churches. However, as with every book in the Bible, the teaching contained here is also relevant and applicable to all churches (and individual believers) in every age. One of the indications we have that these were not private documents, which were meant only for the eyes of Timothy and Titus, is found in the benediction at the end of each of the three letters. Both letters to Timothy end with the words, 'Grace be with you', and the one to Titus concludes, 'Grace be with you all.' In all three cases the word 'you' is in the plural, so obviously the instructions and encouragements are destined for 'you all' — that is, the whole congregation of God's people, then and in every age.

The author

This is clearly stated to be the apostle Paul. The New Testament tells us a great deal about this particular apostle, whose special responsibilities were to the Gentiles. Three times his conversion to Christ is described in Acts (chapters 9, 22 and 26). In addition to this, from Acts 13 onwards we see Paul emerging as the dominant character in the story of the early church. We can also learn much about who he was and the way he conducted himself by reading the thirteen New Testament letters that bear his name.

From all of this information we see that Paul was one who gave himself entirely to God. He devoted his life to spreading the gospel message everywhere he went. He set up churches in numerous places and he served his Lord, and the people of God, unstintingly, despite many periods of illness, persecution and imprisonment.

Paul describes himself as **'an apostle of Christ Jesus by the command of God our Saviour and of Christ Jesus our hope'** (1:1). By saying that he was *'an apostle'* he means that he was someone who was sent out with a specific task. In the ancient world the word which is translated 'apostle' meant an 'envoy' or 'ambassador'. An ambassador is one who represents his country and its rulers. He is the connecting link between his own country and the land to which he has been sent as an ambassador.

In a very real sense every Christian man, woman and child is an ambassador of the Lord. Therefore, it is our task to represent our King (the Lord Jesus Christ) to our workmates, relatives, friends and acquaintances. We should be the means whereby Christ is made known to other people. It is an easy thing for me to write about our need to witness to the Lord, and for you to read about it, but I suspect that most of us are not performing this role very diligently.

Paul also said that he was 'an apostle *of Christ Jesus*'. John, Peter and James usually described the Lord as 'Jesus Christ' but, particularly in these Pastoral Epistles, Paul almost always reverses the order to 'Christ Jesus' — a phrase which he uses three times in these two opening verses. Why did he write 'Christ Jesus' instead of 'Jesus Christ'? It may have been because he, a devout Jew, first perceived the Lord (on the Damascus road) as the Messiah — the fulfilment of all the hopes of Israel. It was only secondly that he saw him as the one who was sent to take away sin. Things were different for John, Peter and James. They had all been among the circle of those most closely associated with the Lord during his earthly life and ministry, and it was firstly by his human name, Jesus, that they knew him. Only later had they come to recognize him as the promised coming one (the Messiah — Christ).

Paul then added that he was 'an apostle of Christ Jesus *by the command of God*'. He is saying that he did not represent himself. His own ideas and views on various matters did not count for anything. He was an apostle of Christ Jesus. It was the Lord Jesus Christ who controlled everything that he did, said and thought. Each instruction which he received came from his King — the one who commanded his loyalty (the word 'command' occurs over and over again in this epistle). But Paul did not just obey Christ because it was his duty to do so. He obeyed because he loved Christ and it was the aim of his life to please him. William Barclay wrote, 'It is always a privilege to do even the humblest and most menial thing for someone whom we love and respect and admire, for someone whom we hero-worship.'[1]

Like Paul, we too should always remember that we are constantly on the King's business. People are watching us all the time, so we must never let down the good name of Christ by becoming involved in anything which is dishonouring to our Lord. We should regularly ask ourselves, 'Can I take

Christ with me to the particular place, or event, which I propose to attend?'

Paul continues by saying that he was 'an apostle of Christ Jesus by the command of God *our Saviour*'. We do not find God described as 'our Saviour' in any of Paul's earlier letters but, as a Jew, he would have been brought up to recognize God as the Saviour — the one from whom all blessings flow. In Psalm 24:5 the psalmist spoke of the godly man who 'will receive blessing from the Lord and vindication from God his Saviour'. The Virgin Mary sang, 'My soul glorifies the Lord and my spirit rejoices in God my Saviour' (Luke 1:46-47). And to the Ephesians Paul wrote that their salvation is not because of their own good works; it is the gift of God (Eph. 2:8-9).

Another reason why Paul called God 'our Saviour' can be found in the background of the people who lived in Ephesus, to whom he was writing. The title 'Saviour' was often on the lips of men in those days. The Greeks called Asklepios, the god of healing, 'the Saviour'. The Romans had called Scipio, their great general, 'our hero and our salvation', and the current Roman Emperor, Nero, had taken upon himself the title, 'Governor and Saviour of the World'.[2]

A fifth thing that Paul tells us is that he is 'an apostle of Christ Jesus by the command of God our Saviour *and of Christ Jesus our hope*'. The people of those days, like many today, must have often felt their situation to be hopeless, but Paul reminded those believers that Christ Jesus is our hope. This word 'hope' is not something which is a vague wish which may, or may not, come to pass. In the New Testament the believer's hope is something which is sure and steadfast. Just as a great sailing ship is prevented from being driven onto the jagged rocks because it is firmly held in place by a strong anchor, so hope in Christ is something which keeps us from falling into danger. The writer to the Hebrews tells us, 'Because God wanted to make the unchanging nature of his purpose very clear to the heirs of what was promised, he confirmed it with an oath. God did this so that, by two unchangeable things in which it is impossible for God to lie, we who have fled to take hold of the hope offered to us may be greatly encouraged. We have this hope as an anchor for the soul, firm and secure' (Heb. 6:17-19).

The recipient of the letter

The letter is addressed to Timothy. We first come across this great worker for God in Acts 16:1. This was on Paul's second missionary journey. Timothy was at Lystra in Asia Minor (modern Turkey). He had a Jewish mother, Eunice (see 2 Tim. 1:5) who was a believer, and a Greek father (who apparently was not a Christian). He also had the privilege of having a godly grandmother called Lois (2 Tim. 1:5). Obviously he was brought up in the Jewish tradition because Paul tells us that 'from infancy' he had 'known the holy Scriptures' (2 Tim. 3:15). This is a wonderful blessing for anyone, so what a great pity it is that few children today are brought up to know and believe the Bible's teaching! From this New Testament information it seems likely that Timothy had been converted during Paul's first missionary journey.

Apparently Paul must have been very struck by the sincerity and enthusiasm of young Timothy, because he wanted to take him along with him (Acts 16:3). However, before doing so, he circumcised him. This was not because Paul thought that this rite was necessary for his salvation (see Gal. 2), but because he wanted to make sure that there was nothing about Timothy that would prevent him from being accepted by the Jews (Acts 16:3).

This was a very sensible action for Paul to take. There may well be customs which we do not feel are absolutely necessary for our Christian lives, but we should not hesitate to submit to them if our doing so will further the spread of the gospel (unless, of course, these customs are contrary to the spirit and teaching of the Scriptures). When we wish to help people, or win them over to our cause, it is necessary to bear in mind their cultural standards. I once heard of an English Christian lady who was visiting an evangelical church in Greece. She believed that she had freedom in Christ to go to church wearing trousers, but it was pointed out to her that she would give offence to the Greek believers if she did so. None the less she still insisted on attending the service in trousers because, as she said, 'I am sure there is nothing wrong with such behaviour, so the Greeks will just have to accept me as I am.' It would have done her no harm to have conformed and worn a dress or skirt, but her persistence caused some embarrassment to the local believers.

From the time of Paul's second journey, Timothy became a companion of Paul and a great helper in furthering the gospel. Later, when Paul was in prison in Rome for the second time, the apostle was to send for him saying, 'Do your best to come to me quickly' (2 Tim. 4:9).

Paul describes Timothy as **'my true son in the faith'** (1:2). He obviously means that Timothy was his spiritual son. As we have already seen, Timothy's natural father was a Greek who probably lived at Lystra, while Paul was a Jew and came from Tarsus. However, Paul may have been the one whom God used to bring about Timothy's second birth (his conversion to Christ).

The apostle said that Timothy was a genuine son — he was not illegitimate; he was true born. Timothy was not someone who had decided to 'give Christianity a try'. He was a genuine child of God. He was someone whose spiritual birth was so real that he would not flinch from his loyalty to Christ. He was firm in the faith. He was no Demas who, when the going got tough, would forsake the apostle (2 Tim. 4:10).[3] The word for 'son' which Paul used was not the usual one (which appears some 380 times in the New Testament), but a more affectionate word which suggests 'tenderness and endearment'.[4]

Finally, the apostle wishes Timothy **'Grace, mercy and peace from God the Father and Christ Jesus our Lord'** (1:2). Paul usually starts his letters with 'Grace and peace' (e.g. Gal. 1:3; Eph. 1:2; Phil. 1:2 etc.), but in both of the letters to Timothy he adds 'mercy' to his usual list (see 2 Tim. 1:2).

'Grace' is a Christian variation on the normal Greek greeting. It means 'the free, unmerited favour of God'. None of us did anything to make God decide to save us. It was of his own good will and pleasure that he made us his children. This is what grace means.

'Peace' is the Hebrew word *'Shalom'* — the regular greeting given to anyone who might be met in the street. However, Paul endowed it with a spiritual meaning by making it stand for the whole well-being of a person 'in the widest sense of the word'.[5]

'Mercy' is that which is extended to those who have committed great wrong, but have been shown wondrous compassion and forgiven for all of their misdeeds.

Bernard sums up these three blessings like this: 'Even grace will not give peace to man, unless mercy accompany it; for man needs pardon for the past no less than strength for the future.'[6]

The meaning for us today

We must remember that we are all called, in some way or other, to represent the Lord Jesus Christ. Paul tells us that 'If anyone is in Christ, he is a new creation; the old has gone, the new has come' (2 Cor. 5:17). He goes on to say that we are Christ's ambassadors (2 Cor. 5:20). Therefore, we need to ask ourselves, 'How faithfully have I have carried out my divine task?'

We must remember that Christ is our hope. Is he the object of our being? Do we keep him in view wherever we go, whatever we do and whatever we say? If we are his true sons and daughters in the faith, then we will want to live like God's children and tell others about the grace, mercy and peace which can only be found by trusting in Christ alone for salvation.

2.
The antidote to false teaching

Please read 1 Timothy 1:3-17

Leaders of churches are sometimes tempted to give up because
of the many pressures which come upon them. Every so often
they stand up on a Sunday to preach God's Word and they see
that there are not so many people in church as there used to be,
and those who do come seem to be bowed down with so many
problems that their desire to seek the Lord is feeble. This is just
one sign that the kind of apathy which exists in the world regularly creeps into the church. On other occasions there seems to
be nothing but trouble in the fellowship, and sometimes it gets
so bad that unbelievers taunt the people of God saying, 'All the
problems in the world stem from religion.' They cite troubled
places across the globe and blame God's people because so
often these disputes have religious overtones.

Timothy must have been very bowed down with the weight
of his work and felt like leaving the church because Paul
addressed this issue right at the beginning of this first letter to
his young colleague at Ephesus.

Remain firm

Paul had been Timothy's great example. For many years the
apostle had been his guiding light. The young man had

accompanied the great apostle on his evangelistic missions to Macedonia and Achaia (Acts 17:14-15; 18:5). He had been with Paul during much of his long preaching ministry at Ephesus (Acts 19:22). He had come to rely on Paul's presence and encouragement, but now he was on his own. Not only that, but he had the leadership of the Ephesian church resting upon his shoulders, and how heavy that was!

Paul had obviously left Timothy in charge of the church. Ephesus was a huge city which occupied an important position at the centre of a heavily populated area in the Roman province of Asia (now part of Turkey). It would seem that the weight of the responsibility for the welfare of this church was getting Timothy down. When Paul left Ephesus what he had said to the young man could be summed up in two simple words: **'Stay there'** (1:3). However, that was not an easy task for Timothy to fulfil. He felt his own inadequacy. Up till that time Paul had been taking the lead. The people had come to rely on his great wisdom and sound teaching, but now that the apostle had departed, maybe the Evil One had tempted Timothy to think, 'The church won't find my ministry acceptable. They are used to Paul, and who am I in comparison?' We can imagine that Timothy must have often felt like running away from the problems of this strategically placed church. But over and over again he could hear Paul's words ringing in his ears: 'Stay there.'

What excitement there must have been flowing through Timothy when a messenger announced that a letter had come from the apostle, Timothy's dear friend and mentor! Perhaps Timothy hoped that the letter would contain instructions which would order him to leave Ephesus and go elsewhere — anywhere. Certainly he would have hoped that this was the case if he believed that he was making a mess of things. He may well have thought that the church at Ephesus would be much better off without him.

However, if that is what Timothy had been thinking, he was disappointed. The letter said, **'As I urged you when I went into Macedonia, stay there in Ephesus'** (1:3). What must have gone through Timothy's mind when he received this word from Paul? Perhaps he was dismayed because he wanted a fresh start — he longed to go somewhere where his mistakes would not be known by everyone. But Paul said, 'Stay there.' So far as we know, Timothy, unlike Jonah, had not tried to run away from his God-given task, but as the word of the Lord came to Jonah a second time, 'Go to the great city' (Jonah 3:1), so Paul said to Timothy a second (or maybe even a third or fourth time), 'Stay there in Ephesus.'

Perhaps a pastor, or other Christian worker, who is disillusioned with his work is reading these words and feeling as Timothy seems to have been at that time. He would give anything to escape from the people for whom he is responsible, but he cannot because God is calling him to stay at his task. In fact, God may not just be calling him to maintain his witness where he is; he may even be calling him to do some more difficult work for the Lord, right in the place where he is now. If that is the case we can be sure that the Lord will equip him for that mission, and also commission him for it by giving him the authority and the power to do it — even if his natural instinct is to run away to some other sphere of service.

Important work to do

Timothy was instructed to speak in the name of God. Paul uses a military term. He has just said that he was 'an apostle of Christ Jesus by the command of God'. Now, by virtue of the authority given him by the Lord, he instructs Timothy to **'command certain men not to teach false doctrines any longer'**.

Paul does not name these 'certain men', but he probably knew who they were and phrased the letter in this way so that these false teachers might be shamed into repentance. Paul knew that his letter would be read out to the church members at Ephesus and, because of this, Timothy's task would be made much easier if the apostle did not name names.

This false teaching had evidently been going on right there in the church and Timothy's job was to stamp it out. Churches must be run in an orderly way and sound doctrine must be taught at all times.

The apostle was often concerned about false doctrine. In 1 Timothy 6:3 he condemns those who gave wrong teaching 'and [do] not agree to the sound instruction of our Lord Jesus Christ'. In Galatians 1:6-7 he says, 'I am astonished that you are so quickly deserting the one who called you by the grace of Christ and are turning to a different gospel — which is really no gospel at all.'

By 'false doctrines' Paul meant any teaching which was contrary to that which was taught by the apostles. Following the Day of Pentecost Luke tells us that new believers in the early church 'devoted themselves to the apostles' teaching' (Acts 2:42). Anyone who teaches anything other than this teaching of the apostles was giving instruction in another gospel; such people should not be listened to. This is why we should all be very careful what we read — and also what we sing in our hymns and choruses. It is so sad when the tune and the rhythm become more important to us than the words of the song. The truth of God is what should always be displayed. Warren Wiersbe writes, 'In many places today the pulpit and choir loft are places for entertainment, not enlightenment and enrichment.'[1]

Timothy was instructed by Paul not to shy away from this task; he was to expose the folly of wrong teaching. Men who **'devote themselves to myths'** were to be stopped from teaching these things in the church (1:4). We do not know what these myths were, but Paul also wrote to Titus saying that he was to pay no attention to Jewish myths (Titus 1:14). These myths seem to have been stories which had been invented about various characters and cities which are named in the Old Testament, yet we know nothing about them. Many fanciful stories had grown up about them which had no basis in fact.

The other thing which Timothy had to stop was teaching which arose out of **'endless genealogies'** (1:4). We have numerous lists of names in the Bible which trace the ancestry of certain people (including the Lord himself — see Matt. 1:1-16; Luke 3:23-37). But other people had developed lists of their ancestors and these went on endlessly because they were just works of fiction. It is said that Alexander the Great even made up a list of his ancestors which purported to prove that he had a direct line back to the Greek gods and heroes.

So what benefit could that kind of thing possibly be? That is always the test which we should bring to bear upon any teaching. What is the point of it? Does it carry us forward in our love and devotion to God and his people? Does it strengthen our faith in Christ, and does it promote the glory of Christ?

Paul said very plainly, **'These** [things] **promote contro-versies'** (1:4). Our universities are producing graduates who have developed the love of arguing; they are taught to question everything which is put before them. This may be a good learning method for many subjects, but when it comes to the Bible a reverent approach is required. Many students seem to love to argue about words. They like controversial discussions. They delight to delve into the rarefied air of philosophy. But, in the long run, what does that achieve — apart from intellectual arrogance? Churches are not debating societies where everyone's views are as valid as everyone else's. God's Word, and what it declares plainly, is what should override everything else. Believers should not set their standards by the demands of society; rather they should look to the Bible for their instructions for living.

The thing that Paul wanted to see being accomplished through all teaching was **'God's work'**. It should be the aim of each of us that God's work must occupy our energy. 'What does God want me to do?' should be the question on all of our lips. God has a plan for the salvation of sinners and the wise stewardship of the household of God. We need to ask ourselves, 'Do all of my activities further the spread of the gospel? Is the way I live my life encouraging love, unity and peace among the people of God?'

But how can ordinary Christians like ourselves promote God's work? We can only do it as we have faith in God and his plan for mankind, and as we exercise that faith by serving God with all of our heart, soul and strength.

The purpose of Timothy's work

The purpose of all this was not just to maintain the numbers. It is comparatively easy to get more people to come to church. All that has to be done is to find out what interests the people living around the church building, and then supply it. That is what advertisers are doing all the time. But that is not what churches are for. In fact when they try to copy the world's activities they usually do it very badly (as Dr Martyn Lloyd-Jones often used to tell those of us who attended the Westminster Fellowship). The goal of Timothy's work was the multiplication of love.

Paul says that Timothy should command false teachers to stop what they are doing. He does not want them to cease their activities just because they are not following Paul's method of presenting the message. He demands that that they be prevented from spreading their teaching because it does not promote love — love for God or love for their fellow men and women.

'Love, which comes from a pure heart' is what the gospel message is all about. 'For God so loved the world that he gave his one and only Son, that whoever believes in him shall not perish but have eternal life' (John 3:16). Some decades after Paul wrote this letter it seems that the church at Ephesus had forgotten (or ignored) this command from Paul, because we find that the Lord Jesus Christ himself says of them, 'You have forsaken your first love' (Rev. 2:4). Love which proceeds 'from a pure heart' is love which is wholehearted, unmixed with any selfishness and which takes up the whole of our being.

Our love should also leave us with **'a good conscience'** (1:5). Everyone has a conscience. It is that still, small voice which tells each of us whether we are doing right or wrong. Unfortunately sometimes the voice of conscience is deliberately stifled, or even seared, but we should make sure that we love God and our fellow human beings with 'a pure heart and a good conscience'.

Our love should also be with **'a sincere faith'** (1:5). There should be no mixed motives about it. We should never show love just so that we might get something out of it for ourselves. In other words, we should never help old ladies over the road in the hope that they will leave us a fortune. We should do all our acts of kindness out of a genuine love towards all people.

Timothy was to encourage love in order to restore backsliders to the paths of God. Paul told him that **'Some have wandered away from these and turned to meaningless talk'** (1:6). It was Timothy's job to expose those who had wandered away — and to stop them leading others into wrong paths.

These foolish talkers were people who were puffed up with a sense of their own importance. Yet they did not realize that they were not capable of being teachers. Paul puts it very bluntly when he declares that **'They do not know what they are talking about or what they so confidently affirm'** (1:7).

If anyone is to be a teacher of God's Word he must be humble and submissive. He must concentrate only on the pure gospel of salvation, through faith alone. That, in fact, is what all of God's people should be doing throughout the whole of our lives. We should show forth the love of God by the way we live, the things we say and the things we do. If we all lived in this manner, every moment of our lives, then not only would we know more of the joy of our salvation, but the whole world would be transformed.

3.
Obey the Ten Commandments

Please read 1 Timothy 1:8-11

I knew an old lady many years ago who, one Sunday evening, went up to the policeman who was on duty near her chapel and said, 'Young man, if it wasn't for sin you'd be out of a job.'

There does not seem much possibility that the men and women in our police force will be redundant in the near future — indeed they have more demands made upon them than ever before, because a greater number of people are now breaking the law. In fact, those who indulge in lawlessness are more numerous and their crimes more varied than at any time in the past. In these days it is not only the 'Bill Sykes' type of person who does wrong; sometimes it is a smart city 'gent' (maybe even a peer of the realm) who is active in insider-dealing or some other business fraud.

Lawbreaking goes on at an alarming rate, as it always has done. There is a great need for people to be taught to know right from wrong. Unfortunately many parents do not seem to be doing this any more, and those in power tend to blame the church for not teaching people to be honest.

In Ephesus Timothy not only had to deal with lawbreakers; he had to reprimand those who were aspiring to be teachers of the law.

God has given the law

Human beings have always been prone to lawlessness. Our
first parents, Adam and Eve, broke God's law (Gen. 3). They
ate of the fruit of the tree which was in the middle of the Garden
of Eden, even though they had received strict instructions not
to do so. There were plenty of other fruits and vegetables
which they could have eaten, but they foolishly listened to the
voice of Satan, and did what he said.

As a result of their disobedience they were cast out of the
garden. Not only were they punished by being banned from
that lovely place but, because of their folly, they then had to
engage in painful toil to produce food for themselves and their
children.

This inclination to disobey God's clear commands has
passed right down through the centuries to each one of us.
There is no one who, in some way or another, does not find
disobedience attractive. If we are honest we have to admit that
there are pleasures in sin (see Heb. 11:25), otherwise we would
not want to break God's laws. But this does not mean that
everything which is pleasurable is sinful. There are many gifts
(like good food and sex) which God has given to us for our
enjoyment, but we must make sure that we make good use of
these things. We must never abuse them. Many things are
lawful for us if we follow God's clear instructions, and these
are all summed up for us in the Ten Commandments.

Some people treat these commandments as though they
were merely ten suggestions which God has given to us to
make our lives a little more bearable. However, they are not
recommendations; they are commandments which must be
obeyed if we are to know peace with God. There is no point in
our saying that we love God if we do not do what he says. Jesus
explained it when he said to his disciples, 'If you love me, you
will obey what I command' (John 14:15).

God gave the Decalogue (the Ten Commandments) to Moses so that all might know how they ought to conduct themselves. These rules have not been given to us with the intention of making life difficult. Their purpose is to enable us to live in peaceful and God-honouring ways. This is why Paul says, **'We know that the law is good'** (1:8). The word 'good' here means, 'excellent in every way'. The apostle says this because he does not want to detract from the force of the law in any way. But we need to remember that the law is only good **'if one uses it properly'**.

The problem is that, so often, we do not use the law correctly. In fact, we do not use it at all. We ignore it and pretend that it does not apply in our particular case. Christians sometimes think, 'Now that I have become a Christian I have been freed from the condemnation of the law. Since I have been washed from my sin in the precious blood of Christ none of the penalties of the law applies to me any longer.'

This statement is true for believers in the Lord Jesus Christ because if anyone belongs to the Lord, then Christ has taken away their sin. He has died on the cross to pay the price for all of their iniquities and they are now free from the condemnation of the law (Rom. 8:1). So, in this sense, believers are no longer under the law; they are under grace.

The value of the law

What, then, is the purpose of the law? It is to show us all how we should live. Some people do not like to think about the law of God because they see it as something which is full of 'Thou shalt nots'. However, the law is not just something which consists only of prohibitions; it outlines our duties. The first four of the Ten Commandments speak about our responsibilities towards God, and the last six show us how we should behave towards our fellow men and women.

Even though we are no longer bound for hell if Christ has paid the punishment for our sins, these laws still have to be obeyed. If we murder someone, we must be brought to justice; we have broken the law of the land and, even more importantly, we have broken God's law.

But there is a further aspect to the Ten Commandments. Paul says, **'We also know that the law is made ... for law-breakers and rebels, the ungodly and sinful, the unholy and irreligious; for those who kill their fathers or mothers, for murderers, for adulterers and perverts, for slave traders and liars and perjurers — and for whatever else is contrary to the sound doctrine that conforms to the glorious gospel of the blessed God, which he entrusted to me'** (1:9-11).

The apostle puts it like this in Galatians 3:24: 'The law was put in charge to lead us to Christ.' That is the very reason why Timothy, and all preachers, Sunday School teachers and youth workers must stress the importance of the law. It is not until we have been brought, by the convicting power of the Holy Spirit, to realize that we have offended against God's holy law that we see ourselves as we really are. Paul also said, 'I would not have known what sin was except through the law' (Rom. 7:7).

So we see that the law demonstrates to us that we are all hell-deserving sinners. The reason why God wants us to know that truth is in order that we should understand that there is no hope for us as long as we remain in our natural condition; the only thing that we can do to gain salvation is to cast ourselves upon God's mercy.

The amazing thing about our gracious God is that he always receives, forgives and cleanses all who come to him, pleading nothing of their own good works. The sinner merely has to ask to be received because of what the Lord Jesus Christ has accomplished for him or her when he died upon the cross.

What amazing love there is in the heart of God, to devise such a plan of salvation for such sinful people as us!

The folly of ignoring the law

Why does Paul say that **'The law is made not for the righteous...'**? (1:9). Does this mean that Christians do not have to obey God's law? Of course it does not mean that. Paul implies that some of the people of his own day were saying, 'Now that I am free from the law, because God has shown his grace towards me, I can carry on sinning and this will enable God to demonstrate to everyone how gracious he is.'

However, Paul would have nothing to do with such erroneous teaching. He said, 'We died to sin; how can we live in it any longer?' (Rom. 6:2). He meant that no one who by faith has seen the face of Jesus Christ can bear to look at the filth of sin. The believer who is living in close fellowship with the Lord finds sin to be abhorrent. Yet, sad to admit, there are still occasions when he feels the tug of his sinful nature gaining strength in his mind; he discovers that sin constantly tries to drag him down. But, if he is a true Christian, indwelt by the Spirit and with a sincere love for the Lord, then he will feel deeply grieved every time he slips into any sinful way. He knows that the sinful life brings dishonour upon the name of his Lord.

I believe that when Paul said, 'The law is not made for the righteous,' he was talking about self-righteous people who thought that because they carried out the ceremonies of religion there was something special about them. The Lord Jesus Christ said, 'I have not come to call the righteous, but sinners' (Matt. 9:13) and the false teachers in Ephesus had forgotten the Lord's teaching. 'The reason why they wasted their time on all kinds of fanciful tales regarding ancestors was that they had never learned to know themselves as sinners before God.'[1] They were full of pride because they thought they were 'a cut above all other men' simply because they claimed to be followers of Jesus.

Paul has a great deal to say in these Pastoral Epistles about such people. He tells Timothy, 'If anyone teaches false doctrines and does not agree to the sound instruction of our Lord Jesus Christ and to godly teaching, he is conceited and understands nothing' (6:3-4); 'There will be terrible times in the last days. People will be ... boastful, proud...' (2 Tim. 3:2); and to Titus he writes that 'There are many rebellious people, mere talkers and deceivers' (Titus 1:10).

So from this teaching we can learn that every true believer in the Lord Jesus Christ ought to live in humble obedience to, and dependence on, the Lord. He or she should have a quiet, gentle spirit and a strong desire to follow the Lord always and obey him constantly.

Details of the Ten Commandments

We can imagine that Paul had the Ten Commandments in mind as he drew up the list of evil-doing in verses 9-10. He picks out extreme cases of sin, but he also includes other sins which we tend to think are not so serious. But we must all constantly remember that, to God, every violation of his law is sin.

In drawing up this list Paul describes the evil behaviour which was rife in his day. He groups these sins in pairs and there are both negative and positive emphases.

Sins against God

The first six are also sins against God (just like the first four commandments). Paul speaks of **'lawbreakers and rebels'**

(1:9). These were the kind of people who behaved as if the law did not exist. They totally ignored what God had to say. They were lawbreakers because they did not recognize any obligation on their part to obey the law. They were also rebels because they blatantly refused to obey God himself.[2]

Next Paul says that they were **'ungodly and sinful'**. He means that their thinking was not right. They had no reverence for God or for his laws and, because they were wrong inwardly, they were automatically defiant in many outward acts of rebellion as well. Their wrong-thinking led to wrong-doing.

These people were also **'unholy and irreligious'**. Nothing was sacred to them. Their god was self. They did not see the need to acknowledge the holiness of God because they thought he was irrelevant to them. The word 'irreligious' was used for those who desecrated the temple. These were the sort of people who trampled underfoot everything that belonged to God. Those of us who are concerned about the Word and law of God will recognize that these people did not die out with New Testament times; there are many like this who are still alive and active today!

Sins against others

The whole of the next section ties up with the second table of the law (our duty towards our fellow men and women). The fifth commandment says, 'Honour your father and your mother' (Exod. 20:12) and here Paul speaks about those who **'kill their fathers or mothers'** (1:9). We may not always agree with our parents, but the law says that we must respect them, and certainly not kill them, or treat them with violence. In fact, any failure to honour our parents is as serious a sin in God's sight as murdering them.

As Paul continues with his list, he speaks about **'murderers'**. To murder someone is to break the sixth commandment:

'You shall not murder' (Exod. 20:13). We should not kill any person, or even 'murder' someone's character or reputation by speaking untruths or unkindness about him. Next Paul speaks about **'adulterers and perverts'** (1:10). There was a great deal of this kind of behaviour going on in Paul's time. His epistles are full of the condemnation of such practices (e.g. 1 Cor. 5:1; Eph. 5:5). The seventh commandment says, 'You shall not commit adultery' (Exod. 20:14). But how up-to-date this passage from 1 Timothy is! The word translated 'perverts' really means homosexuals. It was this sin, among others, which brought down Imperial Rome (see Rom. 1:26-27). At the time of writing there is something called the 'Gay Christian Movement'. According to the passage before us (and other scriptures) those who support such behaviour have no respect for the Bible, which clearly denounces such unhealthy practices. Those who say that Christians should be tolerant of people who indulge in such activities must remember that Paul says that those who do such things will not inherit the kingdom of God (1 Cor. 6:9). It is our duty to warn such people that they are disobeying God's law.

We may find it strange that Paul includes **'slave traders'** in this list. We do not have slave traders in our days (or do we?), but the word really means 'kidnappers'. Kidnapping is a gross violation of the eighth commandment, 'You shall not steal' (Exod. 20:15). We may feel that we are excused on this point, but the fact is that 'Everyone who has ever infringed the rights or liberties of his fellow-men' is guilty of this sin.[3]

Next Paul condemns **'liars and perjurers'**. Geoffrey Wilson comments, 'Those who break the ninth commandment ['You shall not give false testimony against your neighbour', Exod. 20:16] usually contradict, distort, or suppress the truth to gain some dishonourable end.'[4]

Teaching that conforms to the gospel

Paul ends his catalogue of evil by saying, **'and for whatever else is contrary to the sound doctrine'** (1:10). This covers everything which does not conform to the teaching of the Word of God. Sound doctrine is 'wholesome teaching'. The word 'sound' literally means 'hygienic'; the pure teaching of the Bible is hygienic 'because it promotes spiritual health'.[5] Sound doctrine is also teaching which **'conforms to the glorious gospel of the blessed God'** (1:11). We are all required to live lives which are holy, but our sinful nature loves to think we are keeping God's laws because 'Rules and regulations enable a person to appear holy without really having to change his heart.'[6]

Teaching which 'conforms to the ... gospel' is that which the apostles taught. This tells us that we are all sinners by nature and by practice — we have broken God's law time and time again. But the good news is that Christ Jesus has died on the cross to pay the penalty for our wrong-doing; and those who confess their sin and repent of it are forgiven when they trust Christ and believe 'the glorious gospel of the blessed God'. 'Law and Gospel go together, for the Law without the Gospel is diagnosis without remedy; but the Gospel without the Law is only the Good News of salvation for people who don't believe they need it because they have never heard the bad news of judgement.'[7]

Finally, Paul said that this gospel had been **'entrusted'** to him. He often used this expression (see 1 Tim. 6:20; 1 Cor. 9:17; Gal. 2:7; 1 Thess. 2:4; 2 Tim. 1:14). He means that this good news is not something that he has made up. The message of salvation which he preached was first of all given to him by the Lord Jesus Christ himself. It had been entrusted to his care.

His clear instructions were to preserve it, unaltered in any way. He was to keep it pure and to make sure that no one else perverted any part of it. This is why he was so concerned to 'muzzle' false teachers.

This task of preserving the message of salvation by faith alone is ours too. We are to do everything in our power to safeguard sound doctrine. And we are to teach, to everyone who will listen, the good news of salvation. The law has been given to make people realize that they are lost, hell-deserving sinners; and the gospel has been entrusted to us so that we will declare that God has taken the initiative and provided the perfect cleansing and cure for iniquity. He has sent the Lord Jesus Christ to pay the penalty for our sin and save us from the consequences of it.

4.
Give a good testimony

Please read 1 Timothy 1:12-14

It is always a great blessing to listen to people telling how they came to believe in the Lord Jesus Christ and how the Lord is continuing to help them in their daily lives. It is an especially effective testimony when a believer is able to explain how his life has been completely transformed because of his personal encounter with the Lord Jesus Christ. We love to hear someone who had been a thief, or a villain of some sort, recounting how he has been converted. The change in a person's life is one of the most powerful evidences for the validity of his or her salvation.

However, there can be a number of dangers with that kind of testimony. It may be that those who have become Christians in a gentle and quiet way, without any dramatic display, might begin to doubt their own salvation, simply because they cannot tell about similar exciting things which have taken place in their lives. Also there is a danger that a person who has lived a comparatively blameless life before conversion might wish that he, too, had been a drunkard or had lived an immoral life so that he could tell everyone a similar sensational story. A third problem which can occur when a believer gives an exciting testimony is that, unless great care is taken, the person telling the story becomes the centre of it, rather than the Lord Jesus Christ.

Paul had a very sudden and spectacular conversion on the road to Damascus. It came about when he was setting out to hunt down and kill as many 'followers of the Way' as he could (Acts 9:1-4; 22:4-7; 26:10-15). However, when he told Timothy about his conversion it was Christ who was lifted up, not Paul. In fact the apostle felt so ashamed of his former life that he calls himself 'the worst of sinners' (1:15,16).

The blessings Paul had received

The Lord Jesus Christ *had given Paul strength* (1:12). Before he was saved Paul thought that he was a stable, religious man. He assumed that, as a teacher of the law, he could achieve much for God. But, when Christ met with him, he discovered that he had no strength to serve God effectively. He was helpless.

He came to see that none of his good works could accomplish anything of any lasting value (Phil. 3:7). He saw that his efforts to keep the law of the Lord were useless. He realized that he was just like the people he had described in verses 9-10 of this chapter.

But after Paul had become a follower of Christ he was given strength to do all things. The Lord said to him, 'My grace is sufficient for you, for my power is made perfect in weakness' (2 Cor. 12:9). In another place the apostle declares, 'I can do everything through him who gives me strength' (Phil. 4:13). And writing again to Timothy he was later to say, 'The Lord stood at my side and gave me strength, so that through me the message might be fully proclaimed and all the Gentiles might hear it' (2 Tim. 4:17).

Secondly, the Lord Jesus Christ *considered Paul to be faithful*. God found him faithful because he was trustworthy. He had been given work to do for the Lord and he got on with it, and he did it well.

Thirdly, the Lord Jesus Christ *appointed Paul to his service*. He was appointed an apostle by Christ himself. He was not one of the original twelve disciples who accompanied Jesus throughout his earthly ministry. In fact during the time that Jesus was preaching and performing miracles, Paul was living as a strict Pharisee. But while he was on the Damascus road, travelling to destroy all those who were of 'the Way', a great light shone down upon him, his eyes were opened and he saw the Lord (even though he was physically blind for some time after that event).

At his conversion Paul was given strength, he was given the ability to be trustworthy and he was called to the work of the ministry. But did this call to serve God make Paul behave in a proud way? No. It humbled him to be considered worthy to serve the Lord. The ministry to which Paul was called was that of a servant.

Although he was a chosen apostle, the word which he uses to describe his work is the Greek word which is usually translated as 'deacon'. Paul was humble enough to be called a servant, or slave, of Jesus Christ (Phil. 1:1). He had the same lowly attitude as the psalmist who said, 'I would rather be a doorkeeper in the house of my God than dwell in the tents of the wicked' (Ps. 84:10). We, too, should be glad to do whatever the Lord calls us to do, regardless of our own feelings in the matter.

When we consider this humble life to which God's servants are called, we realize that it must grieve the heart of the Lord to look down and see so-called leaders of the church dressed in beautiful robes, sitting on gilded thrones and allowing other men to kneel before them! However, it is not only in the ceremonial 'churches' that pride can be demonstrated; it must pain the Lord too, when a deacon or elder, or other office-holder, constantly expects to have his own way in the affairs of a church.

The life Paul had lived before his conversion

Whenever Paul wrote about his former life he tended to give
his testimony (1:13-14). Three times in the book of the Acts we
are told details of his conversion to Christ (Acts 9:1-22; 22:1-
21; 26:9-18). We can also see his personal experiences of
conversion detailed in passages like Galatians 1:13-17 and
Philippians 3:6.

Here, as Paul writes to Timothy, he is overcome by the
wonder of the great love which God had towards him and is
conscious of being unworthy of God's grace. If the hymn had
existed in his day he would have joined with great feeling in
singing:

I know not why God's wondrous grace
To me he hath made known,
Nor why, unworthy, Christ in love
Redeemed me for his own.[1]

John Newton expressed similar sentiments when he penned
the words:

Amazing grace, how sweet the sound
That saved a wretch like me!
I once was lost, but now am found,
Was blind, but now I see.[2]

When he contemplated what the Lord had done for him the
apostle was filled with tremendous praise to God. Whenever
he considered the awfulness of his past life it amazed him that
God should have had mercy upon him. This is why he says, '[I
have been saved] **even though I was once a blasphemer**'
(1:13). A blasphemer is one who shows disrespect for God.
But Paul was a Pharisee! Pharisees were very strict in their

behaviour. From this we know that Paul had kept the hundreds of religious rules which had been laid down for religious people to observe (see Phil. 3:4-6). Yet he did not know that this Jesus, whom he persecuted, was God himself who had come to earth in human form. He realized, therefore, that he had spoken against the Lord. In fact he was fanatical in his opposition to the Lord Jesus Christ and everyone who followed him. He denied Christ, and he even tried to force others to speak against him. We know this happened because Paul tells us, 'Many a time I went from one synagogue to another to have [the saints] punished, and I tried to force them to blaspheme. In my obsession against them, I even went to foreign cities to persecute them' (Acts 26:11).

However, not only had Paul been a blasphemer, he said that he had been **'a persecutor'** as well. When he set out on the Damascus road his aim in life was to destroy all traces of Christ, his teachings and his followers. This is how he put it in his own words: 'I persecuted the followers of this Way to their death, arresting both men and women and throwing them into prison, as also the high priest and all the Council can testify. I even obtained letters from them to their brothers in Damascus, and went there to bring these people as prisoners to Jerusalem to be punished' (Acts 22:4-7).

And, as if that were not bad enough, Paul adds, **'and** [I was] **a violent man'**. He had an outrageous disregard of other men's rights.[3] He went to the high priest for letters of authority so that he could go all the way to Damascus with the sole purpose of destroying the people who followed Christ. Luke tells us that 'Saul was ... breathing out murderous threats against the Lord's disciples' (Acts 9:1). He really thought that he 'ought to do all that was possible to oppose the name of Jesus of Nazareth' (Acts 26:9).

So what did God do about this man who had behaved in such a dreadful way towards the early Christians? If we had been given power over Paul we would almost certainly have cut him off from everything respectable. We would have said, 'This man deserves nothing, except eternal damnation.' But God did not do as man would have done.

Paul was shown mercy

God is so unlike men. He sees our hearts, and he knows our thoughts. Though Paul was persecuting the people of God, he thought he was doing God a service (see John 16:2). Even though he sinned, he acted in **'ignorance and unbelief'** (1:13) and, therefore, God showed him mercy (see Num. 15:22-31).

Mercy, like grace, is something which is not deserved. When God shows mercy to someone he displays his divine pity and compassion towards that person. Why was it that God showed mercy to Paul? To the human mind it does not seem right, because he had fought against God, and had even tried to stamp out Christianity and stop its spread. But God showed mercy to Paul solely because he chose to set his love upon him.

We have a picture of God's love like this in the Old Testament. Israel had sinned against the Lord time and time again, yet God chose them to be his people. In Deuteronomy 7:7 we read, 'The Lord did not set his affection on you and choose you because you were more numerous than other peoples, for you were the fewest of all peoples. But it was because the Lord loved you.' The Lord Jesus Christ put it like this. He said to his disciples, 'You did not choose me, but I chose you and appointed you to go and bear fruit — fruit that will last' (John 15:16).

None of us who belong to the Lord are Christians just because we made a decision to follow Christ. We are believers because God has chosen us in Christ 'before the creation of the world' (Eph. 1:4). That is the amazing thing about God's love

— he shows mercy to the most unlikely people. God showed mercy to Paul, who had been a blasphemer, a persecutor and a violent man.

Paul was so overwhelmed at the love of God that he was full of praise for his Lord. He said, **'The grace of our Lord was poured out on me'** (1:14). He felt as if he was being drenched with the blessings of God. He said that God's grace was poured out upon him **'abundantly'**. He was constantly using language like that. In Romans 5:20 he said, 'Where sin abounded, grace abounded much more' (NKJV). He wrote to the Thessalonians of faith that 'grows exceedingly' and love that 'abounds' (2 Thess. 1:3, NKJV). He spoke of his joy knowing no bounds (2 Cor. 7:4) and of the 'peace of God transcending all understanding' (Phil. 4:7).[4]

Paul says that the grace of the Lord issued in **'faith and love'** to those who are in Christ Jesus. He is telling us that the effect of grace upon our lives is that we are filled with faith and love. We cannot show real Christian love to anyone unless we have been truly born again. We can show a natural compassion to another person but we cannot display the love of Christ until we have been born again. For Paul grace kindled faith and love. Hendriksen puts it like this: 'Grace is ever the root, faith and love are the trunk, and good works are the fruit of the tree of salvation.'[5] And none of these blessings is to be found anywhere else except **'in Christ Jesus'** (1:14).

5.
Honour God

Please read 1 Timothy 1:15-17

One of the things which seem to hold many people back from becoming Christians is the fact that the Bible insists that the only way to eternal life is through faith in the Lord Jesus Christ. The 'religious' people of this pluralistic age are often very much taken up with multi-faith worship and the search to find the best in all religions. It is considered intolerant for an individual or a church to insist that there is only one way to heaven.

But this is the exact message which Paul, and the other apostles, went everywhere proclaiming. It is not only in the passage which is before us that Paul spoke of Christ coming into the world to save sinners. To the Ephesians he wrote similar words: 'By grace you have been saved, through faith — and this [grace and faith are] not from yourselves, it is the gift of God — not by works, so that no one can boast' (Eph. 2:8-9).

However, despite it being spelled out so definitely in the Bible many people still will not accept this message. They say, 'That's too easy. I don't like something for nothing. I want to pay for what I get. What you are saying sounds too much like a charity hand-out to me.' Yet the biblical fact is that God's salvation can never be earned. It is free, and it is graciously, and fully, given to all those who come to Christ in simple faith, confessing their sins and seeking God's forgiveness.

In the first chapter of Paul's first letter to Timothy, the apostle is writing about the grace of God which had been poured out on him (1:14). He knew that he did not deserve any of these blessings, but he rejoiced in this glorious fact that God had shown him mercy.

The importance of the message

Paul was not giving Timothy a new message; he was reminding him of the things he already knew. We, too, need to recall the truths of God's Word because we forget so easily. That is why teachers constantly reinforce the lessons they are trying to instil into their pupils. Also it is one of the reasons why the Lord instituted the communion service. Every time we meet around the Lord's Table it is to remember him. We take the bread, break it and eat it in remembrance of his sacrifice for us upon the cross of Calvary. We drink the wine, which has been poured out from a bottle, because Christ's blood was freely poured out to wash us from our sins. And we do these things in remembrance of him and his atoning death on the cross for us.

This is why Paul writes, **'Here is a trustworthy saying'** (1:15). Five times the apostle uses this same phrase in his letters — each time in the Pastoral Epistles (1:15; 3:1; 4:9; 2 Tim. 2:11; Titus 3:8). Why does Paul use this phrase? He writes these words to identify a key saying. What follows on from this formula is highly important. It is reliable. The reason why the message which Paul gave could be trusted is because it can be traced back to the lips of the Lord Jesus Christ himself (see John 3:19).

Paul emphasizes the message of salvation by saying that it **'deserves full acceptance'**. The good news of salvation is vitally important. Yet so many people today, even those who call themselves Christians, consider that it is of little consequence. They think, 'There is plenty of time to consider what will happen when I die,' and they live their lives without any real thought about God, or what he wants them to do. However, these glorious tidings of God's love deserve full acceptance. We cannot just take part of this message and ignore the rest. This is what people do when they say, 'I try to live my life by the standards of the Ten Commandments and the Sermon on the Mount, but I can't accept all that talk about the shedding of Christ's blood. I don't think that God wants us to go overboard in our religion. We must have some part of our lives to ourselves, so that we can do what we want to do — provided we're not harming anyone else, of course.'

When Paul used these words he meant that the gospel deserves our 'complete acceptance in every way, without reservation, without hesitation, without the least doubt'.[1]

The content of the message

'Christ Jesus came into the world' (1:15). It is God himself who came into the world, but he came in human form. He, God's Son, is the chosen and anointed one. He is Jesus, the Saviour of sinners. This wonderful God-man left heaven and came right down into this sinful world. The Lord of glory took upon himself human flesh. He voluntarily placed upon himself the limitations of humanity. This meant that as a man he could only be in one place at one time. He knew what it was to be tired, to be hungry and to be sad (Luke 8:23; Mark 11:12; John 11:35). He also knew what it was to be tempted (Luke 4:2). An old hymn puts it like this:

> He knew what sore temptations mean
> For he has felt the same.[2]

He also knew what it was to suffer the agonies of death. All of these human attributes the Lord Jesus Christ freely took upon himself, knowing why he was entering the world, being fully aware of what was going to happen to him.

Why should Christ take upon himself human form? Paul tells us that he came into the world **'to save sinners'**. Think about that word, 'sinners'. Paul had been a strict Pharisee, and all Pharisees had a very clear definition of what a sinner was. Sinners were people like tax collectors and prostitutes. Throughout the Gospels Jesus upset the Pharisees and other religious people because he had contact with those whom they called 'sinners'. On one occasion, 'The Pharisees and the teachers of the the law muttered, "This man [Jesus] welcomes sinners and eats with them"' (Luke 15:2).

With that in mind, is it not amazing that Paul describes himself as a sinner — in fact as **'the worst of sinners'**? (1:15,16). Why did he use this word to describe himself when everyone knew that Pharisees regarded themselves as righteous people? They thought they were holy because they kept the law of God very rigidly, and they tried to make sure that everyone else did so too. In addition they kept well away from those whom they considered to be 'sinners'. This is why they were called Pharisees (the separated ones).

So why, then, did Paul think of himself as the worst of sinners? He tells us that it was because he 'persecuted the church of God' (1 Cor. 15:9).

But a further thing about this verse also surprises us. Paul did not say, 'I *was* the worst of sinners, but I *am* the worst of sinners.' He meant what he said; he was not guilty of false humility. He knew he was a great sinner because his eyes had been opened so that he saw the Lord Jesus Christ in all his beauty. He had come to realize that none of his own righteous deeds had made him cleaner. He became aware of the fact that, up against the purity and holiness of Christ Jesus, he was filthy. He was like Peter when he saw the glory and majesty of the

Lord Jesus Christ for the very first time. The huge fisherman fell down at Jesus' knees and said, 'Go away from me, Lord; I am a sinful man!' (Luke 5:8). Of course, Peter did not really want Jesus to leave him, but he felt so unworthy of Christ's love that he did not consider it right that he should be anywhere near the Saviour. He was like many in the Old Testament before him. 'He felt that God was so powerful and holy that in contrast he was worthless' (see Gen. 18:27; Job 42:6; Isa. 6:5).[3]

Paul had come to understand that all of his righteous acts were of no more value than filthy rags (Isa. 64:6). He would have known, too, about the words of the Lord himself who said, 'It is not the healthy who need a doctor, but the sick' (Luke 5:31). Jesus proceeded to explain how that thought applied to the spiritual realm: 'I have not come to call the righteous, but sinners to repentance' (Luke 5:32).

People who think they are righteous, and are therefore under no obligation to repent, will never turn to Christ until they realize their need of him and his salvation. On the other hand, those who desire Christ's salvation are those who have become aware that, on their own, they are nothing and can do nothing to achieve their eternal salvation. However, when the Holy Spirit works on their hearts and minds they have a great desire to call on the name of the Lord and seek his mercy. It was for that reason that Christ said he had not come to call the righteous, but sinners (Matt. 9:13). Fernando puts it like this: 'The more Paul understood the magnitude of grace, the more conscious he became of his sinfulness.'[4]

The purpose of the message

Paul says that Christ was very patient with him. In former days he had tried his hardest to stamp out the Christian gospel, but God had displayed **'unlimited patience'** towards him (1:16).

Now that he had been saved Paul still could not understand why God did not strike him down dead — particularly as he had been 'a blasphemer, a persecutor and a violent man' (1:13). He could only conclude that the patience of Christ is vast and endless. He told the Roman Christians that God exercised tolerance and patience towards them, despite all their wickedness. This was because the kindness of God was designed to lead them to repentance (Rom. 2:4).

Our God never changes. These 2,000 years further on in time God is still waiting to be gracious towards sinners. He longs that they should repent of their disobedience to his laws. He desires that they leave their wicked ways and evil thoughts, and turn towards the Lord Jesus Christ for salvation.

Then Paul told Timothy why God had saved him, despite all his sinfulness. It was so that he could be **'an example'** to all **'those who would believe'**. Paul is a kind of pattern which is held up to show God's mercy and love towards sinners. If God could save Paul, who was (and continued to be) the chief of sinners, then he can save all kinds of people. There is but one stipulation: they must believe on the Lord Jesus Christ. If they do this then they will **'receive eternal life'**.

It is no wonder that the apostle then launches into one of his characteristic outbursts of praise to God (1:17; see also 6:16; 2 Tim. 4:18; Rom. 11:33-36; 16:27; Gal. 1:5; Eph. 3:21; Phil. 4:20). He says, **'Now to the King eternal...'** He is emphasizing that God is King of all ages; he is *all-powerful*. He overrules all evil, and causes it to turn out for good. Also God's 'kingdom is an everlasting kingdom', and his 'dominion endures through all generations' (Ps. 145:13). Because this is all true we can still pray today, 'For yours is the kingdom, the power and the glory, for ever and ever, Amen.' Not only the kingdom, but God himself is *eternal*. His arms never become tired (Deut. 33:27). He never grows weary (Isa. 40:28). Decay and death are not applicable to him (Ps. 103:15-17). He never changes (Mal. 3:6).[5] The Lord is **'immortal'**. The grass, the flowers of the field and men's bodies will all fade away eventually, but our God lives for ever. He is **'invisible'**. He 'lives in unapproachable light, whom no one has seen or can see' (6:16). Finally in Paul's list, we read that he is **'the only God'**. There is no one else (1 Cor. 8:4).

To all of this our response should be a thunderous **'Amen'**. We should be so taken up with the wonders of God's grace that we gladly and willingly cry out, 'Amen — so be it'. As Paul cries out 'Amen', so he invites us to set our seal upon the truths which he has been proclaiming. 'God's gracious dealings with us should fill us with admiration of his glorious attributes.'[6]

6.
Avoid shipwreck

Please read 1 Timothy 1:18-20

We are always saddened when we hear of people who started out well, only to end up in the gutter. Why is it that some fine, upstanding young people commence their lives in a blaze of glory, but finish them in disgrace and ignominy? Sometimes the reason is because they become 'hooked' on drugs, and for others it is alcohol which wreaks havoc in their lives. On occasions it is the lust for power and fame which takes people over to such an extent that they neglect their health and the welfare of their fellow men and women. But, sadly, it is often fascination for another man's wife which leads a husband into degradation and shame.

The popular newspapers never tire of placarding these affairs for everyone to read about. However, many people who eagerly devour this kind of filth not only bring discredit upon themselves; they can, if they get very involved, drag the whole of their families down with them.

The verses which we are now studying refer to two men who, to use Paul's picture language, made shipwreck of their faith. He means that instead of sailing gracefully on the seas of life, as they were meant to do, they have neglected to use their rudders to steer straight courses and, as a consequence, they have both been smashed to pieces on the jagged rocks of a dangerous spiritual headland. Human nature is still the same today. Those who live their lives in such foolish ways not only wreck their own lives, they also cause other people to suffer much pain. More than that, they are so devastated that they are usually unable to proceed on their chosen course.

A fight to be fought

However, before Paul introduces this seafaring imagery, he uses a military analogy. He uses this frequently in his epistles to Timothy. In chapter 6:12 he exhorts him to 'Fight the good fight of the faith'; in 2 Timothy 2:4 he reminds him that a soldier 'wants to please his commanding officer'; and, finally, writing at the end of his life, the apostle could say, 'I have fought the good fight, I have finished the race, I have kept the faith' (2 Tim. 4:7).

So why does Paul use military terminology? It is because the work of a Christian is, in some respects, like that of a soldier. Being a follower of the Lord Jesus Christ is hard work. It requires persistence and it demands an immediate and wholehearted discipline. Are these the kind of things which come automatically into our minds when we think of the duties of a Christian — and the requirements of a church member? When we look at the language Paul uses here we are forced to ask ourselves questions like, 'How active am I in the work of the Lord?' and 'How much effort do I put into our task of fighting in God's army against sin and Satan?'

Christians, like soldiers, ought to be quick to respond to the orders issued by those who are over them in the Lord. Let us examine the decisive language used by Paul. He says to Timothy, **'I give you this instruction'** (1:18). He had used this sort of wording before when he declared that he was an apostle of Christ Jesus 'by the *command* of God our Saviour' (1:1), when he urged Timothy to '*command* certain men not to teach false doctrines any longer' (1:3) and when he spoke of 'the goal of this *command*' as 'love' (1:5).

However, Paul was not like the sergeant-major who drilled me when I was being put through my basic military training in Catterick Camp in Yorkshire in 1953. The apostle spoke to Timothy in terms of endearment. He called him his young friend (which was not exactly how my drill instructors addressed me!). And here he calls him **'my son'** (1:18), just as he had addressed this letter to 'Timothy my true son in the faith' (1:2).

Paul's teaching was in keeping with **'the prophecies'** which had once been made about Timothy. There is no record of the wording of these prophecies, but Paul makes reference to one of them later in this letter when he says, 'Do not neglect your gift, which was given you through a prophetic message when the body of elders laid their hands on you' (4:14). However, we do know that some years earlier the Holy Spirit had given the prophets and teachers at Antioch a message to set Paul and Barnabas apart for missionary service (Acts 13:1-3) and this may have been something similar.

So it would seem that the Holy Spirit spoke regularly through the New Testament prophets. Of course, it was very important for the church to have some way of knowing what God was saying to them. In those days the believers did not have the New Testament; much of it had not yet been written. When Paul wrote about the Scriptures he meant what we call the Old Testament. Although we cannot be certain what these prophecies were, we can be sure of one thing: they were in line with the teaching of God's Word. We know this because the Holy Spirit is the author of the Bible and it is inconceivable that he should teach anything which is contrary to Holy Writ.

These instructions of Paul, which were **'in keeping with the prophecies once made about'** Timothy, were concerned with fighting. This is why Paul now again takes up the theme which he had begun in verses 3-5. In giving directions to Timothy, Paul says that he must not allow any false doctrine to be taught in the Ephesian church. But that was not all: Timothy was to launch a crusade against all wrong and dangerous teaching.

He was to **'fight the good fight, holding on to [the] faith'**. In other words, Timothy must make sure that he did not depart from the pure teaching of God. Paul encourages us all to realize that the faith of the gospel is something which is worth fighting for. In fact Jude tells the recipients of his letter, 'I felt I had to write and urge you to contend for the faith that was once for all entrusted to the saints' (Jude 3).

How vital it is, then, in these days, when many are perverting the true gospel, to have a great concern to ensure that the purity of the Word of God is upheld! None of us should ever let go of any part of the teaching of the Bible. One of the ways in which we can make certain of this is to 'guard what has been entrusted to [our] care' and also see that we 'turn away from godless chatter and the opposing ideas of what is falsely called knowledge' (6:20). Not only that, but we must speak out against all those who pervert the gospel and deny the truth of God's Word.

Secondly, Timothy was commanded to hold on to **'a good conscience'**. This phrase occurs a number of times in these Pastoral Epistles. In verse 5 of this chapter we read, 'The goal of this command is love, which comes from a pure heart and *a good conscience* and a sincere faith.' Also in 3:9 Paul says that deacons 'must keep hold of the deep truths of the faith with *a clear conscience*'. We see from both of these passages that faith and conscience are often linked together.

What does Paul mean when he speaks about our consciences? He is talking about that which lies within each of us and which tells us what is right and what is wrong, and how to tell the difference between the two. When Paul said that

Timothy 'should be armed with a good conscience' he meant
that he must be sensitive to God's voice.[1] Right beliefs must
show themselves in right behaviour. A person who says that he
believes the Ten Commandments, the Sermon on the Mount
and the Thirty-Nine Articles of the Church of England and yet
does not live a morally upright life is a hypocrite. Paul, and
indeed the whole of the Bible, teaches that every believer
should hold on to the faith and a good conscience because he
is seeking to live a life which is holy, godly and honouring to
the Lord in every way.

Dangers to be avoided

Not everyone who claims to be a Christian lives his life in this
godly way. Some have rejected these things. They have turned
aside from the faith. One of the things which such people say
is that the virgin birth was only a story for first-century ears.
They also teach that Christ did not rise from the dead with a
physical body. They maintain that the Bible can only be
interpreted through human reasoning. They think that men's
minds have grown so sophisticated in these modern times that
miracles can no longer be accepted as actual events. They tell
us that we should not ask about any event recorded in the Bible,
'Is this true?' For them the only important question is: 'What
does this mean?'

   We would not be surprised if someone who claimed to be
an atheist or an agnostic made such assertions. But those who
propound these heresies today are often people who claim to
be ministers or clergymen and women. Sadly, there are comparatively few lecturers now in Britain's theological colleges
who teach that the Bible is the inerrant Word of God.

   Paul spoke very harshly against such people in his day, so
how much more should we attack those who fail to uphold the

teaching of God's Word today! The apostle said that because these men have rejected the teaching of God's Word (by turning away from it) then they have, in effect, made shipwreck of their faith. This was not just a picturesque phrase; Paul knew from personal experience what it was like to be on board a ship which was being smashed to pieces against the rocks. When a ship is wrecked it is completely destroyed, or, even if part of it is saved, it is in a very poor condition by the time it reaches the shore. Paul meant that this is what the lives of these people are like when they reject the Bible.

Not only do these people turn aside from the clear teaching of God's Word, they usually slide morally. We have an example of this in the so-called 'Gay Christian Movement'. These people have rejected many of the doctrines of God's Word. They have let their feelings and desires override their adherence to the Bible. And, as a consequence, their lives are morally corrupt. They do not worry that their lifestyle is in clear opposition to the teaching of Romans chapter 1 and other scriptures. If we are to avoid spiritual shipwreck in our lives then we must make sure that we all hold on to faith and a good conscience.

Paul next gives a specific example of two such men. It would seem that they were known to Timothy. They appear to be just two of many who had turned their backs upon God's Word and God's requirements for holy living. Their names are **'Hymenaeus and Alexander'** (1:20). While we are given more details about Hymenaeus in 2 Timothy 2:17-18, Alexander was such a popular name that no one can be sure which man of this name Paul is writing about.

We are told that Hymenaeus was among those who indulged in 'godless chatter' (2 Tim. 2:16-17). If we were to use this expression about the people of this world they might well be upset by our accusation that they were guilty of such talk. However, they are often sniggering about some smutty joke or other. The thing for us, as God's people, is to ask ourselves, 'Do I listen to such things?' It is salutary to see if our talk (and our 'hearing') is always full of Christ. If it is not then it could certainly be called 'godless chatter'. We have to remind ourselves that Jesus says that 'Men will have to give account on the day of judgement for every careless word they have spoken' (Matt. 12:36).

We are further told that Hymenaeus was a false teacher who had 'wandered away from the truth' (2 Tim. 2:18). This is an interesting phrase. There are very few people who claim to be Christians who suddenly stop believing the truths of God's Word. Instead they become careless over seemingly small things, and then they gradually drift, or wander away, from the truth. But when Paul writes to the Galatians we see that the movement away from the pure gospel on the part of his readers was not something which happened bit by bit. Paul says that he is astonished that they had *so quickly* deserted the one who called them by the grace of Christ, and, in fact, they were already turning to another gospel (Gal. 1:6).

This is why it is so important that we insist that the whole of the Bible is the inerrant Word of God — despite what the liberal scholars might say. Jesus certainly believed it was; therefore so should we. If we are to doubt even a tiny part of the Scriptures then those small uncertainties are liable to spread and affect all of our thinking about the Bible.

In 2 Timothy 2:18 we are given a specific example of one of the doctrines which Hymenaeus denied. He maintained that the resurrection had already taken place. No doubt he said things like this: 'Because we were all raised with Christ at our conversion, then there will be no further physical resurrection of the dead.' However, this is certainly not the teaching of God's Word. Paul declared, 'Listen, I tell you a mystery: We will not all sleep, but we will all be changed — in a flash, in the twinkling of an eye, at the last trumpet. For the trumpet will sound, the dead will be raised imperishable, and we will be changed' (1 Cor. 15:51-52).

The apostle declares that all who have departed from the Lord's ways have made shipwreck of their faith. Therefore they have to be dealt with. They have done harm to themselves and, by their beliefs and teaching, they are liable to damage other believers. The result of their activities might well lead some of God's people to have doubts about their salvation. All that Paul could do to those who had rejected the faith was to hand them over to Satan. He probably meant that they were to be turned out of the church. Certainly they were not to be allowed to teach any more in the congregation because they were speaking against God (which is blasphemy). This is the reason why they were to be excommunicated.

Satan's kingdom is this world (at least for a while longer). This is probably why Paul said that he had handed them over to Satan. He had told the Corinthians to do the same thing to the immoral man who was in their assembly (1 Cor. 5:5).

So why were Hymenaeus and Alexander to be punished in this way? Was Paul saying that they had been cast out of the kingdom of God? Certainly not, if they were true believers. Once we are saved we remain God's children, but that does not mean that we can behave as we like. Discipline has to be applied. But it is important to remember that discipline is always to be administered in order to bring the individuals concerned to repentance so that they can eventually be restored to full fellowship with the people of God. In 2 Thessalonians 3:14-15 we read, 'If anyone does not obey our instruction in this letter, take special note of him. Do not associate with him, in order that he may feel ashamed' (see also Titus 3:10). This discipline was so that the backslider might repent and again come back within the full fellowship of the people of God. And it was for this same reason that Hymenaeus and Alexander were to be handed over to Satan.

Paul wanted them to see the folly of their ways, repent and, in due course, be received back into the church.

Being a Christian is tough. It requires military discipline. It demands a strong adherence to the teaching of God's Word. It calls upon us to take a firm grip upon the rudder of truth so that we might not be driven onto the jagged rocks of unbelief. 'The church is a haven of protection from Satan's power.'[2] As Calvin said, 'If we wish to reach port with our faith intact, we should make a good conscience the pilot of our course, or otherwise there is a danger of shipwreck; faith may be sunk by a bad conscience as by a whirlpool in a stormy sea.'[3] We each of us need to ask ourselves what steps we are taking to avoid making shipwreck of our faith, and our lives. None of us should be so proud as to think that we cannot fall.

7.
Be prayerful

Please read 1 Timothy 2:1-2

The topic of worship is often written and spoken about. We hear people talking about their church and saying, 'We love to come together for a time of worship.' What do they mean by that phrase? Is it a period of joyful singing which the congregation engage in before they get down to the 'thinking' part of the service? Or does the term 'worship' refer to everything that happens during the hour or so of a church service?

I think that if we read the New Testament carefully we shall see that it everywhere speaks of worship as something which ought to occupy the whole life of a believer. It has been said that 'If we are not already worshipping God when we meet together in church, that meeting will be in serious trouble.'[1]

At the beginning of the second chapter of this letter, Paul is starting to deal with the subject of the public worship of God. Before discussing such issues as qualifications for leadership (in chapter 3), or what to do about widows (in chapter 5), the apostle writes about the most important item in the whole spectrum of worship — prayer.

Prayer should pervade all of our worship

Prayer is often the missing element in worship. It is true that we do have prayers in our religious gatherings, but they can be very mechanical. We give the impression that we pray because it is the correct thing to do in church. But how often are we really filled with a spirit of prayer as we come into God's house? Do we pray before we come to church? Are we in an attitude of prayer during the meetings? And is it our habit to beseech the Lord that he will come down upon us in mighty blessing as we join together in worship?

Paul writes to Timothy, **'I urge, then, first of all, that requests, prayers, intercession and thanksgiving be made'** (2:1). He puts this as first in importance. He is not necessarily saying that prayer should be the first thing to happen in a service, although it is a good habit to open meetings with prayer. The apostle is saying that whatever else is done, prayer (in all its aspects) must be given utmost priority.

The question for us is: how much emphasis do we put on our individual prayer life and on the prayer life of our church? It is as we come together to pray that we are drawn closer to God. It is as we draw near to God in prayer that we become conscious of a sense of the holiness of God and our own unimportance. C. H. Spurgeon said, 'We shall never see much change for the better in our churches in general till the prayer meeting occupies a higher place in the esteem of Christians.'[2]

Prayer should be mufti-faceted

We should not pray just because it is the correct thing to do. Our periods of prayer should be times of real, heartfelt communion with God. This is why Paul urges Timothy (and the church at Ephesus) to place such great importance upon this work of prayer.

First of all, we are told that we should come to God with *requests*. But these should never be selfish. They should first of all be for other people. We should pray that God will meet the needs of our fellow men and women — those who are ill, bereaved, troubled, or having to make difficult decisions. It is only when we have made requests for others that we should pray for ourselves.

The word translated 'requests' has to do with the meeting of specific needs. When we come to make requests of God, what kind of things do we ask for? I would suggest that, before anything else, we should ask for our spiritual needs to be met. It is very easy to think of all the things we would like and then to ask for those things. Supplication in prayer is not the same as reciting to God our birthday present list! It is seeking God's face about our spiritual needs — which are our real needs. After that, of course, there are our material needs, which are essential if we are to live helpful, holy lives.

Next on the list is the word *'prayers'*. This is the general word for prayer. It is used in a sense of wonder as we approach God, who is holy. There are always needs in any congregation, so we should pray that these requirements may be met by our gracious Lord. We should pray for God's blessing on the witness of his people throughout the world. We need constantly to pray for wisdom in the ordering of our daily lives and in the corporate work of the church. We need to cry out to God that we might live our lives in ways which are more honouring to him than they have been in the past. And we should pray regularly that justice will be done in all places.

Thirdly, Paul exhorts Timothy to make sure that *intercession* is carried out. This word does not necessarily mean interceding on behalf of other people. 'Requests' include that idea. The word 'intercession' (which is only used here and in 4:5) conveys the idea of 'drawing near to God'. It means 'gaining entrance to the presence of a king in order to submit a petition'.[3]

Does our prayer life, both as individuals and in the church where we belong, have about it an awareness of drawing near to our glorious, holy God, so that we can speak confidently with him? We should examine our hearts and ask how real our prayer life is. It is no wonder that missionaries often feel neglected if we do not draw near to God in prayer on their behalf. I need to ask myself, 'How much is the work of the gospel held back because I do not draw near to God in prayer as often and as fervently as I should?' John Newton, the ex-slave trader, wrote:

Thou art coming to a King;
Large petitions with thee bring;
For his grace and power are such,
None can ever ask too much![4]

Finally, all these prayers should be offered in the attitude of *thanksgiving*. How little we stop to thank God for all his blessings! If he did not give us the ability to breathe, we should die. How often do we thank him for giving and maintaining our lives? If he did not provide food, drink and shelter for us, then we should be in a desperate situation. How often do we thank him for giving us the necessities of life? If he had not provided a country for us where, by and large, we can live in peace, then we should be in great distress. How seldom do we stop to thank him for the fact that our land is peaceful? Those who remember the stress and anxiety of the Second World War will realize how grateful we should be for the peace which we enjoy.

We should also thank God for answers to our prayers. God always answers our prayers. Because he is a wise Father he does not give us everything we ask for. However, he always provides us with what we need. Sometimes God answers our prayers by saying, 'Yes'. Sometimes he says, 'No', and at other times he says, 'Wait'. Yet all of these are gracious answers to prayer, and we should thank God for them. Paul said to the Philippians, 'Do not be anxious about anything, but in everything, by prayer and petition, with thanksgiving, present your requests to God. And the peace of God, which transcends all understanding, will guard your hearts and your minds in Christ Jesus' (Phil. 4:6-7).

Prayer should be for everyone

Selfishness in prayer is very wrong. Paul brings this out here. The Jews had been taught by their leaders that God's blessings were only for their nation. They 'regarded the whole Gentile world as excluded from covenant mercies'.[5] But Paul writes very clearly that he wanted the church to pray for **'everyone'**. In fact all through the opening verses of this section Paul hammers home this point. In verse 3 he writes, 'God ... wants *all men* to be saved'; and in verse 5 he says that 'Christ Jesus ... gave himself as a ransom for *all men*.' So we are required to pray for everyone — to whatever nation they may belong. Obviously this does not mean that we should pray for every individual in the whole world. We could never do that because we do not know everybody, but we do know all sorts of people. And, whoever they are, we should pray for them. I often say to people who tell me that they do not want anything to do with the gospel, 'Well, you can't stop me praying for you.'

Then Paul gave another command. He said that the church at Ephesus should pray **'for kings and all those in authority'**. This is in line with New Testament teaching elsewhere. In Romans 13:1 Paul says, 'Everyone must submit himself to the governing authorities, for there is no authority except that which God has established.' And Peter writes, 'Submit your-selves for the Lord's sake to every authority instituted among men: whether to the king, as the supreme authority, or to governors, who are sent by him to punish those who do wrong and to commend those who do right' (1 Peter 2:13-14).

Paul says all this because he does not want anarchy to break out. God is a God of order, and peace and quiet can only come about where there is obedience to the proper authorities. It is one thing to submit to those who rule over us (we can grit our teeth and put up with things which we do not like); it is another thing entirely to pray positively for these people. Yet we should offer requests, prayers, intercession for everyone, including kings and all those in authority — even if we did not vote for them. And we should be thankful in our prayers.

It is comparatively easy for us in Britain today to pray for our queen and the prime minister, but what would we do if our rulers were of the same calibre as Nero? He was Emperor of Rome when Paul wrote these words. That cruel tyrant fiddled, or at least recited poetry, while Rome burned, and then he blamed the fire on the Christians. Despite all of that Paul said, 'Pray for him.' Nero was so cruel that he murdered even his own mother (who had used her influence to bring him to power) and then he killed his wife Octavia. He lived a life of debauchery, extravagance and tyranny, and once, in a fit of passion, he murdered another of his wives, Poppaea, by kicking her when she was pregnant. Yet Paul said, 'Pray for him — and all like him.'

Why does Paul say that we should pray for people like this? It is so that **'we may live peaceful and quiet lives'**. The word 'peaceful' refers to a life which is 'free from outward disturbance',[6] and the word 'quiet' seems to refer to our inward being. Paul's desire, then, is that churches should be able to worship God without any interference from outside — either from state intervention, or from hooligans who cause trouble. He also desires that God's people should be calm within their own spirits. This is one of the reasons why he required of the church at Corinth that 'Everything should be done in a fitting and orderly way' (1 Cor. 14:40).

Paul also says that we should pray for everyone so that peace will facilitate the spread of the gospel. One of the ways that this can be done is by believers living lives in **'all godliness and holiness'**. When we live our lives reverently, exuding holiness, then people will automatically be influenced to find out what makes us devote our lives to God and his ways. We should not only do these things so that the gospel may spread, but also because **'This is good, and pleases God our Saviour'** (2:3).

8.
God's go-between

Please read 1 Timothy 2:3-7

There are many passages in the Bible which tell of God's greatness and splendour. They declare that God is in heaven and that he is very holy. There must be few people who have no inbuilt realization of the greatness of God. All heathen nations certainly felt compelled to acknowledge that their destiny was in the hands of a powerful being; otherwise they would never have offered such precious sacrifices to appease his wrath.

Anyone who goes out into the open countryside on a beautiful day and considers the vast expanse of the earth and the sky has to accept that God is so very great. I have never been to Canada, but I would love to stand near the foot of the Rocky Mountains and stare, in awe, at the grandeur and majesty of those ancient heights towering all around and above me. But we do not have to go to Canada; we can just stand in the dark, clear crispness of midnight and look up at the sky. How can anyone gaze upon such a sight and fail to think:

> When I consider your heavens,
>   the work of your fingers,
> the moon and the stars,
>   which you have set in place,

what is man that you are mindful of him,
the son of man that you care for him?

(Ps. 8:3-4).

In the light of all of this there is a question which has puzzled millions of people for centuries. It is: 'How can I draw near to God?'

In Psalm 8, which we have just quoted, we have the problem clearly stated. God is so great, but we are so small and inadequate. How can we reach up to such a Creator God as this? However, it is not just that we are insignificant and tiny. Things are far worse: we are sinners. All of us, however good we might think we are, have sinned against a holy God in word, in thought and in deed, and we have done so again and again.

So we have two extremes here: on the one hand there is God, in all his holiness and purity; and on the other hand we have ourselves, in all our poverty and filth (because that is what sin does to us). It is so patently obvious that we have no power or authority to reach up to God, but the wonderful news is that God can reach down to us, and hear us.

Isaiah tells us this when he says:

Surely the arm of the Lord is not too short to save,
nor his ear too dull to hear.

Then the awful problem is stated, with icy coldness:

But your iniquities have separated
you from your God;
your sins have hidden his face from you,
so that he will not hear

(Isa. 59:1-2).

Job was very much aware of this problem too. He cried out concerning God, 'He is not a man like me that I might answer him, that we might confront each other in court' (Job 9:32). How, then, could a way be discovered to bring Job and God together? There was only one solution. It needed someone to stand between God and man who could be able to unite them. We hear the anguish in Job's voice as he cries:

> If only there were someone to arbitrate between us,
>   to lay his hand upon us both,
> someone to remove God's rod from me,
>   so that his terror would frighten me no more
>
>   (Job 9:33-34).

And the good news is that there is a go-between, a mediator, who can reconcile man to God. The Lord Jesus Christ was sent to this earth for that express purpose.

God desires the salvation of all

Paul has been encouraging Timothy to urge that the church pray for everyone. He says, **'This is good.'** He means that to draw near to God in prayer is a good thing in itself. We should not just pray so that we can obtain things. We should commune with God because it is a good thing to do. The word 'good' is one which Paul uses over and over again in these Pastoral Epistles (1:8,18; 2:3; 3:1,7,13; 4:4,6; 5:4,10,25; 6:12,13,18; 2 Tim. 1:14; 2:3; 4:7; Titus 2:7,14; 3:8,14).

Prayer is not only good, it **'pleases God our Saviour'**, and we should want to do things which please God. The Lord delights to hear the prayers of his children. Once again Paul describes God as 'our Saviour' (see 1:1). The salvation of sinners lies at the heart of God because he is full of goodness. It is in his nature to save from sin and degradation.

In fact his desire to save sinners is as rich and broad as it possibly can be. He **'wants all men to be saved'**. This is reflected throughout the Bible. In Ezekiel 33:11 God says, 'I take no pleasure in the death of the wicked, but rather that they turn from their ways and live.' John tells us that 'God so loved the world that he gave his one and only Son, that whoever believes in him shall not perish but have eternal life' (John 3:16). And Jesus sent his followers 'into all the world' to 'preach the good news to all creation' (Mark 16:15).

'God ... wants all men to be saved and to come to a knowledge of the truth.' His desire is that people come to 'the full knowledge of the truth as this is embodied in Christ (John 14:6; Eph. 4:21)'.[1] Paul does not mean that he wants all men to know *about* Christ. He means that he wants all men to come into a personal relationship with the Lord Jesus Christ and to know him as their own Lord and Saviour. He has already explained much of what that means in 1:15-16.

The trouble is that many do not want to humble themselves and come to a full knowledge of the truth. They are not prepared to confess their sinfulness. They do not want to come to the foot of Christ's cross and lay their burden there. They are too proud and self-sufficient. They would rather carry on being 'the masters of their own destiny' (so they think).

God could save everyone in the world. He could issue a decree that all must be saved — and they would be. But God does not want us to be like robots. He has not given an order that everyone must be saved, but he has sent forth a command that all people should repent of their sins. Instead of giving instructions, he has stated his *desire* that all men be saved. But, like the inhabitants of Jerusalem whom Jesus longed to gather 'as a hen gathers her chicks under her wings' (Matt. 23:37), they were not willing. Matthew Henry puts it like this: 'He has a good will to be the salvation of all, and none perish but it is their own fault.'[2]

Christ died for all

The Jews thought that salvation was something which was only for them. But Paul had refuted that in Romans 3:29-30. There he said, 'Is God the God of Jews only?' and the answer came back with a resounding 'No'. He is the God of the Gentiles as well. When the Jews wanted to speak about all kinds of people on the earth they talked about Jews and Gentiles (non-Jews). When it came to salvation Paul said that all those who have faith like Abraham's faith (he believed God) are saved; it matters not what nationality they belong to.

Then Paul refers to the fundamental principle of all Judaism. He quotes from the *Shema*: 'Hear, O Israel: The Lord our God, the Lord is one' (Deut. 6:4). Every Jew still confesses this belief in the oneness of God every day. This too is a basic, fundamental tenet of Christianity. So Paul reminds his readers that the principle of the Old Testament still holds good: **'There is one God.'**

However, God is in heaven, and far off, and in order for us to communicate with him we need someone to bridge the gap between him and us. Habakkuk said of the Lord, 'Your eyes are too pure to look on evil; you cannot tolerate wrong' (Hab. 1:13). So to meet this need God sent the man Christ Jesus to be the **'one mediator between God and men'**. As there is one God, there only needs to be one arbiter to bring God and man into communion. It matters not how saintly a person might be, no mere human being can fulfil this task of acting as a go-between. The Lord Jesus Christ, the only one who is God and at the same time a perfect, sinless man, can intercede on our behalf. It needed a human being to pay the price of our salvation.

This mediator, by his death on the cross, has redeemed us from the curse of the law, having become a curse for us (Gal. 3:13). Because Christ stands between us and the curse of the law (which is God's just anger against sin) the curse fell on him and we are thereby saved.[3] The writer to the Hebrews also speaks of Christ, our heavenly High Priest, as mediator (Heb. 8:6; 9:15; 12:24). This wonderful middleman brings peace between God and men.

Throughout this passage Paul constantly refers to **'men'**, or **'all men'**. He is contrasting this with the Jews. Had salvation been intended only for the Jews the apostle would have written, 'There is ... one mediator between God and men, the Jew Christ Jesus.'[4] But he is **'the man Christ Jesus'** because he stands between God and all sorts and conditions of men.

This is why we are told that Christ **'gave himself as a ransom for all men'** (2:6). A ransom was the price paid to redeem a slave. Paul had written to the Romans that he (like all mankind) was 'sold as a slave to sin' (Rom. 7:14). Sin has such a grip upon us that we are in slavery to its corrupting influences. But here is the wonderful news: 'Christ has redeemed us.' We have been 'bought at a price' (1 Cor. 6:20; 7:23). And that price was the precious blood of the Lord Jesus Christ which he shed on the cross of Calvary.

This ransom has been given, freely, by the Lord Jesus Christ for all men. The words 'all men' here evidently mean *all kinds of* men — otherwise Christ's death would have been ineffective because, quite clearly, not all men, without exception, come to know the Lord in a personal, loving way. So we can say, God did not save all men *without exception*, but he did save all men *without distinction*. Those who hear and respond to the saving call of the gospel come from all kinds of backgrounds. It is a wonderful thing to find in a church fellowship people from all walks of life, everyone enjoying the blessings of being 'all one in Christ Jesus' (Gal. 3:28).

The **'testimony'** (the witness) of this salvation was given at the **'proper time'**. In Galatians 4:4 we read that 'When the time had fully come, God sent his Son, born of a woman, born under law, to redeem those under law, that we might receive the full rights of sons.'

The good news must be told to all

Paul said that we must declare the good news on every possible occasion. This good news is that, through his death, Christ has bridged the gap between God and man, and has opened up a way for sinners to be saved. The apostle is amazed that he, of all people, should be given the wonderful privilege of being called to go and tell this good news. He had been a violent opponent of the early Christians. He really thought that he should hound them out of the country and put them all to death. But not only did God have mercy upon his soul and grant him the gift of salvation, he also called him into his service to go and tell the gospel to all who would hear. That is why Paul says, **'I am telling the truth, I am not lying'** (2:7).

The apostle uses three words to describe his task. He says, **'I was appointed a herald.'** He did not appoint himself (see 2 Tim. 1:11). John the Baptist heralded Christ's coming (John 1:23). A herald was someone who went before the king and told the people that he was coming. In the same way, Paul was an ambassador proclaiming to the nations, 'We implore you on Christ's behalf: Be reconciled to God' (2 Cor. 5:20).

Secondly, he says, **'I was appointed ... an apostle'** (see also 1:1). An apostle was one who was sent with a special mission. Paul had God's delegated authority over the church. This is why he was able to lay down rules for the belief and the conduct of the church. It is for this reason that all his letters are divinely inspired and inerrant.

Thirdly, he was **'a teacher of the true faith to the Gentiles'**. Warren Wiersbe puts it like this: 'The Good News is not for Jews only, but also for Gentiles.'[5] In Acts 9:15 we read that God said to Ananias, at the time of Paul's conversion, 'This man is my chosen instrument to carry my name before the Gentiles and their kings and before the people of Israel.'

All people need to hear the herald of God preaching the gospel of salvation. For them to trust it, they must be certain of the authority of the messenger and what he says, and they require someone to teach them the meaning of this good news. For this message of God to be effective all these things have to be carried out, and the whole work watered by much prayer.

9.
Men and women in church

Please read 1 Timothy 2:8-10

There is one major thing which is often forgotten in all the discussion which takes place about the content of public worship. That is the need for God's people to approach the Lord in a holy and reverent manner. It used to be said that worshippers ought to prepare themselves for the Sunday services on Saturday evening. However, so many young believers today seem to spend Saturday evenings (and even the early hours of Sunday) in hectic activities. It is not surprising, in such cases, that they often have difficulty in keeping their eyes open during the preaching of God's Word. If the liveliness of the previous night has dominated all their thoughts and energy, then it is no wonder that they are not in a fit state to come before the Lord in a solemn manner at the time of worship.

Paul is very concerned about the attitude of believers when they gather for public worship; this is his theme in this passage. First of all, in these three verses, he addresses men, then he speaks to women and finally he challenges all of God's people.

The men

Initially Paul addresses those who are heads of households. He says to them, **'I want men everywhere to lift up holy hands**

in prayer' (2:8). It was the Jewish custom for the men to take the lead in the synagogue services. In fact the women had to sit at the back, or in the gallery — and keep quiet! The main responsibility of the ladies was to look after the children and observe what was happening at the meetings. All of the teaching and public praying was done by men. So it is not surprising, then, that many of these Jewish customs were automatically incorporated into the worship of the early church.

Paul gives a very careful description of the kind of men who should do the praying in church. He says, 'I want men ... to lift up holy hands in prayer.' He is referring to all kinds of men (as in verse 4). The praying in the church meetings was not confined to the elders, deacons or other recognized leaders; it was open to all kinds of men. They did not have to have received a particular standard of education. They were not required to have been believers for a certain length of time. There was no necessity for them to have passed an examination in churchmanship. They merely had to be men in good standing — whose hands were holy. In other words, they had to be men whom everyone acknowledged to be dedicated wholly to God and his service.

Some people teach from these verses that all women are forbidden to take part in public prayers. However, we know that this is not the case because Paul speaks in 1 Corinthians 11:5 about women praying in church. He cannot mean that they are only to pray silently, because he also speaks about these same women prophesying, and that must have been a public act!

Paul had a strong desire that men *everywhere* should lift up holy hands in prayer. Public worship need not only take place in consecrated religious buildings. By using the word 'everywhere' he means that he wants men to pray in every place where believers meet together for the public worship of God. This may be a hired hall (as Paul used in Ephesus — Acts

19:9), or it may be in someone's home (as the church fellowship met in the house of Philemon — Philem. 2). It may even
have been in the open air. From the New Testament letters we
can see that it is not the place where believers meet that
matters; it is the desire of their hearts which is important.

Why does Paul say that he wants these men to *lift up their
hands* as they pray? It is because it was the custom of the Jews
to raise their hands in the air whenever they prayed in the
synagogue. However, the apostle is not stipulating that this is
the only valid stance for prayer. We can read in the Bible of
many different attitudes adopted in prayer. Some people stood
with outstretched hands (1 Kings 8:22). Others knelt in prayer
(Daniel 6:10). Some just stood where they were (Luke
18:11,13). Some bowed their heads (Gen. 24:26). Others lifted
up their eyes to heaven (John 17:1) and some fell to the ground
(Gen. 17:3). There is only one recorded instance in the Bible
of someone sitting in prayer (2 Sam. 7:18; 1 Chron. 17:16) —
the position adopted by most nonconformists today in public
worship. However, 'The important thing is not the posture of
the body but the posture of the heart.'[1]

This brings us to the three things which Paul says are
essential for God-honouring prayer in public worship. He says
that the hands lifted up must be *holy* hands. We use our hands
for practically everything that we do; that is another reason
why Paul speaks about hands. Hands are a symbol of daily
activity. On board ship the call sometimes goes out: 'All hands
on deck!' Today we think it derogatory to talk of working
people as hands, but that is how they were viewed in the past.

Holy living is something which is vital to our spiritual
growth. If we are not seeking to devote ourselves to the Lord,
then we are not living holy lives. If we are not constantly
repenting of our faults and failures, and endeavouring to turn
from them, then we are not living holy lives. And if we are not
making a conscious effort to grow spiritually and lead healthy

inner lives, then we are not living holy lives. The psalmist said,
'If I had cherished sin in my heart, the Lord would not have
listened' (Ps. 66:18).

Secondly, the person praying must do so **'without anger'**.
He must be someone who gets on well with his fellow
believers. We all have different temperaments, but even if we
have a tendency to flare up in temper, we are required by
Scripture to keep it under control if we are to be fit to lead in
the public prayers in church.

Thirdly, the men leading the prayers must do so **'without
… disputing'**. When we are angry it is usually a sign that we
have an open disagreement with another person. The word
which is translated 'disputing' is one which has to do with a
disagreement regarding an account.[2] What Paul is saying is
that we must not have any disagreements with God or with our
fellow-believers, about anything, when we lead others in
prayer in public worship. Warren Wiersbe says, 'Christians
should learn to disagree without being disagreeable.'[3]

The women

The first thing which Paul says about the ladies is that they
must dress modestly. He links what he says about the women
in public worship with what he has just said about the men. Just
as the men must come to church with prepared hearts, so the
women must give evidence of the same spirit of holiness. In
fact they must do this while they are 'still at home, getting
ready to attend the service'.[4]

What did he mean when he wrote that the dress of women
at public worship must be modest? He did not mean that they
should dress in a dowdy way; rather their appearance should
be with decency and propriety. In other words, they should
take care to dress in a way which is appropriate for the

occasion. No lady (or gentleman, for that matter) should dress in a way which is designed to draw undue attention to herself. Church is not a fashion parade, but neither is it a place where people should come without giving any thought to their appearance.

Paul followed up this statement by giving the ladies some guidelines on how they should *not* dress. He said that they should **'not'** attend public worship with **'braided hair or gold or pearls or expensive clothes'**. This does not mean that ladies should never have their hair cut or styled. What Paul was doing was to warn the ladies not to go to the extremes to which Roman women went in those days. They spent many hours plaiting gold and precious stones into their complicated hair-dos. Rather than giving a total ban on the wearing of jewellery or braided hair, Paul was expressing 'caution in a society where such things were signs of extravagant luxury and proud personal display'.[5]

Finally, Paul tells the women *how they should dress*. In Jewish society women were regarded as having a fairly low status, and it was lower still in Greek thinking. But the gospel changed all of that. Paul himself said that 'There is neither Jew nor Greek, slave nor free, male nor female, for you are all one in Christ Jesus' (Gal. 3:28). Contrary to the opinion of some people, there is no evidence to suggest that Paul was against women. He knew that there were devoted women who ministered to Jesus in the days of his earthly ministry (see Luke 8:1-3) and he must have been aware that there were many godly women in the church (e.g. Acts 9:36; 16:14-15; 17:4,12; 18:1-3; Rom. 16:1-2,6,12).

To sum up the apostle's teaching on the clothing of women, he said that they should dress themselves with good deeds (not instead of clothes, of course!). Peter uses the same contrast in 1 Peter 3:3-4 where he wrote, 'Your beauty should not come from outward ornament, such as braided hair and the wearing of gold jewellery and fine clothes. Instead, it should be that of your inner self, the unfading beauty of a gentle and quiet spirit, which is of great worth in God's sight.'[6]

These are the kind of 'clothes' which are **'appropriate for women who profess to worship God'**. The word 'profess' is a very strong one. It means 'to convey a message loudly and clearly'.

A challenge for every believer

With what kind of spirit do we, each of us (whether male or female), go to religious services? Do we always take the time and make the effort to prepare ourselves adequately to meet with God and his people when we come together for public worship, or do we just manage to rush into the meetings at the last minute?

If we were being welcomed by the queen at Buckingham Palace we would make lengthy preparations to see that we were properly prepared to enter her presence. We should do the same when we come into the presence of God, in the holy assembly of God's people. We ought to remember the words of the Lord Jesus Christ when he said, 'Where two or three come together in my name, there am I with them' (Matt. 18:20). We need to be conscious that he is present in our times of worship and, in every way possible, behave in a reverent and holy manner.

10.
The role of women

Please read 1 Timothy 2:11-15

I have been in membership with several churches over the years, and everywhere I have found that the majority of the congregation are women. In my first pastorate there was a problem over this. It had been a tradition that only men prayed publicly in the prayer meetings but, at the time I went to the church, there was only one man who could attend the week-night service. As a result of this they made the decision that, as there were so few men present, ladies could take part in the prayer sessions.

It has often been said that Paul was a woman-hater because he wrote such things as: 'Women should remain silent in the churches. They are not allowed to speak, but must be in submission, as the Law says' (1 Cor. 14:34). A similar attitude is expressed in verses 11-14 of the passage which we are currently studying.

Does this mean that women are of little use and that no lady can take an active part in church meetings? On the face of it, that does seem to be what Paul is saying. However, we need to look at this subject more closely. What, in fact, was Paul's attitude to women? Had he really got a 'down' on them? If we read his letters carefully we see that Paul had quite a different attitude to them.

Take Lydia, for example. The Lord opened up her heart to respond to the message which Paul preached, and Paul and his friends gladly stayed at her home (Acts 16:15). Paul also willingly lodged in the home of Aquila and his wife Priscilla (Acts 18:3) and a number of prominent women joined Paul and Silas at Thessalonica despite the opposition of the Jews. When Paul wrote his great letter to the Romans he greeted at least eight women in chapter 16 and he even entrusted Phoebe, who is described as a deaconess in a local church, with the task of carrying this important letter to the Roman church.

So we can see that Paul was not against women taking an active part in the life of the church; he was merely pointing out that there are God-given roles assigned to women — and to men.

Women must be submissive

Peter says that husbands must be considerate and treat their wives with respect. He gives his reason for saying this: the wives are the weaker partners (1 Peter 3:7). He does not mean that women are weaker morally, nor that they have inferior characters to their husbands. He is probably just making reference to their physical strength. We can observe that, generally speaking, the man has more muscle!

Paul also takes up the same theme when he writes, '**A woman should learn in quietness and full submission**' (2:11). It may have been that at Ephesus some of the women, conscious of their undoubted freedom in Christ, had raised themselves up as teachers, thus taking over that task from the men of the church. Here Paul was merely trying to redress the balance. He was not saying that women are inferior. In fact, to the Galatian church he had stated categorically that 'There is neither ... male nor female, for you are all one in Christ Jesus'

(Gal. 3:28). However, it is usually the task of the women to take the lead in bringing up the little children and in the running of the home.

Calvin could write, in the 1579 edition of his commentary, 'Let women study this lesson day and night that first of all they may play the housewifes.'[1] Earlier he had said, 'Let us learn ... that if a woman be among her household, and be busied about her children, to wipe them, and comb them, and dress them: or if she be a nurse and be up day and night, and suffer cold and heat to give them suck, if she bear it patiently knowing that this is God's good appointment, and he allows of it, this is a sweet smelling sacrifice to him.' And later he commends women for taking pains about housewifery, 'to make clean her children when they be arrayed, to kill fleas, and other such like'.[2]

Today we see things rather differently. But probably we would still say that the ideal situation is that the husband is normally the breadwinner and the wife the homeworker. Sometimes, because of employment difficulties, the roles are reversed, but that does not alter the principle.

Paul also teaches that it is not only wives who must be submissive to their husbands: children should be submissive to their parents (Eph. 6:1); employees should submit to their employers (Eph. 6:5); citizens should submit to government authorities (Rom. 13:1-7; 1 Peter 2:13-17); wives should submit to the Lord, and to their own husbands (Eph. 5:22); and we should all 'submit to one another out of reverence for Christ' (Eph. 5:21).

To the Philippians, this same apostle wrote, 'Do nothing out of selfish ambition or vain conceit, but in humility consider others better than yourselves. Each of you should look not only to your own interests, but also to the interests of others' (Phil. 2:3-4)

So, with all this in mind, we can see that 'Submission is recognizing God's order in the home and the church, and joyfully obeying it.'³ Submission is the key to spiritual growth. Above all, we must all submit ourselves to the Word of God. The Scriptures are very clear at this point.

One Christian young lady challenged me on this rather 'old-fashioned teaching'. I had to say to her, 'If you don't agree with what I am saying, then your argument is not with me, but with Paul and Peter — and ultimately with God himself, who wrote the Bible. The only way to avoid these conclusions which I am teaching is to rip these verses out of your Bible.' At the time of writing, she is still wrestling with this point — not wanting to disbelieve the Bible, but wondering why the Church of England now allows women priests and why Salvation Army officers' wives have always been able to preach in their meetings.

However, to concentrate upon the Scriptures, we see that the woman's role, generally speaking, is to 'learn in quietness and full submission' — as, indeed is the case with each one of us (male, as well as female). We must *all* have quiet minds when we come to hear God's Word. That means that we should not find fault with what God is saying to us.

Another young lady also challenged me at the same meeting as the one I have already mentioned. Although she too was unhappy with this teaching that the women should 'learn in quietness and full submission', her conclusion was: 'I don't like it, but I have to accept it because it is the Word of God.'

In writing these things, I am not saying that everyone should necessarily agree with everything that a preacher says. We must never forget that preachers are fallible human beings, and they can make mistakes. So they have to be careful that they do not lead people astray. To minister the Word of God is a very serious matter. It should not be done without earnest thought, prayer and preparation, because eternal realities are being handled every time the Bible is faithfully preached.

Women must not be teachers

This is clear from this passage, yet merely to state it, without any explanation, is likely to make three-quarters of all Sunday School teachers want to resign, but that would be to misunderstand what is being said here. The context in this passage is public worship. Paul elsewhere tells us that women can teach other women (Titus 2:3-4). It is obvious to all who know their Bibles that women can, and must, teach their children the truth of God. Paul reminds Timothy how that from infancy he had known the Holy Scriptures (2 Tim. 3:15). Who was it who taught him these things? Obviously his mother Eunice and his grandmother Lois attended to these duties (2 Tim. 1:5). That, after all, was the normal task of all Jewish women; they taught the little ones the Word of God.

But it goes further than that: not only can women teach children, in certain circumstances they can teach men as well! An illustration of that is found in Acts 18:26 where we read that Aquila and Priscilla invited Apollos into their home 'and [both of them] explained to him the way of God more adequately'.

So what Paul is saying here is that a women 'must not be an authoritative teacher of doctrine in the church ... she should not exercise dominion over men'.[4]

When I was preparing to preach on this passage I asked a good friend of mine, who is a lady canon in the Church of England ministry, what she thought it meant. She had no hesitation in telling me that it referred to a particular local situation at Ephesus, which no longer applies to the church today. She said, 'There were some women there who were obviously getting very domineering, and Paul needed to correct the balance; so he had to order that the women should not teach.'

But there are a number of difficulties with that answer. First of all, we should be very wary of saying that any part of the Scriptures does not apply to us today. The whole of the Bible is God's Word. This is why Paul wrote to Timothy, 'All Scripture is God-breathed and is useful for teaching, rebuking, correcting and training in righteousness, so that the man of God may be thoroughly equipped for every good work' (2 Tim. 3:16-17).

Secondly, Paul says a similar thing to the church at Corinth (which lay many miles across the other side of Aegean Sea from Ephesus). If the women had to remain silent in the churches, then they obviously could not teach in public worship (1 Cor. 14:34).

But the most telling reason why we can see that Paul is not just dealing with a difficulty in the Ephesian church is that the apostle gives us two illustrations from the book of Genesis to show why women should not teach in an authoritative manner — certainly in services of public worship.

He refers his readers to the creation and the way that Adam was formed first, before Eve. We can see, then, that Paul is talking about the order in which these things happened. He is not talking about importance; he is referring to roles. We can illustrate this by examining the way in which the army structures its discipline. A colonel is higher in rank than a private, but that does not necessarily mean that the colonel is a better person than the private; in God's eyes they are both equal. The difference is that the colonel has to bear more responsibility than the private.

If we keep these things in mind we can gain a clearer understanding of the teaching that Eve was made as 'a helper' for Adam; she was taken out of the man (Gen. 2:20,22). We can conclude from this that, although husbands and wives should always discuss things with each other and decide on their actions together, when no unanimity can be reached then it is the husband who ought to take the responsibility for making a decision. That is often where things go wrong. So many husbands fail to act responsibly and sometimes this can indicate that a marriage is beginning to break up. I suspect that very few wives really like to always 'wear the trousers'! Almost all of them want their husband to be 'a man' and face up to things which need to be done.

Another reason that Paul gives for men taking the lead is because all of us are affected by the Fall. He gives us the teaching: it was the woman who was deceived by Satan. Eve was misled by a snake. Adam was not fooled by a snake; it took a woman to lead him astray! Eve ate the forbidden fruit and in doing so she sinned against God. But then she seduced Adam into also disobeying God's command. In other words, instead of being the follower (as was her role), the woman became the leader. And look where her leadership led: it led Adam into sin! Paul is not teaching that women always lead men astray, he is merely saying that, in certain circumstances it is God's order that the man should take the lead. This is why Adam took the responsibility for bringing sin into the world; Eve is not blamed. Elsewhere Paul tells us that 'In Adam all die' (1 Cor. 15:22; see also Rom. 5:14).

We must not deduce from this that women have no part to play in the work of the church — far from it. Where would the missionary societies be without women workers? Where would so much of the work of God be without the ladies? However, women must not have authority over men.

A positive note

Paul ends this section by pointing Timothy to the glorious role of women. He says that they are to be good mothers. Not all women are called to this task. Some are set apart by God to lead a single life and some married women are not able to have children, but Paul points to the principle. God always has his exceptions. There have been women preachers who have been mightily used by God. And Calvin, who believed that the woman's place was in the home, points out that Deborah was not only a prophet, but also a ruler in Israel![5]

However, generally speaking, women will be kept safe in child-bearing (there certainly have been exceptions to this) and they will receive spiritual blessing through the joy of bringing children into this world, and in bringing them up in the ways of God. This is conditional upon their continuing **'in faith, love and holiness, with propriety'**. The women Paul speaks of here had already been saved; they were believing members of the church at Ephesus. But, he says, they will receive much more blessing as they bring up their children in the training and instruction of the Lord.

Some of these children will be males, who will grow up to be great teachers and preachers in the church of Jesus Christ. It is as these women live faithful, loving, holy lives, filled with good sense, that they will be a great influence for good on many who take notice of the way in which they live their lives. Therefore, each one of us, male and female alike, young and old, should always seek to continue in faith, love and holiness with propriety!

Men and women are equal, but they are different from each other — and I, for one, say, 'Praise the Lord!'

11.
The role of elders

Please read 1 Timothy 3:1-7

The way in which a church is organized can make a tremendous impact upon those who are outside of its membership. If a church is run in a chaotic way it not only leads its members to grumble and misunderstand things, but it causes confusion to unsaved people and brings disrepute upon the name of Christ. When Paul wrote that 'Everything should be done in a fitting and orderly way' (1 Cor. 14:40), he was saying that God is a God of order. There is, therefore, no excuse for poor arrangements in church affairs; Paul gives us very clear instructions on how churches should be run.

We only read in the New Testament of two offices in a local church. These have been ordained by God so that God's people should be cared for efficiently. These leaders are called 'elders' (called 'overseers' in the NIV) and 'deacons'. The letter to the church at Philippi is addressed to them: Paul writes 'to all the saints in Christ Jesus at Philippi, together with the overseers and deacons' (Phil. 1:1).

These two groups of people are dealt with in the first part of 1 Timothy 3. In verses 1-7 the apostle especially speaks about the qualifications and duties of elders and in verses 8-13 he writes about deacons (and maybe deaconesses).

Except for churches like those of the 'Brethren' persuasion, almost all other evangelical churches have made a distinction between the pastor, or senior pastor, and the other elders. Usually this minister is paid (preferably on a full-time basis) and the remaining elders fulfil the office in their spare time. However, Paul makes no distinction here, or elsewhere, between those who are pastors and those who are other elders. Timothy and Titus were certainly pastor/teachers but they did not have responsibility for only one congregation. No other pastors are mentioned individually in Paul's letters.

The importance of elders

Paul starts with the second of his five 'trustworthy sayings'. When we looked at 1:15 we saw the first one; the others are found here in 3:1 and in 4:9; 2 Timothy 2:11 and Titus 3:8. Nowhere else in the New Testament does Paul use this expression. These statements appear to be sayings which were in common use among the believers at that time.

'If anyone sets his heart on being an overseer, he desires a noble task' (3:1). As we have already noted, the NIV translates this word 'overseer', but other translations of the word are 'superintendent' or 'bishop' (AV/NKJV). These officials are people who have responsibility for the spiritual care of the people in the churches. We can learn more information about them in Acts 20:17-38, where Paul called for the leaders of the church at Ephesus to meet with him. After speaking to them about his work as an apostle he gave them this injunction: 'Keep watch over yourselves and all the flock of which the Holy Spirit has made you overseers.' In calling them 'overseers' he is indicating that they were shepherds who were in charge of a flock of God. Another word for shepherd is 'pastor' and that is why ministers are often called pastors. Sometimes these men are called 'elders', and sometimes they have the description 'overseers'.

When we turn to the Greek words which Paul uses, we see that the first one is transliterated from the Greek as *'presbyter'* (and often translated as 'elder'). This word is applied to someone who is older and well-respected. This is why the men who were in charge of Jewish synagogues were called elders. We have a similar word in Britain which is used for those who have responsibility for the ordering of the affairs in large cities: they are sometimes called aldermen (which is a rendering of 'elder men').[1]

The other Greek word which can be translated 'elder' is the one from which we get the word 'episcopal', meaning 'having to do with a bishop'. This word is also often translated 'overseer', or 'pastor'. It describes the work these people do. However, we need to realize that in New Testament times a bishop was not a senior pastor who was in charge of lesser clergy in other churches (as he is today). In those days each church had several bishops within its own membership. In fact the Authorized Version of the Bible translates the letter to the Philippians as one which was written to 'the bishops [plural] and deacons' who had responsibility in Philippi. So we could say of a church today which, for example, has four elders and seven deacons that it has 'four bishops' in its leadership team.

Paul says that 'If anyone sets his heart on being an overseer, *he desires a noble task.*' He means that it can be good to have ambitions provided that we are setting our hearts upon something which is honourable. However, we must remember that no one should become an elder just to satisfy his pride. Those who wish to be thought of as important have no right to be appointed as elders. Much more rigid requirements are to be observed.

In New Testament times it was not an easy thing to become an elder of a church. In those days church leaders were often persecuted, and many of them were even executed because of their position in the church of Jesus Christ.

Furthermore Paul says that eldership is not a job for a lazy man. This is why he says that those who aspire to be overseers desire 'a noble task'. He uses a word which means that it is an onerous task; it is hard work. Being an elder of a church requires much mental, physical and spiritual stamina. The job is not for the faint-hearted, nor for the hard-hearted. Often a pastor will find it difficult to sleep at night because he is worrying very deeply about a difficult relationship within the church fellowship. All elders need much strength to be able to cope with the many problems which the devil hurls at them.

The qualities of elders

Paul commences with a blanket statement which covers almost everything else which he has to say. Notice these solemn words: **'Now the overseer must be above reproach'** (3:2). He does not say, 'An overseer should never be criticized.' That often happens. I have sometimes caught myself wrongly criticizing other pastors for the way they are conducting themselves. What Paul is saying is this: 'There must not be anything in an overseer's life which can justifiably give cause for criticism.' This is not to say that overseers must be perfect, or that they must possess in exceptionally large measure all the qualities neeeded for them to carry out their responsibilities well. Pastors are not supermen; no one fits into that category perfectly in every particular. What Paul means is that elders should strive to live blameless lives. They should be morally pure. They cannot carry out their tasks efficiently if they behave improperly.

Paul then lists some of the qualities an overseer ought to be displaying in his life. Many of these characteristics are also required of deacons. They, too, should live lives which are honouring and glorifying to Christ — just as every Christian man, woman and child should do.

Firstly, Paul tells us an overseer should be **'the husband of but one wife'** (3:2). This does not mean that he must be married. However, in those days, it was very unusual for a respected older man not to be married. Some scholars translate this verse as 'someone who has only been married once', but Hendriksen and other commentators say that there is no justification for reading the text in that way.[2] The Scriptures do not require widows or widowers to remain unmarried when their partner dies (see Rom. 7:2-3).

What Paul is teaching is that overseers should live morally upright lives; they should be faithful in their marriage bond with their one wife. They must not adopt the pagan fashion of immoral relationships with other women, and they certainly must not have more than one wife at a time — that is, they must not be polygamous.

There is one thing which is beyond dispute: this passage clearly teaches that an elder must be a man. We know that eldership is male because we are told here that these men have authority in the church and, as we have already discussed in our consideration of chapter 2:12-14, women are not permitted to exercise such authority.

The next requirement which Paul lays down is that overseers should be **'temperate, self-controlled'** and **'respectable'** (3:2). A pastor should be one who always acts sensibly and exercises wise judgement. Some versions of the New Testament use the word 'sober' here. What these words tell us is that an elder must be able to control his behaviour. He should never act in a foolish way which would cheapen the office he holds. He must have a serious attitude to the work of the ministry. And he should be orderly in his thinking and his living because a disorganized pastor is an inefficient minister. The Greek word for 'respectable' is the same one which is rendered 'modestly' in connection with women's clothing in 2:9.

Paul also says that overseers should be **'hospitable'**. In those days inns were dangerous, expensive and immoral places. So no travelling believer would want to stay in such a place. This is why Paul says that church leaders should set an example in showing hospitality to other believers. The word 'hospitality' means 'loving strangers'. Where I live in southeast England we are very reserved, and we tend to be suspicious of people we do not know. But that is not the case in other countries. I visit evangelical churches in Greece regularly and many of the church buildings there have guest-flats built into their upper floors. They have been put there to provide a place for visiting believers who are travelling through the area. In Greek the word for 'guest' and the word for 'stranger' are the same— *'zenos'*. William Barclay wrote, 'The Christian leader must be a man with an open heart and an open house.'[3]

After mentioning teaching, Paul then lists some of the things which a pastor should not be guilty of. He should **'not [be] given to drunkenness, not violent but gentle, not quarrelsome, not a lover of money'** (3:3).

While alcohol is not condemned in the Bible, *drunkenness* most definitely is. No Christian should ever have so much to drink that he loses control of his senses. All pastors, and indeed every believer, should always be self-controlled (3:2). What a disgrace it would be for a well-known Christian to be convicted of driving a car while over the alcohol limit! Likewise no believer should ever be the cause of encouraging anyone else to drink strong drink. How would it rest on your conscience if a young man or woman became an alcoholic mainly (or even partly) because he or she once saw you drinking?

Another thing we must bear in mind is that drunkenness can often lead to violent behaviour (as sometimes occurs at football matches). Paul is most insistent that an elder should never be violent; rather he should be 'gentle'.

Also he should not be *quarrelsome*. It is not only drink which makes some people quarrelsome. C. H. Spurgeon once said to some ministerial students, 'Don't go about the world with your fists doubled up for fighting, carrying a theological revolver in the leg of your trousers.'[4] It seems that some Christians go out of their way to find theological fault with others. Warren Wiersbe helpfully reminds us: 'Pastors should be peacemakers, not troublemakers... Short tempers do not make for long ministries.'[5] Certainly pastors should fight for the rights of others but they should not be quick to stand up for their own rights. Many years ago I heard a pastor say that one morning a young man burst into his study saying, 'I'm nothing but a doormat in this church.' The pastor then stood up, stretched out his hand to the young man and said, 'Well, from one doormat to another, Good morning. Sit down.'[6]

Paul added words to this effect: 'Don't let *the love of money* control your thinking and behaviour' (see 1 Tim. 6:10).

Then he declared that an elder must **'not'** be **'a recent convert'** (3:6). In the Authorized Version this is translated as 'not a novice'. The word actually means someone who is 'newly planted'. When we plant a new bush, or a small tree, in our gardens we often have to put a strong stake next to it, and tie the plant to it. This is because strong winds will buffet the tree and may damage it (even when it is several years old). So a newly planted tree needs to be well supported, and allowed to grow and put down its own roots firmly into the ground.

Elders, then, must be people who have had time to mature as Christians. They must have had the opportunity to learn some of the challenges (as well as the joys) of church life. A pastor friend of mine, who had been in the ministry for many years, told me that he once ignored this injunction and appointed a fairly new, but very keen, Christian to the eldership. He told me, 'He didn't stand the test, and very soon he resigned.' When a new convert is appointed to leadership in a church he sometimes becomes puffed up with pride and, like Lucifer, he falls (see Isa. 14:12, AV).

There is one final quality which is required of an elder: he must be someone who has **'a good reputation with outsiders'** (3:7). If, for example, an elder does not pay his bills on time, then he will bring the name of the church into disrepute. If he is constantly carping and complaining about things, he will give outsiders the impression that the church takes a purely negative view of everything. If he keeps himself apart and will not speak to anyone who does not belong to the church, then he is creating the impression that believers think themselves superior and have no concern about the welfare of those outside.

A good elder is one who is held in high esteem by the people of the world as a man of integrity and a good citizen. Be sure that the devil will do everything in his power to prevent any of the believers from having a good name in the district where they live. This is one of the reasons why Peter tells us that the devil goes around like a roaring lion, looking for someone to devour (1 Peter 5:8): he wants to bring down the people of God.

The work of elders

In all of this long list, Paul only mentions two duties of elders. They must have the ability to teach the Scriptures, and they must have a concern to care for the people of God. A pastor must be **'able to teach'** (3:2). Paul does not say that a pastor must be able to give scintillating sermons, or that his preaching must be such that it uplifts his hearers. The only requirement he gives is that the overseer must be 'able to teach' (see also 2 Tim. 2:2,24). Naturally no one wants to hear boring sermons, and there is certainly a place for an uplifting one. But there is room, too, for sermons which cause people to stop and consider their ways. Pastors should be very diligent in their work of teaching the Word of God. Warren Wiersbe says, 'The pastor who is lazy in his study is a disgrace in the pulpit.'[7] A pastor wants to see people come to the foot of the cross and find salvation in Christ. Then he desires to feed them upon the teaching of the pure Word of God so that they will grow up to be mature Christians.

Secondly, a pastor must have a constant concern for the welfare of the people whom God has placed under his care. This is why Paul says, **'If anyone does not know how to manage his own family, how can he take care of God's church?'** (3:5). I once heard about someone being turned down as an elder of a church because his children behaved badly during the services. This seems a little hard on a very gifted, and otherwise well-qualified man, but being an elder of a church means being able to give wise and firm leadership. If a father is not strong enough to be able to ensure that his own children behave as they should, then that is a very clear indicator that he is likely to be weak in his care of the people of God. Hendriksen says, 'Though authority must be exercised, this must be done "with true dignity", that is, it must be done in such a manner that the father's firmness makes it advisable for a child to obey, that his wisdom makes it natural for a child to obey, and that his love makes it a pleasure for a child to obey.'[8]

Facing up to the challenge

How can anyone measure up to these demanding standards? First of all, an elder must examine this list very rigorously and ask himself, 'Am I qualified to be a pastor?' Obviously many will fail in some respects, but these high standards must be aimed at. An elder must have a pastor's heart. He must have a constant concern to care for the people of God. He weeps when he sees any believer growing cold in his relationship with the Lord Jesus Christ. He grieves when any of the congregation are showing signs of losing their first love for the Lord (Rev. 2:4).

An elder also should be constantly encouraging all of the people of God to live up to these standards of godliness which are outlined in this passage. He will ask himself these questions: 'Is my behaviour above reproach? Am I temperate, self-controlled, respectable and hospitable? Am I gentle? Do I have a good reputation with those outside of the church?'

Finally, he will make sure that he has a loving concern for the welfare of all of God's people — wherever they are.

12.
The role of deacons

Please read 1 Timothy 3:8-13

I once belonged to a church where a lady stood up in a business meeting and said, 'If you're not a deacon's wife in this church you're nothing.' She obviously felt neglected. She assumed that nobody cared about her and that she did not count. Unfortunately it can sometimes happen in churches that people do get overlooked. Often the reason is that the minister has so many things to deal with that he cannot be aware of the needs of everyone.

But whose job is it to go and drink tea with lonely old ladies in the afternoon? Who has the responsibility for doing the shopping of someone who is shut in all day? And how can arguments over these more social ministries be sorted out?

That was a problem which the early church had to face. As the number of believers increased, certain groups of people began to feel that other sections of the church were getting preferential treatment over them. One difficulty which came to the fore quite quickly was a disagreement over the distribution of food aid. Apparently it was felt by the Greek-speaking Jews (who had been born outside of Palestine) that the wives of the Hebrew-speaking Jews (who had preserved their Jewish culture and customs) were getting a larger share of the food hand-outs than they were.

Obviously a call had gone out for the leaders of the church to arbitrate in this dispute. We can imagine what some people were saying to their leaders: 'Here, Peter, can you stop preaching for a minute and come and sort out this dispute? They will take much more notice of what you say than they will of me — after all, you are an apostle.'

It is clear that this kind of thing could not carry on without some arrangements being made to deal with people in a compassionate and fair way. The apostles were very stretched in their work of instructing the people in the Word of God because so many were coming to faith in Christ! So, in the end, the twelve convened a meeting.

The reason for deacons

The apostles addressed the believers and spoke sound sense: 'It would not be right for us to neglect the ministry of the word of God in order to wait on tables' (Acts 6:2). Everyone could see that they had more pressing work to do. It was not that they considered that the distribution of food was unnecessary, or unimportant. They knew that it had to be done. In fact it would be very wrong if it was not done. But the problem was: who was going to be responsible for carrying out this task? Who would make sure that these matters were dealt with fairly? The apostles had the authority to do it, but if they spent time doing that, then they would have to leave off instructing the new believers about the truths of the Christian faith.

Moses had the same problem in his day, when the people came to him from morning till evening so that he could sort out their disputes. However, Moses had a wise father-in-law, Jethro. Jethro saw that Moses was wearing himself out with their comparatively minor problems, so he said to him, 'What you are doing is not good. You and these people who come to you will only wear yourselves out. The work is too heavy for you; you cannot handle it alone' (Exod. 18:17-18). Jethro therefore advised Moses to 'select capable men from all the people — men who fear God, trustworthy men, who hate dishonest gain — and appoint them as officials over thousands, hundreds, fifties and tens' (Exod. 18:21). The job of these people was to cope with the straightforward cases so that Moses could concentrate on the more difficult ones. The result was that Moses was able to stand the strain, and all the people who had come with a grievance went home satisfied.

While it is unlikely that the apostles had to deal with the vast numbers that Moses had to adjudicate between, the principle was the same. Because the apostles were occupied in sorting out comparatively minor difficulties, they were not able to get on with their real work. They were using their valuable time in dealing with problems which others were quite capable of resolving.

So they proposed a solution to the problem. They said, 'Brothers, choose seven men from among you who are known to be full of the Spirit and wisdom' (Acts 6:3). These could then lighten the load of the apostles by taking over tasks like 'waiting on tables'. By this they meant all the practical affairs of the church.

The apostles were not saying that these practical things were beneath them and of less importance. They were merely saying that others were more fitted to deal with them. They themselves would then be free for other vital things, which they had been in danger of neglecting.

They said that if others dealt with the practical matters then they would be able to give their attention 'to prayer and the ministry of the word' (Acts 6:4). We have already seen that spiritual duties are primarily the responsibility of the elders in a church, and the work of 'waiting at tables' is the task of deacons. This passage does not directly call these seven people 'deacons', but it is generally recognized that these verses describe the calling of the first deacons. This is highly likely because the word 'deacon' means 'servant' (literally, 'slave').

The qualifications of deacons

At first sight there appears to be very little difference between the qualities required of deacons and those demanded of elders. This is why Paul says, **'Deacons, likewise, are to be men worthy of respect'** (3:8). He uses the word 'likewise' to link them with what he has been saying in verses 1-7. Deacons must have the same standard of spiritual life as the elders. The main difference is that elders must be able to teach, and they have a special responsibility to exercise a spiritual and caring rule over the people of God.

Deacons must be worthy of respect and they must be **'sincere'**. This means that they must have a wholesome attitude towards others. They should not say one thing to one person and something else to another. They must not 'kow-tow' to important people and ignore those who have no money or position in society (see what James has to say about this kind of behaviour in James 2:1-4). The word which is translated 'sincere' means that deacons 'should not be double-tongued'. They must not be like the parson of Bunyan's town of Fair-Speech; he was called Mr Two-Tongues. Mr Smooth-Man, Mr Facing-Both-Ways and Mr Any-Thing were also inhabitants of Fair-Speech. Deacons should not be like that. They should be people who are perfectly open, honest and sincere in all that they do, say and think. William Barclay says that this word means that deacons should be 'straight'.[1]

Paul also says that deacons should **'not [indulge] in much wine'**, nor should they be those who spend their time **'pursuing dishonest gain'** (3:9). Anyone who has too much to drink is going to be impaired in his judgement. There was a good reason why alcohol used to be called 'the demon drink'! Deacons, like elders, must remember that they are never off duty. If they drink any alcohol at all they must be careful how they use this dangerous substance and be aware that they might be leading other, weaker people, astray by their actions.

Next Paul mentions money. One of the tasks of deacons is to take charge of the care and distribution of the church's money to the poor and needy. To some people money is a temptation. If they have money belonging to others they are tempted to pocket some of it. John tells us about one occasion when Judas Iscariot complained about the expensive perfume which was poured over the feet of Jesus. He said, 'Why wasn't this perfume sold and the money given to the poor?' Then John gives us a revealing insight into the character of Judas. He tells us that Judas did not say this because he cared for the poor, but because he was a thief. 'As keeper of the money bag,' he had, and took, opportunity to 'help himself to what was put into it' (John 12:5,6). Someone has commented, 'Judas was not the last treasurer who betrayed his Lord for a few pieces of silver.'[2] This means that people elected to the diaconate must be scrupulously honest.

Another stipulation for deacons is that they must be men who are known to be spiritually-minded: **'They must keep hold of the deep truths of the faith with a clear conscience'** (3:9). In other words, they are required to be those who know and love the teaching of the gospel, the deep truths concerning the life, death and resurrection of Jesus Christ — the things which are sometimes called 'the mystery which has been revealed'. Those who do not know the Lord Jesus Christ as their Saviour have not yet been let into the secret. They have not experienced the joy of God's salvation and they are, therefore, unqualified to hold office in the church.

Paul is very serious about these things. He says that deacons must be people who have put these gospel truths into practice. For them, the Christian life is more than believing in a set of doctrines; it is living a life worthy of the name of Christ. It is keeping the faith with a clear conscience because they live holy and godly lives.

However, deacons must be put to the test. Paul does not mean that they have to pass a formal written examination before they can be appointed to office in the church, but that they have to be observed by all the members of the church to see whether they are suitable for the office of deacon. This does not mean that everyone should be spying on everyone else. On the contrary, the apostle is teaching that those who are appointed as deacons are to be those who have demonstrated, by the way they live, that they are worthy of that office.

I was once a member of a church where one of the young men dropped a hint that he and his wife might soon be leaving to join another church. When he heard this, the senior deacon (who was a businessman) said, 'Let's make him a deacon and perhaps he will change his mind about leaving us.' Although that might be a way of keeping good people in a firm, it is not a reason for making anyone a deacon. People have to prove that they are qualified according the scriptural pattern laid down here before they can join the diaconate.

So why does Paul not also say that elders have to be tested? I assume that he does not require this because most elders have first of all been deacons in the church. In any case, it is clear from the qualifications listed in 3:1-7 that before a person is called to the eldership he must have proved himself to be someone worthy of the office and capable of carrying out the onerous task of shepherding the people of God.

The work of women (or deaconesses)

Without changing the subject Paul speaks about the qualities of women workers in the church. The words which are

translated **'their wives'** can be rendered 'deaconesses' (or
'servant-women'). It is likely that this is the sense in which
Paul uses the word. If he had meant that those women who
were married to deacons automatically had an office in the
church, then why did he not also outline a role for the wives of
elders?

When we read the Scriptures we can see that women served
the early church in various ways. Phoebe is described as 'a
servant of the church in Cenchrea' (Rom. 16:1). In this passage
the word 'servant' is the feminine form of the word for
'deacon'. There are also records of how many other women in
the New Testament performed a role in the church similar to
that of the deacons.[3]

Paul tells us that these lady deacons are **'to be women
worthy of respect'** (3:11). They must be ladies who are
looked up to by all the members of the church. They are
required to live their lives in such a way that those outside the
company of the believers should think highly of them because
of their good works and seemly behaviour.

Furthermore, they must not be **'malicious talkers'**, but
'temperate and trustworthy in everything'. This is very
similar to what is required of male deacons (see verse 8). In
those days, and indeed today, women could visit certain
homes which it would be unwise for a man to enter. However,
they were required to be on their guard lest they get caught up
in doing the devil's work. The Greek word for 'not slanderous'
is *'me diabolous'*. This means that a lady deacon must not be
thought of as a 'she-devil'. She must avoid improper speech;[4]
some commentators suggest that women are more prone to
gossip than men![5] Whatever the case, all of us, men as well as
women, must be careful that we only speak that which is
helpful (Phil. 4:8).

The reward of deacons

'Those who have served well gain an excellent standing and great assurance in their faith in Christ Jesus' (3:13). No deacon should serve just to be well thought of, but those who serve the people of God faithfully receive the Lord's 'Well done, good and faithful servant' (Matt. 25:21,23). Their reward might be to go on to become elders, but they do not look for material rewards; they look for spiritual blessings in the work of the Lord. Because they have an excellent standing then they will also have 'great assurance in their faith in Christ'.

We are all called upon to be servants of Jesus Christ. We may never occupy a formal, public office in any church, but we are required to live our lives as servants of our Master. And we do that best by loving him, honouring him, living lives to his glory and helping our fellow-believers in their life of faith in this dark world.

13.
Upholding the truth

Please read 1 Timothy 3:14-16

People often seem lost today. They are wandering through this world not knowing what to believe, or whom to trust. What such people need more than anything else is certainty. Like children, they want to know where they stand. They want to know what they are allowed to do and what they must refrain from doing.

The sad thing is that the church does not seem to be able to help them. When they listen to church leaders on the radio or television they become more and more confused. No one seems to give any certain direction. What many harassed unbelievers need to know is how they can get through the next Monday morning. Instead all they hear about is the seemingly petty squabbles of the various churches. Someone who is desperate to learn how he or she can find security is not helped by a discussion on women priests, or whether gays and lesbians should hold office in the Anglican Church. Such a person wants to know what he or she should believe and where to find sound guidance on the pressing problems of life.

At the point we have reached in our studies we see that Paul is laying down instructions so that people might know how to conduct themselves in the church of the living God.

Correct conduct

Paul had been wanting to see Timothy and he hoped that his visit could take place soon. However, in case he became delayed he wrote down his instructions for Timothy. These were not mere suggestions; they were clearly orders which had to be obeyed. They had to do with the appointment of elders, deacons and deaconesses. Paul wanted his young missionary friend (and everyone else) to know how churches should be governed.

In verse 15 he gives a number of pictures of the church. First of all, he says that the church is God's family. Because all church members belong to a family, then it is important that they should treat their fellow members as though they were their own blood relations, or relatives by marriage. Paul gives some examples of how they ought to do this a little later in the epistle: 'Do not rebuke an older man harshly, but exhort him as if he were your father. Treat younger men as brothers, older women as mothers, and younger women as sisters, with absolute purity' (5:1-2).

How should we treat our families? We should see that they are cared for and their needs are met. We should make sure that they have good protection, shelter and clothing, and that they are fed properly. In a church family the deacons should look after the physical needs of the people and the elders should provide their spiritual needs. Warren Wiersbe comments, 'A church does not grow by addition, but by nutrition.'[1] God's people need to be fed with the pure Word of God. Correct teaching is absolutely necessary in the church of Jesus Christ. This is what every member should be concerned about. We should make sure that we attend a church where the unadulterated Word of God is taught in the church services, in the Sunday School, in the Bible studies and in every activity of the church fellowship. We should also make sure that we feed ourselves by our private study of the Word of God.

The correct basis

Paul goes on to use another picture. He describes the church as the **'pillar and foundation of the truth'** (3:15). The truth is what matters above all things and we need to be certain that what we believe to be the truth of God is indeed that which is found in the Scriptures.

If our religious beliefs are founded upon anything that is not in the Bible then we are likely to be wrong. There should be no room in the church of Jesus Christ for speculation. None of us should ground our beliefs upon sentimental reasoning. We should not base our doctrines upon tradition, common practice, or the reaction of the world. Instead we should plant them squarely and firmly on the teaching of the Bible.

It is wrong to think of the church as merely the repository of the truth. The church's task is to display the truth, or, as Paul tells us here, the church is the pillar and foundation (or bulwark) of the truth.

In the ancient world, the temple of Artemis (or Diana, to use her Latin name) was one of the seven wonders of the world. People came to Ephesus from all over the ancient world every year to take part in the great festival which was held in this huge temple. Among the prominent features of this edifice were the 127 pillars which held up its roof and each of which was the gift of a king.

Today you can go to the site of ancient Ephesus and see the spot where this temple once proudly stood, but now all that remains to be seen is a bog with an old stump of a pillar sticking out of the mud. Some idea of the strength of these pillars can be gained by examining the huge base of one of them which was brought to England at the end of the last century, and is now on show in a downstairs room at the British Museum in London.

Every one of these pillars was made of marble; some of them were even studded with jewels and overlaid with gold. The people who lived in Ephesus knew very well, then, how beautiful a pillar could be,[2] so they would have had some idea of what Paul was talking about when he described the church as 'the pillar ... of the truth'. As one of those ancient pillars was there to beautify the temple, so it is the task of the people of God to display the glories of the truth of God. They are also required to hold up this truth against all attacks, just as one of those temple pillars held up the roof of the building dedicated to Artemis (see 1:3-4).

When we think about what Paul was teaching we are forced to ask ourselves how well we, and the church to which we belong, are displaying the truth of God. How powerfully and how soundly is the genuine teaching of the Word of God being declared in our church? None of us has any excuse for saying, 'That is the work of the church leaders; we are not involved.' None of us has any right to say, 'Well, it's the pastor's job to do the teaching — and the Sunday School teachers, and the Bible class leaders, of course. It's nothing to do with me.' If we are saying that to ourselves, then we are disobeying God's commands. It is the task of every believer to study the Word of God, put into practice the results of our learning and then pass it on to other people.

However, the church is not only the pillar of truth, it is the foundation of truth as well. Foundations are what hold a building up, and bulwarks are what buttress it against ferocious elements. We need to ask ourselves, 'Is my life (as part of God's church) built upon the foundation of God's truth?' If it is not, then the church fellowship is being weakened. Solid foundations are vital for any building; so the church, and the efforts of its members, can only be effective if it is built firmly on the foundation of the truth of God.

Correct belief

Paul then wrote about the greatness of **'the mystery of godliness'** (3:16). The pagans were taken up with the greatness of the goddess Artemis. However, when many became Christians the trade in silver images of Artemis declined and this loss in sales was blamed on Paul and his preaching. The traders decided to stir up trouble for Paul and as a result a riot took place. Such a large crowd of people barracked Paul's friends that they were shouting in the Great Theatre at Ephesus for some long time, 'Great is Artemis of the Ephesians!' It is instructive to read Acts 19:23-34, while standing in that Great Theatre and looking down towards the left. There can be seen the *agora* (the market-place). It is easy to imagine the crowd rushing from their shops along the marble road and up into the theatre.[3]

This incident must have remained in Paul's memory for the rest of his life. Perhaps with this in mind, he writes to Timothy, now in Ephesus, about something much greater than the goddess Artemis. He speaks about the greatness of the mystery of godliness. In those days the pagans had many mystery religions. They were called 'mystery religions' because the followers claimed that no one could know the truth until he was let into the mystery to which they alone held the key. These religions were for a select few. However, the mystery of godliness which Paul declared was great and is one which is revealed to all who believe in the Lord Jesus Christ.

In chapter 2:2 Paul had urged that prayers be made that 'we may live peaceful and quiet lives in all godliness and holiness'.

He meant that a godly life is something which has been revealed in Christ. None of us should boast about our holiness. It is not our experiences of Christ's presence that we should be showing off to others, but the wonders of his grace. Hendriksen tells us, 'The more we know him, the better we will be able to discern the mysterious unfathomable character of his love and of all his attributes.'[4]

Then follows what is thought to be part of an ancient Christian hymn. It is about the Lord Jesus Christ but it makes no mention of the cross or the resurrection. This is certainly not because they are unimportant, but it may well be that they have been mentioned in other verses which Paul has not quoted and which have not been preserved for us.

Six statements are made about the Lord. The first, fourth and fifth are centred on this earth, and the second, third and sixth refer to heavenly exaltation. The hymn tells us that Christ was both fully human and fully divine, at one and the same time.

The hymn starts with the incarnation: **'He appeared in a body.'** This is what we especially remember at Christmastime: 'Veiled in flesh the Godhead see.' In human form God came down to this earth. 'He partook of our humanity.'

Secondly, it says that **'He ... was vindicated by the Spirit.'** Most commentators agree that this refers to the Holy Spirit. So how was Jesus vindicated by the Holy Spirit? There are three obvious ways. When Jesus was baptized the Spirit of God descended upon him like a dove and a voice from heaven said, 'This is my Son, whom, I love; with him I am well pleased' (Matt. 3:17). Then we can see that through his resurrection the Holy Spirit declared him to be the Son of God (see Rom. 1:4); and also when he ascended into heaven God sent the Holy Spirit to convict the world of 'sin and righteousness and judgement' (John 16:7-8).

Thirdly, this hymn says that Jesus **'was seen by angels'**. We have numerous accounts of the angels witnessing to Christ: at his birth (Luke 2:9-14); at his triumph over Satan's temptations (Matt. 4:11); after his ascension into heaven (Acts 1:10-11) and as they welcomed him back into heaven (Rev. 7:12).

Fourthly, he **'was preached among the nations'**. It was not just the Jews who were invited to enter into the joy of the Lord. All peoples received the invitation to come and find rest in him. This call still goes out today through the preaching of the gospel message.

Fifthly, he **'was believed on in the world'**. Through the preaching of the cross of Christ all sorts of men, women and children, from all the nations of the world, come to faith in him. It should be the task of all of God's people now to 'Go into all the world and preach the good news to all creation' (Mark 16:15). It should be their aim to do everything in their power to bring many to faith in Christ.

Sixthly, he **'was taken up in glory'**. At the end of all of his earthly ministry Jesus was taken up into glory. He was faithful in all that the Father gave him to do, and he entered into his glory.

We need to ask ourselves, are we faithful to our calling? If we are then we too shall be taken up to the glory of heaven and God's immediate presence one day.

The implications of being a member of Christ's church are not things which we should consider only on occasions. They ought to have a great impact upon the whole of our lives. Paul wrote to Timothy in order to explain how God's people **'ought to conduct themselves in God's household'** (3:15). Are we behaving as we are commanded?

14.
Combating false teaching

Please read 1 Timothy 4:1-8

What do you do when you come across people who are peddling false doctrines? Do you merely try to get rid of them as soon as possible, or do you try to show them the error of their ways?

Many of us find it difficult to be abrupt with such men and women because so often they appear to be very nice people; sometimes, too, they are very smartly dressed, which makes it more difficult to be rude to them. They also seem to have all the answers to the questions of life. They are not vague about what they believe, and when we question them they reply by giving us clear and concise explanations of their beliefs, as though they have learned them off by heart (which, in fact, they have).

But it is not only members of false sects who come to us with wrong teaching. Sometimes even among Christians people are found spreading unscriptural ideas. This is obviously the kind of thing that Paul had in mind as he wrote this section of his letter.

The fact of false teaching

God had warned that this kind of thing was going to happen. Jesus told his followers that 'Many false prophets will appear and deceive many people' (Matt. 24:11). Also Paul said something similar when he bade his final farewell to the Ephesian elders at Miletus. He told them, 'I know that after I leave, savage wolves will come in among you and will not spare the flock. Even from your own number men will arise and distort the truth in order to draw away disciples after them' (Acts 20:29-30).

However, in addition to these things, Paul seems to have received a special revelation from God about the imminent appearance of these false teachers. He told Timothy that **'The Spirit clearly says that in later times some will abandon the faith'** (by 'the faith' he means the body of beliefs which had been accepted by the apostles and the church). Paul had previously had experience of some people who had started well, but then they had turned their backs upon the teaching of God's Word. He mentions two such people at the end of his second letter to Timothy and says that they had caused him a great deal of heartache. First, there was Demas, who had deserted Paul 'because he loved this world' (2 Tim. 4:9), and then there was 'Alexander the metalworker' who, he said, 'did me a great deal of harm'. Paul's conclusion about this wicked man's behaviour was that 'The Lord will repay him for what he has done.' The apostle then goes on to warn Timothy, 'You too should be on your guard against him, because he strongly opposed our message' (2 Tim. 4:14-15). The message of the apostle was God's Word. Also, when Paul writes of 'later times', he means that whole period between the first and second comings of our Lord Jesus Christ (see Heb. 1:1-2).

What kinds of people are guilty of deceiving Christians? They are those **'whose consciences have been seared as with a hot iron'** (4:2). The picture here is of cauterizing. This was what was done to wounds which had been inflicted on the battlefield. The burning sealed off the gaping cut to stop it bleeding and to prevent infection from getting into it. It also had the effect of making the part which had been cauterized lose all sensitivity so that the pain was dulled.

So Paul was saying that those people who taught wrong doctrine knew what the truth really was, but instead of obeying God's Word they had deliberately and continually refused to listen to the voice of conscience within them. With their consciences sealed off they would be totally insensitive to correct teaching and behaviour.

Some commentators also think that the searing of these people's consciences means that they had the mark of Satan upon them; these are **'things taught by demons'** (4:1). The apostle called these people **'hypocritical liars'** (4:2). He meant that they were pretending to be teachers of God's truth while, in fact, what they were advocating was contrary to God's Word.

Not only did these false teachers propound wrong doctrines, they also advocated erroneous practices. They were deceiving God's people by implying that real Christians have little to do with this world. They were trying to build a race of super-spiritual Christians. They were saying that all bodily urges should be resisted. They were suggesting that the truly spiritual person does not need human companionship (4:3). For them, the celibate life was the one which is truly dedicated to God. They thought that it is only spiritual weaklings who give way to the needs of the body. In effect, they were saying, 'Sex is sinful — or only suitable for lesser mortals.'

But that is not the teaching of the Bible. They ought to have been teaching that the *misuse* of sex is wrong — desperately wrong — but marriage has been ordained by God. God blessed Adam and Eve and said to them, 'Be fruitful and increase in number; fill the earth and subdue it' (Gen. 1:28). The writer to the Hebrews states very clearly, 'Marriage should be honoured by all, and the marriage bed kept pure, for God will judge the adulterer and all the sexually immoral' (Heb. 13:4).

These hypocrites also said that people should **'abstain from certain foods'** (4:3). However, Paul said that this was nonsense because God has created these foods to be **'received with thanksgiving'**. In the Garden of Eden God had said to Adam and Eve, 'I give you every seed-bearing plant on the face of the whole earth and every tree that has fruit with seed in it. They will be yours for food. And to all the beasts of the earth and all the birds of the air and all the creatures that move on the ground — everything that has the breath of life in it — I give every green plant for food' (Gen. 1:29-30). God also revealed to Peter that he should not call impure anything that God has made (Acts 10:15; see also Mark 7:19).

Of course, we should remember that, like marriage, food should be used correctly. Paul was not saying that we all have freedom to gorge ourselves, or to eat unhealthy foods in the wrong proportions. He was saying that we should use marriage and food wisely.

How should we receive these things? We should receive them with thanksgiving. All those who believe and know the truth want to show gratitude to God for all of his good gifts to them. No one should just selfishly take everything that God gives to us. Prayer should surround our acceptance of every good gift which we have received from God. No godly Christian would ever consider being married without reading and considering the teaching of the Bible. No believer would want to be married without prayer being offered on his or her behalf. Even if the believing couple are married in a registry office then prayer and the reading of God's Word would take place at some other ceremony. When we eat our food we say grace — prayer is offered in thanksgiving for God's provision. The Word of God and prayer consecrate these things to God. Paul means that marriage, mealtimes and other good things are set apart for God's glory and for our benefit (see 2 Tim. 2:21).

The antidote to false teaching

When things are beginning to go wrong in a church then the elders must gently point out these things to the believers. Tact is needed. In verse 11 Paul tells Timothy to command and teach certain things, but here he says that wrong teaching must be pointed out **'to the brothers'**. By using the term 'brothers' he means all of the believers. 'He places the emphasis on love. Believers in the Ephesus community are brothers, members of Paul's (and of God's!) spiritual family. Paul loves them. God loves them.'[1]

A good pastor, who upholds the truths of the faith, will not 'wear hobnail boots' when he seeks to lead the people to whom he ministers away from error. He will remember that false teachers are very subtle and believers can easily be deceived by these men. He will also realize that often people become absorbed with one particular issue, to the detriment of all others, and that is the only matter they can think about. This happens especially to those who are young, or immature in the faith. But the minister who enters that situation 'with all guns blazing' is more likely to harden the views of his members who have embraced wrong teaching than to draw them away into the truth. When voices are raised, positions tend to be entrenched and people are less likely to admit that they are wrong.

In these verses Paul deals with both the negative and the positive. He says, **'Have nothing to do with godless myths and old wives' tales'** (4:7). He has already referred to those 'myths and endless genealogies' in 1:4. He now adds that they were godless. He means that these people were teaching things which were contrary to the true character of God. Also they had not backed up what they had said with the teaching of Scripture. He also refers to 'old wives' tales'. We have this expression in English too. Old wives' tales are things which have no basis in fact. They are silly superstitions which some old women try to palm off on to their neighbours or their grandchildren.[2]

How quickly certain people become involved in idle speculation on Christian topics! There are many things which the Scriptures do not make clear to us; so in these cases we should accept that it is not necessary for us to know all the details about them. How often, down through the ages, have people debated about the exact date and time of the return of the Lord Jesus Christ? Equally godly Bible-believing scholars have taken different positions on the timing of these events. I once heard a lengthy sermon entitled, 'Are there animals in heaven?' We are not told the answers to this kind of question, so it is futile for us to construct hypotheses about them. I cannot believe that anyone has ever been strengthened in his faith, or aroused to leave his sin and turn to Christ in faith, by listening to a sermon which takes such topics as its main focus of attention!

Rather than going off at a tangent about numerous philosophical problems, just to show how clever we are, or to exercise our powers of debate, Paul said that we should train ourselves to be godly. He meant that we should concentrate on the things that really matter to our Christian life and witness. Seeking to lead a holy life, to God's glory, is much more important than satisfying a purely intellectual enquiry.

Then Paul takes us, in our imagination, to the gymnasium. He says that physical training is of some value. And, of course, none of us has any excuse for neglecting bodily exercise. I did for the first fifty-two years of my life — until I took up badminton. Now I find it difficult to move quickly and smoothly because in the past I had not trained my body to do so. But Paul was not teaching that people should be so taken up with sport that they neglect everything else. He was putting the emphasis on training for godliness.

To illustrate what he means Paul uses the pictures of a young Greek athlete who is training for the Olympic (and other) games. First of all, an athlete is determined to exert himself to the utmost. And so, by God's grace and power, we too should spare no effort to attain our goal of godly living. Secondly, the Greek youth runs naked. Like him, we are also to disregard everything which is likely to hamper our spiritual progress. Thirdly, in order to complete the course the athlete is determined to keep his eye on the winning post. We too should constantly be aiming for the goal of dedicating ourselves wholly to God and fulfilling his will for our lives.[3]

However, we shall never fully attain our reward until we leave this earth and arrive in heaven. We should live our lives in the light of the prize which is ahead of all those who belong to Christ (see Phil. 3:12-14; 1 Cor. 9:24-27).

Who will reach that goal? Not merely those who have lived a good life, but those who had surrendered their lives into God's hands while they were here on earth. How foolish it is for any to think that they will go to heaven just because they did their best while they lived here on earth! The only way to achieve godliness in the life to come is to experience the value of it in this life. That means coming in humble repentance to the foot of the cross of Christ and laying the burden of our sin at his feet.

15.
Silencing criticism

Please read 1 Timothy 4:9-16

How well do you cope when people are criticizing you? It is not a pleasant thing to be aware that people are speaking against you — especially when you are doing your best, and things keep going wrong. Under such conditions some people just hand in their resignation and leave; they cannot handle the pressure of life and work. Others go quiet and refuse to say anything at all. They go around with a miserable look on their faces all the time. However, the most violent reaction to criticism comes from those who launch into a counter-attack. They not only vehemently defend their actions; they turn in anger on those who are speaking against them.

Obviously Timothy had received some criticism of his work. This had mainly sprung out of the fact that he was considered to be too young for the task of church leadership. C. H. Spurgeon, the great Victorian preacher, had the same kind of criticism levelled at him. When he was only twenty-one years old he became the pastor of a large Baptist church in London. On one occasion a lady who was shaking his hand at the door at the end of a service said, 'Mr Spurgeon, your ministry is so helpful and it does my soul good to hear you preaching the gospel with such power, but, oh, you are so young!' Spurgeon listened carefully to the old lady and then is reputed to have replied, 'Well, madam, I suppose if you give me time, I will grow out of that!'

Hope in the living God

To silence criticism we should put our hope and confidence in the living God and the teaching of his Word. We should never forget those sayings which encapsulate some of the great truths of the Christian message. Paul here gives the third of the trustworthy sayings which we find in this letter. It seems that he is referring back to what he has just said in verse 8 when he writes, **'This is a trustworthy saying'** (4:9) because he then goes on to speak of the value of rigorous spiritual training.

One of the ways in which we can be distracted from unkind criticism is to labour hard and strive after godliness. It is true that people will always find fault with God's servants, but we must make sure that there is no justifiable ground for their accusations. The devil will always try to lead us into ungodly ways, but we should strive to follow the Lord and the teaching of his Word in everything that we do. If we are concentrating on training ourselves to be godly we shall be too busy to become weighed down by unfair complaints made against us.

When I once asked the headmaster of a very large school how he coped with the increasing pressure of his work he said, 'I swim fifty lengths in the swimming baths each morning before I start work.' He added, 'While I am doing that I can think of nothing else but reaching the end of the bath. All my worries are forgotten while I am swimming.'

We too, shall not be dogged by miserable thoughts if we **'put our hope in the living God'** — and keep him before us. Many people in Timothy's day trusted in dead gods, but these could not help them. The fact that many worshippers gathered at the temples of false gods did not mean that these gods had any value. In the same way there are many today who are turned aside from the right way by false cults and sects; these people are pinning their hopes on things other than the living God. We should be those who worship the Lord. When we are feeling cast down let us remember that he is the only Saviour; no one else can rescue us.

Paul then reminds us that God **'is the Saviour of all men'**. He means by this that the Lord saves all men in the sense that he provides deliverance and preservation for them. The land of Britain was saved at Dunkirk in 1940 when vast numbers of our military personnel were able to return to this country. We were saved from Nazi invasion through God's great deliverance.

God also saves everyone in the sense that he gave up his life on behalf of all sorts and conditions of men. We saw that in chapter 2:6. But that does not mean that every man, woman and child will be saved from the fires of hell. Oh that it would! But the Scriptures declare in many places that those who go down to their graves unrepentant will not spend eternity in heaven. We know that during the time of Moses God saved a great multitude from Pharaoh's slavery in Egypt, yet Paul tells us that 'God was not pleased with most of them' (1 Cor. 10:5).

The same kind of thing occurs when we think of people being saved from the punishment of hell. God is the Saviour of all men; in a general sense everyone benefits from the blessings of God's common grace. However, God is only the Saviour of those who believe — in the special sense of washing away their sin and making them his spiritual children. The only ones who will be saved from the punishment of hell will be those who come to Christ believing that he is the Son of God, and casting themselves wholly upon his mercy. Paul says that Timothy is to command these things — as a military commander gives orders to his troops (see 1:1).

Set a good example

Another way in which Paul says that Timothy could silence criticism was to set a good example to others. Timothy must have been in his thirties — perhaps his late thirties — when Paul wrote this letter to him. However, by the standards of those days that was considered to be young to head up a church. Privately Paul had urged Timothy to examine what he believed, and also to put his hope in that teaching. Now he encourages him to show to others that he was capable of doing the work to which he had been called. He was to set a good example for the believers.

His private life

Timothy was to set an example in his private life. His *speech* must always be pure. This is good advice for all believers in every age. We should always be careful what we say. No Christian should engage in unhelpful talk. Elsewhere Paul says, 'Do not let any unwholesome talk come out of your mouths, but only what is helpful for building others up according to their needs, that it may benefit those who listen' (Eph. 4:29). Jesus also said that we shall all have to give an account of ourselves on the Day of Judgement for every careless word we have spoken (Matt. 12:36). Our prayer should be: 'Set a guard over my mouth, O Lord; keep watch over the door of my lips' (Ps. 141:3).

Timothy's *life* should always be exemplary. 'Paul was saying, let the way you behave, the way you go about your daily business, be such that people who were intending to criticize you would end up being challenged by your example.'[1]

Timothy was also to demonstrate *love* to other people. Criticism can be dispelled by showing love in return for unkind words. We should all have a deep love for our fellow believers. That may be comparatively easy, but Jesus says that we should even have a loving concern for our enemies (Matt. 5:43-47).

Timothy's objective should be to show to everyone his *faith in God.* As love to our fellow men and women shows our horizontal relationships (to other human beings), so faith in God exhibits our vertical relationship (to God our Father in heaven).

Timothy was also to set a good example in *purity.* His thought-life should be pure. How uncomfortable we would feel if all of our thoughts were displayed on a large screen for everyone to read! The Christian leader's motives should always be pure; we would feel very embarrassed if the reasons we did some things were known by other people. Indeed, every action which Timothy took should be pure. If he wanted to avoid criticism then he must continually live a life which was beyond reproach.

His public ministry

But not only must Timothy's private life be pure, he was also to set an example in his public ministry. He must not waste his time. Paul was hoping to visit him, but that did not mean that Timothy could do little work until the apostle arrived; he must remember his ministerial duties.

He was to devote himself **'to the public reading of Scripture'.** Many people could not read in those days. Therefore it was very necessary to have portions of the Scriptures (what we know as the Old Testament) read out aloud. The people would then hear the Word of God for themselves.

This injunction of Paul's reminds us that we should not be tempted to pare down the length of the Bible readings in our church services just because the passage may be difficult to understand or there are too many other items to fit into the meeting. The public reading of the Bible is still the most important part of any Christian worship service. Therefore we should give much more weight to what God says, rather than to a preacher's ideas.

Also Timothy was to devote himself to **'preaching'** (the word used is literally 'exhorting'). This is what Paul and his companions were invited to do at the public reading of the Scriptures in the synagogue in Acts 13:15. Exhorting would include warning the people against error (in doctrine and in morals). It would also include giving advice and encouragement.[2]

Timothy was also to devote himself to **'teaching'**. This would mean that the people should be instructed in the truth of God's Word. It does matter what we believe. We should be able to give reasons for the hope we have within us (1 Peter 3:15). The exhortation would be aimed largely at the heart, but the teaching would be most concerned with the head.[3]

Use the gifts God has given

To silence criticism Timothy should use the gifts God had given to him. Paul tells him not to neglect the gift which had been given to him **'through a prophetic message'** (4:14). We have no other details here, or anywhere else, about this prophetic message, but we know that it was given to him when the elders laid hands upon him. This was the usual way in which any leader was commissioned to the service of God in the Jewish community. The laying on of hands was done to signify that authority had been given to that person on behalf of the whole company of God's people; the authority was transferred to him.

It would seem that Paul had also been present at the ceremony when Timothy was officially set apart for the task of leading the church in Ephesus (see 2 Tim. 1:6). We do not know what the prophetic message was, or which prophet (or prophets) gave it, but we do know that before the New Testament canon of the Scriptures had been completed there were prophets who exercised these spiritual gifts (see 1:18).

We do not know what Timothy's particular gift was, but it appears that it was in the area of spiritual leadership. Paul told Timothy to use these skills, the fact of his ordination and the prophecy given in connection with him, to silence those who were criticizing him. Whatever the particular gift was, Paul required Timothy to exercise it. The same thing applies to all of God's people today: those who do not use their gifts may well discover that, eventually, they will lose them.

Not only was Timothy to make sure that he did not neglect this gift, he was to **'be diligent in these matters'**. Paul obviously means that he should take care about the way in which he lived and the public work which he performed. These things mattered above everything else. Timothy was to **'give [himself] wholly to them'**. A minister is paid so that he can spend his time in prayer, the study of the Bible and in the pastoral care of the people. He must not waste his time. If he does so, then any criticism he receives could well be justified.

Paul encourages Timothy to let everyone know how much progress he has made in his pastoral abilities. Success in the ministry (as with everything else) comes about after much hard work. No one can be a good pastor without the calling of God and the power of the Holy Spirit upon his work. But the minister who starts to preach a sermon without having properly prepared both himself and his message is, as one pastor put it, 'nothing but a lazy tyke'.[4] It is hard work preparing a spiritual address, and the faithful preacher spends many hours doing it. Personally I do not find study easy, so I have to force myself to stay in my study until something worthwhile has been achieved. I find it much more enjoyable to go and talk to someone rather than remaining at my desk or computer.

Great attention should be paid by the pastor to his life and his beliefs. Paul put it so clearly when he told Timothy, **'Watch your life'** (4:16). The world is always watching and waiting to trip up any believer who is not behaving as he should. Paul also says, **'Watch your ... doctrine.'** He means that preachers should study the Bible very carefully. They should ensure that everything they teach is based firmly upon the Word of God, and not on men's ideas, or reasonings.

In John Blanchard's book, *Whatever happened to hell?* he quotes a theologian called Clark Pinnock who wrote, 'It just does not make sense, to suppose that, alongside the new creation, tucked away in some corner of it, there exists a lake of fire with souls burning ceaselessly in it.' John Blanchard comments that if we base our doctrine upon what makes sense, rather than on what the Scriptures teach, we are disregarding the truth of God.[5] Before I preach I try to check each of my sermons through thoroughly to see if I can find scriptural justification for what I am intending to say. If I cannot find any then I put a line through the whole sentence (or maybe the whole paragraph).

Finally, Paul writes that if a pastor perseveres in holy living and sound doctrine he will bring the blessings of salvation to himself and to all of the congregation. Salvation has many aspects. When we are born again we are saved for all eternity. No one can rob us of that. But we need constantly to keep ourselves pure from the world and from Satan, and we do this when we concentrate on living for Christ's glory, believing the truth of the gospel.

Paul exhorted the Philippian believers, 'Continue to work out your salvation with fear and trembling' (Phil. 2:12). This does not mean that we earn our eternal salvation because of our good works. It means that we all need to work hard at living close to God. Holy living and holding sound beliefs are expressions of our salvation. Our spiritual growth and progress in the Christian life are an evidence that we belong to God. Calvin tells us that through the diligent preaching of the gospel, by men, God chooses to bestow salvation on sinners.[6]

16.
Caring for the family

Please read 1 Timothy 5:1-2

People sometimes complain about the church they attend. They say things like, 'I don't find anyone helps me in that church,' or 'No one has visited me for the past six months.' At the same time others may say of the same church, 'I belong to a lovely, caring fellowship; I couldn't be happier worshipping there.'

How do people view the church? Do they see it as a largely irrelevant organization which is concerned mainly with perpetuating ancient traditions? Or do they see it as a community of people who love God and care for one another?

There are different kinds of needs

Some people consider that they are self-sufficient. They think there is nothing wrong with their lives. They are aware that other people have problems, but they are seldom conscious of their own inadequacies.

But no one is perfect, and every one of us needs to be corrected if we are going astray. Just because a person has passed his advanced driving test, for example, it does not mean that ordinary drivers should not warn him of dangers on the road ahead.

In this section of Paul's first letter to Timothy he refers to the needs of different kinds of people.

Older men

Timothy was a comparatively young minister, but that did not mean that he had to keep quiet when older men were behaving incorrectly. He had been called by God to be a leader in the church at Ephesus; therefore, it would be quite wrong for him to remain silent when anyone was going astray, even if that person was a respected older man.

This is why Paul encourages Timothy to take action in such circumstances. When necessary it was his responsibility to reprove an older man if he was behaving in an unscriptural way. In fact Timothy would be failing in his duty if he said nothing, and the older believer might well end up in a bad way spiritually.

This kind of situation could not have been easy for Timothy to handle. He had a big problem. Jewish tradition and teaching were very strong in laying down that older people should always be treated with great respect. Indeed, every kind of society in those days required that older people should have great honour bestowed upon them. In view of that, how could Timothy reprimand someone who was much older than himself?

Paul gives him some very careful instructions on how to deal with such a situation. First of all, he tells him what he was *not* to do. He was not to act **'harshly'**. This means that he was never to behave in an arrogant manner. Whatever action he took, it should be done without raising his voice, losing his temper, or behaving in any way disrespectfully to the older man. He should always remember the instructions given in the Scriptures, such as, for example, 'Rise in the presence of the aged, show respect for the elderly and revere your God' (Lev. 19:32).

Then Paul tells Timothy *what he should do*. He was to exhort the older man **'as if he were [his] father'**. The Ten Commandments say, 'Honour your father and your mother' (Exod. 20:12). This is something which is sadly lacking today — especially in Western society. I suppose, if challenged about this, some children would say that they no longer honour their parents because they have lost all respect for them. They may feel that their mother and father have let them down in some way. That sometimes does happen. Or they may feel that their parents have given them unsound advice, and they no longer trust their judgement. However, even if these things are true, the Bible teaching remains that children should always respect their parents, even when they cannot accept their counsel.

Timothy was to bear all this in mind when he corrected any older man who belonged to the people of God. Then Paul explains how he should deal with this older brother. He says that he must **'exhort him'**. In this context that literally means that Timothy should take the older man on one side and have a quiet, gentle word with him. In fact, in the first instance anyone (of whatever age and sex) who is doing wrong should be rebuked *gently* — and in private. It is only if the person refuses to mend his ways that a more public rebuke is needed. That is what Jesus taught in Matthew 18:15-17. However, if the older man is a gracious believer and the young pastor deals with the matter sensitively, then all should be well. Ajith Fernando writes, 'When an elder, who is a sincere person, is admonished in this way, he will realize that the correction comes not from a desire to throw one's weight around but from a just motive. So he will take the leader's word seriously and without dismissing it as one of the zealous excesses of an inexperienced young upstart.'[1]

Younger men

Younger men also need to be chided on occasions. Timothy was especially aware of that because he was a young man too. But although he was comparatively young in years, he was to make sure that no one looked down on him because of his age (4:12). He had been appointed as a leader in the church at Ephesus and he therefore had the authority and the responsibility to correct those who were veering from the straight and narrow pathway. Paul gave him this charge: 'Preach the word; be prepared in season and out of season; correct, rebuke and encourage — with great patience and careful instruction' (2 Tim. 4:2).

But just because he had the power to rebuke those who were wrong, it did not mean that he was to order other young men around as though they were mere private soldiers in an army of which he was the general. Peter wrote to his fellow elders, 'Be shepherds of God's flock that is under your care ... not lording it over those entrusted to you' (1 Peter 5:2-3). We all know that young men sometimes behave as though they know all about everything. But, on the other hand, young men do have valuable insights on occasions (see Acts 2:17). Even though young men 'often show impatience with other people treating them as though they are inferior',[2] yet they, like the older men, are also to be treated with great respect.

They are to be dealt with **'as brothers'**. The picture here is of a family. Paul speaks of older men who must be regarded as fathers, younger men who should be treated as brothers, older women who ought to be cared for as mothers and younger women who should be looked upon as sisters. 'Blood is thicker than water,' is a well-known saying. This means that relatives stick up for one another — even if they do not get on particularly well together. So when a young pastor has to censure someone who is of a similar age, he should deal with him as if he were his brother. In fact, in the family of Christ we are all brothers and sisters. William Barclay wrote, 'Those who are Christians can never be strangers to each other; they must be brothers in the Lord.'[3]

Older women

Paul said that when Timothy had to speak to an older woman about her behaviour he must treat her as he would his own mother. In Jewish life the mother plays an important role. Not only does she look after the home and care for the children, but she also has the spiritual education of the children in her hands. While fathers and the older boys went to the synagogue on Friday evenings (the Jewish sabbath commences at sundown on Friday evening, and lasts till the Saturday evening), the Jewish mothers prepared the sabbath meal. It is the mother who offers the sabbath-day prayers at the beginning of the special meal on Friday evenings. Every Jewish boy would have been instructed to give special affection to his mother. The book of Proverbs tells us that 'A foolish man despises his mother' (Prov. 15:20). Mothers were treated with special respect and affection in Jewish society.

Younger women

There sometimes arose situations where younger women needed to be visited. When Timothy had to make such visits, Paul counsels him to treat these younger women **'as sisters'**. They were never to be thought of as silly young women. Just as Timothy should never let anyone despise him because of his youth, so he, in turn, should never look down on any of the women just because they were young. He was to deal with them as though they were part of his own family, his own younger sisters in fact.

But there was something else that Timothy must be careful about. He was to behave wisely when in the presence of someone from the opposite sex. There has been many a young minister who has started off well, but has ended up bringing shame on the cause of Christ. This has come about because he has not treated the younger lady he has visited with absolute purity, as though she was his sister.

It is often said that a young minister should take a chaperon with him when he visits a young lady who is on her own. All Christians should 'abstain from all appearance of evil' (1 Thess 5:22, AV). There may be nothing wrong in what he is doing, but it behoves all of God's people to 'bend over backwards' to avoid giving opportunity for tongues to wag. Hendriksen writes that **'absolute purity'** means 'in complete conformity in thought and word with God's moral law and is not to be restricted to sexual purity'.[4]

The whole family

Each one of us must remember that, if we have been born again, then we are members of the family of God. Unlike earthly families, the members of God's family should never fall out with one another. Unfortunately that does happen from time to time, and when it does it brings the cause of Christ into disrepute. Each of us has the responsibility to do everything within our power to maintain the family structure and the family love.

We should care for each other. Those who are older and more mature should help those who are younger and weaker. A family should be characterized by love, care, concern for each other's welfare and a desire to uphold the good name of the family of God. How it grieves us when we hear of believers falling out with one another, often over comparatively trivial things! How it must touch the heart of God when his children squabble with one another!

This is how we should all behave as members of God's family: those who are strong should help the weak and those who are going astray should be gently and tactfully brought back into the fold of God's love. Each of us should take to heart these words of Paul, which, are in fact, the word of God to his children.

In Titus chapter 2 Paul outlines further details of how the members of God's family should behave. There he says, 'Teach the older men to be temperate, worthy of respect, self-controlled, and sound in faith, in love and in endurance. Likewise, teach the older women to be reverent in the way they live, not to be slanderers or addicted to much wine, but to teach what is good. Then they can train the younger women to love their husbands and children, to be self-controlled and pure, to be busy at home, to be kind, and to be subject to their husbands, so that no one will malign the word of God' (Titus 2:2-6).

Over and over again the New Testament declares that we should treat each other with great respect. Paul was concerned that the Philippians should be likeminded. He enjoins them:

Do nothing out of selfish ambition or vain conceit, but in humility consider others better than yourselves. Each of you should look not only to your own interests, but also to the interests of others.

Your attitude should be the same as that of Christ Jesus:

Who, being in very nature God,
    did not consider equality with God something to be
        grasped,

but made himself nothing,
  taking the very nature of a servant,
  being made in human likeness.
And being found in appearance as a man,
  he humbled himself
  and became obedient to death — even death on a
    cross!
Therefore God exalted him to the highest place
  and gave him the name that is above every name,
that at the name of Jesus every knee should bow,
  in heaven and on earth and under the earth,
and every tongue confess that Jesus Christ is Lord,
  to the glory of God the Father
                                        (Phil. 2:3-11).

17.
Caring for widows

Please read 1 Timothy 5:3-16

When I was eighteen years old I was called up to do my National Service; for some fifteen years after the end of the Second World War all young men had to serve in the forces. After I had completed my basic training I was sent abroad to Nairobi in Kenya. During my sixteen months' tour of duty there were two Christian families who were especially kind to me. One family opened up their home to me so that I could visit their house whenever I was off duty and at a loose end. I was very grateful for their hospitality, but one thing worried me a great deal: how was I ever going to repay them for all their generosity?

As I thought about it I remembered hearing a radio broadcast by Chester Wilmot, one of the BBC's War Correspondents during the Second World War. I cannot bring to my mind what incident the reporter was telling his audience about but I do recall that it was something to do with a kindness shown to him by a soldier during the conflict. When he thanked the soldier he said, 'I will probably never see you again, so how can I ever begin to thank you?' The soldier replied, 'Pass it on, mate.' Older readers may well remember a song which goes,

Have you have had a kindness shown?
Then pass it on.

In 1 Timothy 5:3-16 Paul outlines for us his teaching on passing on care to others.

Responsibility to widows

A widow is someone who is bereft of a husband. The Scriptures have a great deal to say about widows. For example, Psalm 68:5 tells us that God is 'a father to the fatherless, a defender of widows'. In Bible times widows were in a very difficult situation. There was no such thing as Widows' Benefit available from the state, so a widow had to do what she could to fend for herself. Her plight was even greater if she had no children to work for her.

The Gospels show us how tenderly Jesus dealt with widows. We can see this in the care the Lord showed to the widow of Nain (Luke 7:11-15). She had lost not only her husband, but her only son as well. So this poor lady was in a very sad state. She had received a double blow. Because her only son had died, she had no one on earth to provide for her needs; there was no breadwinner in the house. In those days some widows who could find no legitimate way of earning money were driven to prostitution.

A widow was entirely dependent upon the help of others. She was certainly in a dire situation if she had no other relative to provide for her. She was then a widow who was **'really in need'**. Paul uses this simple phrase three times in this chapter (5:3,5,16).

The apostle points out to Timothy that the Christian community has a responsibility to care for any such widows among their number. Unfortunately people like this can get overlooked today. In some countries they can claim money off the social security system, but even so this is not always enough to meet all of their needs. Others may be so shy and so sensitive that they refuse to take what they think of as 'charity'. This is one of the reasons why it is the church's responsibility to see that the needs of widows are met. I heard about a church which was very active in preaching sound doctrine, but where the elders were unaware that in the congregation there was a widow who had several children and little money to pay for their food and clothes.

It is for this kind of reason that deacons have been called into being; their job is to find out what the needs of the people really are, and to meet those needs as well as they can. Indeed, it was over the very question of the provision for widows that deacons were appointed in the first place (Acts 6:1-3).

However, it is not only finance that widows need. Even more pressing than this may be the desire for companionship, or advice on practical or spiritual matters. Even if they have children, widows often discover that their sons and daughters are too busy with their own affairs to spend time with their mother.

For these and many other reasons, Paul told Timothy to **'Give proper recognition to those widows who are really in need'** (5:3). These are the ones to whom the church has a special responsibility.

Children should care for their widowed mothers

Children owe their mothers are great deal. How sad it is when we hear of mothers (and fathers) whose children will have nothing to do with them! These are the very people who should be facing up to the responsibility of meeting the needs of their widowed mothers. They have a duty to repay them for all the sacrifices they have made over the years, to provide for their education and their welfare when they were young. However, Paul took this principle even further: he said that grandparents are to be repaid as well! (5:4).

Such behaviour **'is pleasing to God'**. It is one of the ways in which children can put their Christian faith into practice. If we really want to commend Christ to the world, then we must obey his commands. God said, 'Honour your father and your mother' (Exod. 20:12). If any of us fails to do that then we are not only letting our parents down, we are also bearing a bad witness to the world. It is impossible to know how many people have been deterred from following Christ because a professing believer has failed to care for his or her loved ones. In fact, Paul said that anyone who does not provide for his relatives, and especially his immediate family, **'has denied the faith'** and he, himself **'is worse than an unbeliever'** (5:8).

But it is not only children who must provide for their aged parents; a woman (perhaps this means a fairly wealthy woman) who has widows in her family should also help those women who are in need (5:16). An example of this may well have been Lydia in Acts 16:13-15. She was obviously someone who had her own business, and a number of women in her household. It is possible that some of them were widows. What is clear is that Lydia provided for the needs of those in her household, whoever they were.

On the other hand, Paul is not advocating a 'scrounger's charter' where lazy people can get free food and provisions. He makes it clear elsewhere that everyone should do something to earn his or her living. These widows might not have been able to go out and work, but there were many household chores which they could do to lessen the burden on others who were busy with other things.

Paul's teaching is very definite: 'If a man will not work, he shall not eat' (2 Thess. 3:10). Clearly he is not saying that the unemployed should be left to rot. But just as certainly he is advocating that those who will not try to help themselves should not be a drain on the limited financial resources of the church (see 5:16). The church's coffers are not a bottomless pit, and the church should not be burdened with those who can legitimately obtain help elsewhere. On the other hand, a church which fails to pay its pastor adequately, so that he has to live on social security, is also violating the scriptural principle that 'The worker deserves his wages' (Luke 10:7). This means that we all have a responsibility to care for the welfare of all those who are less fortunate than ourselves.

Widows have a responsibility to Christ

Paul writes here about a **'list'** (5:9). No one really knows what this was, but it seems that there were some widows who pledged themselves to Christ in a particular way. The outcome of this was that they were set apart for special service in the church. This did not apply to all widows; only certain widows were qualified for inclusion on this list. They had to be over sixty years old; they must have been faithful to their husbands while they were alive; and they should have a reputation in the neighbourhood for good works. These included **'bringing up children, showing hospitality'** and **'washing the feet of the saints'** (following the pattern set by Christ in the upper room — John 13:4-12). This seems to mean that such a person had rendered humble service to travelling preachers, for instance. She would have been known as someone whose whole life could be summed up in terms of **'devoting herself to all kinds of good deeds'** (5:10).

However, younger widows could not be put on this list. This was because a younger woman might well marry again and, therefore, she should not pledge herself to this sacred work and then subsequently turn her back upon it just because she had found someone whom she could marry. Paul was not against the remarriage of these younger widows. In fact, he advocated it. He said, **'I counsel younger widows to marry,**

to have children, to manage their homes' (5:14). These things were all honourable aspirations.

What Paul was very unhappy about was those who promised to serve the church and then changed their minds (for whatever reason). Perhaps some younger women had been put on the list in the past and their lack of experience of life had proved to be a stumbling-block to some. It may have been that these younger widows had gone from house to house, with the object of bringing help and good cheer to the ladies whom they visited, but instead they had became gossips who did more harm than good (5:13).

Paul is not saying that all younger widows waste their time in idle talk, but he is saying, 'Do not divert your natural urges for a healthy married life into prying into other people's affairs.' To transfer this thought into today's situation, Paul would certainly not have been pleased to find believers becoming absorbed in all the sexual scandal which is so often emblazoned across many of our newspapers.

Then Paul writes about one final group of widows — perhaps we can call these the 'merry widows' (5:6). These are those who have lost their husbands and have not remarried. Whether to drown their sorrows, or to celebrate their freedom, we do not know, but these widows lived only for pleasure. And, although (unlike their husbands) they were alive physically, Paul says that spiritually they were dead.

It seems that these people had never been to the cross for Christ's salvation. Outwardly they were having 'a whale of a time', but inwardly they were far off from God. Anyone who is estranged from God must be miserable (deep down) even if he or she always appears to be very jolly in public. So if this group of widows were not real Christians, why does Paul write to Timothy about them? It must have been because they came within the orbit of the church in some way. Perhaps they attended some of the meetings. They probably believed that they were real Christians, yet it is evident that they did not have a living relationship with God. They were 'without hope and without God in the world' (Eph. 2:12)

There is no one more hollow than a person who thinks that he or she is a Christian, but is not; such people are at a great distance from God. The widow described in verse 5 has lost everything: she has nothing to lean upon, but God. She **'puts her hope in God'**. She knows that there is no one else to whom she can turn. He alone is her strength and stay. It is for this reason that Paul tells us that she **'continues night and day to pray and to ask God for help'**. She is like Anna, who was in the temple at the time when baby Jesus was presented to God: 'She never left the temple but worshipped night and day, fasting and praying' (Luke 2:37). People who live like that know that their help can come only from the Lord.

What a contrast this lady is to the widow in verse 6! The latter lives only **'for pleasure'**. Enjoyment is her god. Her motto is: 'Let us eat, drink and be merry; for tomorrow we die.' The sad fact is that one day she will die and, unless she repents and turns to Christ in faith, she will discover what an awful thing it is to die without Christ.

The church has a responsibility to such people. Paul said, **'Give the people these instructions, too, so that no one may be open to blame'** (5:7). 'These instructions' must mean all that Paul was teaching in these verses. Everyone has to accept responsibility for behaving correctly towards God and their fellow men and women. Anyone who refuses to obey the command of God is in danger — in grave danger. If ignorance of the law of the land is no excuse when we break it, then surely failing to observe God's law will place us under his chastisement.

18.
The care of elders

Please read 1 Timothy 5:17-25

No one likes being ignored. Even the most easy-going among us can feel slightly hurt if our needs are passed by as if we do not matter.

We have seen that Paul has been exhorting Timothy to care for all kinds of people in the church community. In chapter 5:1-2 he tells the younger man how to deal with the different kinds of people who make up the family of God; in verses 3-16 the apostle gives many instructions regarding the care of widows and in verses 17-25 he explains that elders should be cared for too.

This is an area which is often overlooked. The pastor and the other elders are so busy trying to meet the needs of all the people in their care that their own necessities are sometimes overlooked. So often there is no one who is willing, or able, to pastor the pastors. Some leaders of churches have become so depressed by the situation in their church fellowships that they give up completely. They feel that the only thing they can do is to shed all the burden of responsibility for running a church because they can no longer cope with the pressures of the work, and they leave the ministry.

It is specifically because of this kind of situation that Paul writes this section of his letter; he is concerned about the needs of the elders.

Honouring elders

Paul begins by speaking about the elders **'who direct the affairs of the church well'** (5:17). They do the job superbly. They are excellent ministers of the gospel. They work hard at it. They do not waste any time. They are very conscientious in carrying out all of their duties and they are well qualified for the work.

The apostle has already explained (in 3:1-7) what kind of people elders (or 'overseers') should be. These elders have passed very rigorous tests. They are those who have the right qualifications. They see that those who need spiritual discipline receive it, but at the same time that these wayward believers are dealt with in love. They make sure that the whole church functions smoothly. In fact Paul tells us that they 'direct the affairs of the church well'. They do not just sit back and say, 'Let's see what happens if we don't intervene in this situation.' They are personally active in governing the affairs of the fellowship.

While the overseers are all spoken of as one body in 3:1-7 and in Titus 1:6-9, here in 5:17 a distinction is made between them. All are spoken of as those who 'direct the affairs of the church well', all are 'worthy of double honour', but Paul then singles out for special mention **'those whose work is preaching and teaching'**. The word 'work' (hard work, toil) is emphasized as though this was a specific task for which these particular elders had been set apart. There is no suggestion that they were to be regarded as more important, or of a higher status, than the rest of the elders, who also had to be 'able to teach' (3:2), and able to 'encourage others by sound doctrine and refute those who oppose it' (Titus 1:9). These elders, whose work was preaching and teaching, are also mentioned in the plural. This does not necessarily mean that Paul was speaking about the one pastor from each congregation in the area around Ephesus; we certainly know that in the church at Philippi there was more than one overseer (Phil. 1:1).

The apostle says that each of these two groups of elders is **'worthy of double honour'**. Different commentators give various interpretations of this phrase. Some say that it means that elders who do their jobs well should receive double pay. However, that explanation does not seem to fit in with 3:3, where Paul writes that an elder should not be 'a lover of money'. In any case the word used here is 'honour'. It is the same word which Paul uses when he is talking about widows (5:3). There it is translated, 'Give proper *recognition* to those widows who are really in need.' So it would appear to mean that elders who oversee the church well should be honoured, first of all, because of the office they hold and then, secondly, because they do their tasks extremely well.

Nevertheless the element of money is not absent because Paul quotes twice from what he calls **'the Scripture'** (5:18). He refers first to Deuteronomy 25:4, which says that when oxen are used to thresh wheat they should not be muzzled. In other words, these animals should be allowed to eat some of the grain they are trampling under their feet. The reason for this is, surely, because they have earned a reward in recognition for all the hard work they are doing. Then the apostle quotes from a saying of Jesus. How did Paul know these words? He may have read them in one of the first pages of Luke's Gospel to be produced; perhaps copies were already being distributed. It is likely that this saying was already well known by the believers in the early church.[1] Whatever the case, Paul is teaching here that elders who work hard should be adequately remunerated.

This was not a 'payment by results' stipulation. The condition was that the elders who worked well should be fairly rewarded, and especially those whose work was preaching and teaching. The people must be taught the Word of God, and they must also be exhorted to apply that word to their own situations. A full-time elder should be paid, not for success in bringing in the crowds, but for faithfulness to the Word of God and expounding accurately and carefully the whole will of God (Acts 20:27). Paul wrote to the church at Corinth (to whom he had sent Timothy — 1 Cor. 4:17), 'It is required that those who have been given a trust must prove faithful' (1 Cor. 4:2).

The discipline of elders

'Don't shoot the piano-player; he's doing his best', is a saying which used to be heard when someone, who was doing his best, was being criticized. Sometimes people complain about their pastors. I suppose one of the most common grumbles which people make about their minister is this: 'He doesn't spend enough time visiting me.' Another complaint which is often made is that the pastor's sermons are too long, too repetitive and too full of 'padding'. Sometimes pastors are criticized for being too tactless in the way they speak to people. Others are faulted because they keep quiet when the people think they ought to 'sort out' someone. If vocal members of a congregation are unhappy with their pastor then they will find some reason why they think that he is not doing the job properly — a task for which they 'pay him'. It is true that on occasions complaints against pastors are justified, but that is not always the case. Good pastors sometimes have accusations made against them.

However, Timothy was not to listen to individuals who made numerous complaints against an elder. He was to realize that sometimes these charges would be made solely for malicious reasons. Timothy was to remember that the person in the front line of the battle is going to draw the fire of his enemy.

President Truman said, 'If you can't stand the heat, get out of the kitchen.' The people who lead churches are certainly going to be attacked severely if they are doing their work well. The sad thing is that it is often a church member who makes the most vicious attacks on the pastor. In such cases Paul outlines the principle which must be followed: **'Do not entertain an accusation against an elder unless it is brought by two or three witnesses'** (5:19). Sometimes an elder is found to be at fault. In such cases he should be spoken to about his behaviour. However, if that is the case then the pastor, or some other suitable person, must make sure that there are a number of people in the church who feel the same way as the one making the complaint. Only in such circumstances was Timothy to investigate the accusations.

Warren Wiersbe says, 'A church member approached me at a church dinner one evening and began to accuse me of ruining the church. She had all sorts of miscellaneous bits of gossip, none of which was true. As soon as she started her tirade, I asked two of the officers standing nearby to witness what she was saying. Of course, she immediately stopped talking and marched defiantly away.'[2]

However, if an elder should really be guilty of some misdemeanour, then action must certainly be taken. Matthew outlines the procedure to be followed in such cases (Matt. 18:15-18; see also 2 Thess. 3:6-16; 2 Tim. 2:23-26; Rom. 16:17-18; Titus 3:10). When an elder, who has great responsibility in the church, sins, drastic measures have to be taken and the rebuke which is given must not be 'hushed up'; it must be given **'publicly'**. Some commentators say that this means that it must be issued before the whole body of elders, but surely the whole force of Paul's statement means that the elder must be rebuked before all the members of the church.

This public rebuke must be given for two reasons. The first is *to bring the sinner to repentance*; that is always one of the reasons for disciplining a wayward church member (see Gal. 6:1). Secondly, this must be done in public *so that others will take warning* and not fall into the same error.

Paul then follows up this command with a solemn injunction. He charges Timothy, **'in the sight of God and Christ Jesus and the elect angels, to keep these instructions'** (5:21). He will use the same formula again in 2 Timothy 4:1. Paul reminds Timothy that not only do God and Christ observe what is happening, but the elect angels also witness these things. Paul had already mentioned the angels as being witnesses of Christ in chapter 3:16. This may well be because angels saw the Lord at his birth (Luke 2:9-14), his resurrection (Luke 24:4) and after he had risen from the dead (Acts 1:10).[3]

Furthermore Timothy was to act impartially and without showing favouritism. If an elder was to be disciplined, Timothy was not to let him escape the proper punishment because he was a good friend of his. Nor was he to receive a harsher punishment if he was not particularly liked by Timothy. Timothy was always to be fair and 'let the punishment fit the crime', regardless of his own personal feelings in the matter

The selection of elders

Elders are needed for the smooth running of churches. When I was rushed into hospital in the middle of the night in November 1991 with a suspected heart attack (which proved not to be so), the church did not abruptly come to a standstill. The remaining elders (and numerous other people) took over the running of the church, and the result was that everything went very smoothly. That is what should happen in churches when the pastor is removed.

However, new elders are needed from time to time to replace those who die, retire, move away or resign from office.

When this happens Paul counsels Timothy to take great care in the selection of further elders. There must be no hasty judgements made, but when a suitably qualified person is found (see 3:1-7) then Timothy is to see that he is ordained to this task. The way in which this was done was for the existing elders to lay their hands upon the new elder at a public service. This was to symbolize that he had been appointed by God and accepted by all of the people. But this act of appointment was not to be undertaken without due care. Paul has already told us in chapter 3:6 that an elder must not be a recent convert. No one should be appointed to this office who has not had time to mature, and prove that he is capable of doing such an important task. If Timothy appointed someone who was unworthy of the office then Paul warns him that he would take a share of the blame. This is why Timothy was to do everything he could to keep himself pure (see also 4:12; 5:2).

At this point Paul breaks off to give Timothy some personal words of advice. Apparently Timothy had been suffering with a bad stomach. Perhaps he had observed that there was much drunkenness in the area and he had decided to refrain from drinking any wine. But the problem was that the water was often polluted and if it was drunk in that state then it would result in upset stomachs. So Paul said to his young friend, **'Use a little wine'** (5:23). Wine, being fermented grape juice, was much purer than filthy water. The emphasis was upon '*a little wine*'; this did not mean that he could take a lot when he became well again!

Finally, the apostle resumes his remarks about appointing elders. He says that sins will often be noticed. Some men are obviously unsuited for the work of eldership because they do not want to live holy lives; others try to cover up their misdeeds. Paul says that these sins trail behind them. However, the important thing to notice is that there is a place of judgement awaiting all sinners (those who sin openly, and also those who try to keep their iniquity hidden). Those who stand before the judgement seat of Christ still in their sins will have to answer for these sins. They will have to recognize that they have sinned against God, who is holy, one who cannot look upon sin. The only destination for those who die in their sins is that dreadful place which Jesus called 'hell'.

What a joy it is, though, to be let into the secret that the Lord Jesus Christ died on the cross to take away the sins of all those who repent of their transgressions and turn to Christ in faith!

'In the same way, good deeds are obvious, and even those that are not cannot be hidden' (5:25). But when we stand before the judgement seat of Christ we shall not be able to say, 'Look at all the good I have done!' This is because our good deeds will never be enough to outweigh the enormity of our sin. Only as Christ comes and takes the load of our sin upon himself will any of us be made free from the guilt and power of our unrighteousness.

19.
The responsibility of slaves

Please read 1 Timothy 6:1-2

Just after the Second World War, when Test Cricket recommenced, the West Indies sent their team to England. At that time a new word came into most of our vocabularies. It was the word 'calypso', because all around the cricket grounds the West Indian cricket supporters improvised songs about the successes of their bowlers, Ramadin and Valentine.

During that period (I suppose I was about twelve years old at the time) I remember the excitement caused to us boys as a very expensive car was driven, very slowly, up the high street of the small town where I lived. All of us were very interested in this car, but the thing that I remember most was that the driver was a black man. I had scarcely seen a coloured man in those days, and the ones I had heard about I associated with the slaves of the cotton fields of the southern states of the United States of America. In all my twelve years I had never felt so resentful of anyone as I did of that smartly dressed West Indian who owned that spectacular car. It just did not seem right to me. I hope that I have now learned not to be so prejudiced against anyone, because of the colour of his skin, or of his social status.

Slavery

In the Roman world it has been estimated that there were something like 60,000,000 slaves. That meant that almost one-third of the people were in bondage. Slavery was built into the social systems of those days. Slaves had no rights of their own and they were often treated little better than cattle, or items of property.

A master (the word used of slave-owners is *'despotas'*, from which we get the English word 'despot') could treat his slaves however he liked, and no one could legally prevent him from doing so. They could be condemned to hard labour. They could be chained up, or severely lashed, branded upon their foreheads (if they were considered to be thieves or runaways), or even crucified.[1] There existed a Roman law which stated that if a master was murdered then all of his slaves could be examined under torture, and they could be put to death if they were considered to be guilty.[2]

However, that is not the whole story; slaves could also hold positions of high responsibility. Not only were they sometimes appointed as barbers, butlers and cooks, but the family physician might well be a slave.

So how did a person become a slave in the first place? Some were in this position because they were prisoners of war. Some were condemned men. Some became slaves because they owed a great deal of money which they had no hope of repaying. Some had been kidnapped, and then sold into slavery. Some had been sold as slaves by their parents, and many had been born into slavery because their mothers were slaves.

Slavery was a cruel yoke which bound the slave to his or her master. A yoke was a piece of wood which had been shaped to sit on the shoulders of two animals and so join them together as they ploughed a field; its use compelled both animals to move in the same direction and at the same speed. Jesus used the same word to describe the way in which his people ought always to be in close contact with him. He said, 'Take my yoke upon you and learn from me... For my yoke is easy and my burden is light' (Matt. 11:29-30).

So we see that slavery was an evil practice which eventually became outlawed in most civilized countries through the efforts of men like William Wilberforce in the last century. But if slavery was such an inhuman evil, why did Paul not condemn it? Several times he writes about slaves (see Eph. 6:5; Col. 3:22 - 4:1; Titus 2:9-10) but in none of these passages does he advocate that the slaves should rise up and seek to overthrow this iniquitous system.

Does this mean that Paul thought that, although it was wicked, nothing could be done about it? It would seem that this was not the case. However, there were various practical reasons why the apostle did not preach against this system. First of all, he knew that to urge slaves to rise up against their masters would only result in a blood bath. There have been numerous novels written in which slaves have banded together to free themselves from their yokes, and often these stories show that the slaves came off far worse as a result of their rebellion.

Paul was convinced that the best method to win people over to the ways of Christ was for believers to bear a good witness by living holy lives. This is why he enjoined Timothy to teach and urge slaves who had become Christians to serve their masters well (6:2).

Slaves owned by pagans (6:1)

Christian slaves should **'consider their** [heathen] **masters as worthy of full respect'** (6:1). This word, translated 'respect', is the same one which Paul uses of other groups of people. In chapter 5:3 the widows who are really in need are to be given 'proper *recognition*' (i. e. respect, honour). In 5:17, 'The elders who direct the affairs of the church are worthy of double *honour*' (or respect); and now we are told that Christian slaves are to 'consider their masters worthy of *full respect*' (or honour).

Paul means that these Christian slaves were not to treat their masters as their masters treated them, if their masters were cruel to them. The slave, for the sake of Christ, should consider his master worthy of all respect. He should behave in the way Christ taught his disciples to act. The Lord said, 'Love your enemies and pray for those who persecute you... If you love [only] those who love you, what reward will you get?' (Matt. 5:44,46). Earlier in the same passage the Lord taught them, 'Do not resist an evil person. If someone strikes you on the right cheek, turn to him the other also' (Matt. 5:39).

There was also another reason why slaves should respect their masters. It was **'so that God's name ... may not be slandered'** (6:1). God's name is often taken in vain in these days. For people to use the name of God as a swear word brings his name into disrepute. The name of God is holy. It stands for the whole being of God and, therefore, the name of God should never be blasphemed. We should do everything in our power to make sure that we do nothing to bring dishonour upon the Lord in any way.

Paul is also concerned that his teaching (the doctrine which had come directly from God, through the Lord Jesus Christ) should not be abused. How sad it is when the teaching of God's Word is treated as though it does not apply any more! Some people prefer to listen to 'so-called' theologians who tell them that the Bible has to be reinterpreted in the light of today's knowledge and understanding. This is the reason why many church conferences debate whether 'gay' men and women should be admitted to the leadership of the church. Presumably those who argue for this believe that Paul's clear teaching in Romans 1 does not apply any more. They say that this teaching has been superseded by one which says that faithfulness to one's partner (even of the same sex) is all that matters.

Slaves owned by Christian masters (6:2)

Paul next turns to slaves who are in the privileged position of being owned by true Christians. Here the relationship is different. In verse 1 the slaves were regarded as pieces of property owned by pagan masters. In verse 2 the slaves are still slaves and the masters are still masters. However, because both slave and master are Christians, they are brothers in Christ. Everything is different in this case. They both belong to the family of God and, in that sense, they are on an equal footing, so far as God is concerned.

But this does not mean that the Christian slave should show less respect to his Christian master than he would if they were not both brothers. No, Paul says that these must serve their Christian masters **'even better'** than they would a pagan master. The reason for this is because it should be counted as a great privilege to serve a fellow-believer; mutual love would flow between them. They would both be dear to each other. In Ephesians 6:5-8 Paul writes, 'Slaves, obey your earthly masters with respect and fear, and with sincerity of heart, just as you would obey Christ. Obey them not only to win their favour when their eye is on you, but like slaves of Christ, doing the will of God from the heart. Serve wholeheartedly, as if you were serving the Lord, not men, because you know that the Lord will reward everyone for whatever good he does, whether he is slave or free.' Likewise Christian masters are to treat their slaves in the same manner: 'And masters, treat your slaves in the same way. Do not threaten them, since you know that he who is both their Master and yours is in heaven, and there is no favouritism with him' (Eph. 5:9).

What relevance has this to us today?

We are all slaves of Christ. If we belong to him it is bcause he has purchased us with his own precious blood. We are owned by him and we should delight to serve him. We should gladly obey him, doing what he says and going where he calls us, because we know that he will equip us for every task that he sends us.

We should treat our heavenly Master with the very greatest of respect. We do that when we honour his name, by exhorting Christ in everything we do, say and think, and by living holy lives. We should always take great care to spend much time in the presence of our Master so that when we go out into our daily lives we may always reflect his glory.

We also treat our heavenly Master with great respect when we honour his Word. The teaching of the Bible should be our daily guide. We should be ever ready to uphold that teaching and defend it against all attack. To do that we need to spend much time prayerfully reading and studying it, and reading helpful Christian books as well.

And we should remember that we are living witnesses of Christ wherever we go. People are watching us. We should always seek to reflect the glories of Christ as we go about our daily lives.

20.
The lure of money

Please read 1 Timothy 6:3-10

Money is the root of all evil.
Money is the root of all evil.
Won't contaminate myself with it.
Take it away!
Take it away!
Take it away!

This is a song which was very popular when I was a boy. That was just after the Second World War, when everything was in very short supply. I suppose the song became well-known because most people did not have very much money, and to make themselves feel better they pretended that money was the cause of all evil and everyone would be better off without it. Naturally this song was sung very much 'tongue-in-cheek' because the majority of the population actually believed that if they had more money then many of their troubles would quickly be over.

The popular song, of course, completely misquoted the text of 1 Timothy 6:10 because Paul is talking about *the love* of money being a danger. The Scriptures recognize that we all need the wherewithall to buy food, clothing and shelter for ourselves and our families, but Paul is highlighting the fact that the person who takes a delight in acquiring more and more money tends to be a miser and a very miserable person.

However, that was not the only thing which was wrong with that song. Paul does not say that the love of money is the root of all evil. He says that it is **'a root of all kinds of evil'**. The Bible also calls bitterness a 'root' that will 'cause trouble' (Heb. 12:15). On the other hand, we do have many examples in the Scriptures where people behaved foolishly because they had set their hearts on acquiring more money than they needed. A rich young ruler went away from Jesus feeling very sad because the Lord encouraged him to give up his wealth (Matt. 19:22). Judas Iscariot betrayed his Master for thirty pieces of silver (Matt. 26:14-15; Luke 22:5); and Ananias and Sapphira told lies to protect their money (Acts 5:1-10).

In this section (6:3-10) Paul is writing to Timothy about the motives of certain false teachers who were travelling around the country, causing trouble in churches. He says that the reason they did this was for **'financial gain'** (6:5).

The character of false teachers

The Greeks were very fond of oratory. There were numerous speakers who went from place to place addressing the crowds on various topics. They would gather a number of people around them and ask their hearers to name a subject they would like them to speak about. The orators would then talk at great length upon the chosen theme, using beautiful words and phrases. They also used to give lessons to people who wished to develop the art of making speeches. The reason they did this was solely in order to earn as much money as possible. The more popular an orator was, the more money he collected. This may be one of the reasons why sometimes Paul would not take any payment for his services (see 1 Thess. 2:3-10).

Paul shows his concern that many people who were false teachers were going around the churches, pretending to speak in Christ's name. They were false because what they were teaching did **'not agree to the sound instruction of our Lord Jesus Christ and to godly teaching'** (6:3). The teaching which is sound (i.e. wholesome, healthy) is that which comes from Christ. This was the very doctrine which Paul and others were taking around to the churches and writing to them about. The apostles' teaching (see Acts 2:42) was what these early church leaders had received from the Lord (1 Cor. 11:23). We know that there were many other things which Jesus did and taught than those contained in the four Gospels. John tells us this (John 21:25). Also during the forty days between Christ's resurrection and his ascension the Lord appeared to the apostles and 'spoke about the kingdom of God' (Acts 1:3) This is 'the sound instruction of our Lord Jesus Christ' (6:3).

Yet, while the apostles spoke the truth, there were many who travelled around the churches speaking falsehood. Writing to the Galatian church, Paul said that this teaching was another gospel: 'I am astonished that you are so quickly deserting the one who called you by the grace of Christ and are turning to a different gospel — which is really no gospel at all. Evidently some people are throwing you into confusion and are trying to pervert the gospel of Christ. But even if we or an angel from heaven should preach a gospel other than the one we preached to you, let him be eternally condemned! As we have already said, so now I say again: If anybody is preaching to you a gospel other than what you accepted, let him be eternally condemned!' (Gal. 1:6-9; see also 2 Cor. 11:1-6).

False teachers went around claiming to be teachers of the truth. The reason they did this was because they were conceited (6:4). They were filled with a pseudo-intellectualism. They wanted everyone to think that they were very clever. They desired that others should look up to them and say (because they used long words and complicated arguments), 'Isn't he brainy? He is so gifted and skilled in dealing with such intricate matters!'

This is how Paul describes these people: with devastating simplicity he concludes that they 'understand nothing'. How sad it is that still today there are those who regard the gospel message as 'too simple' while they, who regard themselves as so intelligent, are heading for a lost eternity at an ever-increasing speed! Elsewhere Paul says that such people are 'separate from Christ ... without hope and without God in the world' (Eph. 2:12).

Phillip Jensen told of an incident which happened to a Christian lorry driver in the United States of America. This brother's vehicle broke down near the home of a millionaire. The very rich man kindly gave the driver a good breakfast. When it became clear that the lorry driver was a Christian the wealthy man said, 'I'm an agnostic.' The millionaire's wife was a little embarrassed by the word which her husband had used in front of such an ordinary man. So the millionaire asked the lorry driver if he knew what the word 'agnostic' meant. The lorry driver said, 'Do you want the dictionary definition or the truth?' The millionaire was caught a little off balance by this reply but he said, 'I'll have the truth.' So the Christian said, 'An agnostic is someone who, deep down in his heart, knows that there is a God to whom he is answerable, but pretends that he doesn't know, so that he can live the kind of life he wants to.' The rich man hung his head and admitted that that was exactly his position. He pretended to be an intellectual who was far above the claims of Christ. Yet he knew that, one day, he would have to stand before the judgement seat of the Lord.[1]

Secondly, the false teachers of Paul's day had an **'unhealthy interest in controversies and quarrels about words'**. In chapter 1:4 Paul had already spoken about these things. However, splitting hairs and making mountains out of molehills were not confined to people of Paul's day. There are always some people who love to argue over things that are not relevant to their particular cases!

The devil uses such tactics to stop people from thinking about the real issues of life. A man who knows that he ought to be right with God will often say something like: 'Before I can believe I must understand why God allows little innocent children to starve to death in places where war is raging.' I have an acquaintance who has been around many churches. Instead of getting his life sorted out, this man will occupy many hours of time asking believers questions like, 'What is the unforgivable sin?' or 'Did Demas ever return to the Lord?' These people are taking an unhealthy interest in controversies and quarrels about words.

Those whose views about Christ are mistaken will, sooner or later, begin to display unholy living. Wrong thoughts will lead to wrong actions. How up-to-date these letters are! A superior intellectualism leads to **'envy, strife, malicious talk, evil suspicions and constant friction between men of corrupt mind, who have been robbed of the truth'** (6:4-5). These people not only present intellectual arguments to those who listen to them in the debating halls (or the open air), but they squabble among themselves. These things are the 'products of fleshly minds, not the fruits of the Spirit'.[2]

It seems that these false teachers once knew the truth. They had an intellectual understanding of Christian teaching, but the gospel did not change their hearts. They had been robbed of the power of the truth. They were so 'completely occupied with themselves and their own interests that in their hearts there [was] neither time nor room for God and his revealed truth'.[3]

Finally, Paul tells us the real reason why they did so much 'preaching'. They **'think that godliness is a means to financial gain'** (6:5). They are just in it for the money. When we read the Christian press we cannot help but think that some people (a few preachers who become very rich) are doing this work with the intention of becoming famous and making a fortune out of their efforts. These people, who have wrong motives for preaching the gospel, do not understand what true 'godliness' is.

The contrast with humble believers

The quest for financial gain is not what characterizes the lives of real Christian men and women. The truly godly person is not interested in amassing huge sums of money. 'He possesses inner resources which furnish riches far beyond that which earth can offer.'[4] That is what real contentment is — a mind at peace with God. Paul has already told us, 'Physical training is of some value, but godliness has value for all things, holding promise for both the present life and the life to come' (4:8). The apostle knew what it was to be content (the word is 'self-sufficient'): 'I have learned to be content whatever the circumstances. I know what it is to be in need, and I know what it is to have plenty. I have learned the secret of being content in any and every situation, whether well fed or hungry, whether living in plenty or in want. I can do everything through him who gives me strength' (Phil. 4:11-13).

The godly person realizes that true riches do not consist of material things. When we were born we did not bring anything into this world, and when we die we shall take nothing out of it (6:7). As Job said, 'Naked I came from my mother's womb, and naked I shall depart' (Job 1:21). Our true riches are already in heaven, where Christ is (see Matt. 6:21).

Nevertheless there are certain basic essentials which everyone needs. These are food, clothing and protection. The Lord is not saying to his people that the needs of the body should be neglected. He is saying that believers should be content with the simple things of life. The humble, godly Christian is not someone who is constantly yearning after additional material possessions; he or she knows that these cannot satisfy the soul. The believer's contentment comes from knowing and doing the will of God.

The consequences of a life given over to falsehood

'People who want to get rich fall into temptation.' Pride goes before a fall. These men, who were so proud of their intellectual accomplishments, quickly went down the slippery slope. The apostle tells us that they **'fall into temptation and a trap'** (the word used means 'a continual falling') **'and into many foolish and harmful desires that plunge men into ruin and destruction'** (6:9). They wander from the faith (6:10); and they pierce themselves with many griefs (6:10).

The person who, above everything else, wants to get rich is faced with many temptations every day. There are always questionable financial deals open to those whose integrity has been seared; what Christian principles they once may have had are quickly pushed to one side.

Elders are told to be careful of the devil's trap (3:7). Here is a picture of a person who is chasing after riches. Once he falls he can be snared like an animal who has been caught and held fast in a trap. He will then find it very difficult to escape from that snare. 'When the devil sees which way their lusts carry them, he will soon bait his hook accordingly.'[5] **'The love of money is a root of all kinds of evil'** (6:10).

But money should not be our God. Some who live only to get more and more money eventually discover that they have **'wandered from the faith'** (6:10). When others look at them they see only successful, hard-working men or women, but inwardly they are those who crave only more money and more success in life. Their desire to build up their business, or advance up the promotion ladder at work, has taken control of the whole of their lives. Without realizing it they soon begin to neglect their families, their friends and, of course, their faith. They become obsessed with the love of wealth. They buy more and larger possessions in order to impress their friends and make themselves feel that they are successful and have 'arrived'. They spend more time with their colleagues, both at work and in their leisure time, than they do with their wives and children. They regard playing a round of golf with their boss as more important than taking their family to the seaside. Before they realize it they have a broken marriage on their hands and they discover that they have **'pierced themselves with many griefs'**.

The fact is that when a person loses touch with his God, then everything else quickly begins to fall apart. If the teaching of Christ and the commands of the Bible are no longer paramount in our lives then moral laxity can begin to creep in as well. How we need to guard our faith! For **'Some people, eager for money** [and power and prestige], **have wandered from the faith and pierced themselves with many griefs'** (6:10).

Few believers make a deliberate effort to abandon their faith. It just happens, very gradually. The sheer pace of life drives Christian things out of their reckoning. Without realizing it they wander off from the paths of righteousness. One person may become dissatisfied with the place where he lives; he feels that his children deserve to be brought up in a more select part of the town. For another person it may be that he finds that he can get overtime by working on a Sunday; he thinks that it will not matter if he misses church once or twice. But those who stay away from church occasionally discover that it becomes increasingly easy to be absent again and again. Soon attending church regularly seems to be an unnecessary burden. For such people it is almost a relief not to be faced with the teaching of the Word of God Sunday by Sunday. Once they stay away from the means of grace they find out that it is very difficult to get back into the habit of meeting with the people of God once again. However, ceasing to attend the church services is not their real problem; it is only a symptom of what is happening inside of them.

Paul is calling us all to be more devoted to our Lord Jesus Christ. We should not let things (money, power, or prestige) come between us and the Lord. We need to ask ourselves some searching questions. How precious is the Lord Jesus Christ to us? How much time we do spend each day speaking with God in prayer and listening to his voice? Is reading the Bible something which delights us, because we hear God speaking to us through it? Do you gather your household together each day to read the Bible and pray together as a family?

If we have the Lord Jesus Christ living within us by faith then we should be godly and contented people. Can we say, with Paul, 'For to me, to live is Christ and to die is gain'? (Phil. 1:21).

21.
Holy living

Please read 1 Timothy 6:11-16

We are not the kind of people we ought to be. God has called us to be holy, as he is holy (1 Peter 1:15), but, time and time again, we fail to live up to the standards which he sets for us.

We have in this passage some guidelines and incentives to holy living. These verses instruct us how to conduct ourselves in a way which is so honouring to the Lord that it causes other people to stop in their tracks and praise God because of our holy lives.

The need for holy living

Paul has just been writing about those whose god was money. They were men of the world who taught false doctrines (6:3), and they found fault with the sound instruction given by the Lord Jesus Christ. They were the kind of people who say, 'We must take what the Bible teaches with a pinch of salt. We are now more sophisticated than those who lived in the first century A.D.; we have grown up and have learned a great deal more than they ever knew.'

How foolish such talking is! How stupid it is to ignore God and go against the clear teaching of the Bible! Those people thought they were very clever, but Paul tells us that they were conceited and, in effect, they understood nothing (6:4). These men spent all of their time in futile pursuits. They had an unhealthy interest in controversies and quarrels about words. They engaged in envy, strife, malicious talking, evil suspicions and constant frictions. The spirit of the world controlled the whole of their thinking and behaviour. For them, everything came down to the selfish question: 'What can I get out of this, for myself?'

When we read the correspondence columns of evangelical magazines we can see that this same spirit is still at work, even among those who have faith in Christ and have a strong allegiance to the Scriptures as the inerrant Word of God.

The foolish thing about these people of Timothy's day was that when they had secured their objectives, they did not know what to do with them. They were just like some individuals in our own day who have obtained wealth, fame and the praise of men, and have made a name for themselves, yet they have been so miserable that they have been driven to commit suicide. The much-acclaimed author Ernest Hemingway did that. He had everything he desired out of life, but he realized that, in themselves, none of these things brought true satisfaction. He was merely a man of this world.

This is one of the reasons why Paul wrote to Timothy of the great dangers of worldliness: **'But you, man of God, flee from all this'** (6:11). The apostle was saying that there ought to be in Timothy's life a contrast with that of the men of the world. God's people are not to be men of this age. On the contrary, Timothy was to be a man of God. He was to be different from those who looked only to the world for their pleasures and satisfaction. This is why Paul described him as a man of God.

We can find this exact description given of the great saints of the Old Testament. Moses was called a man of God (Deut. 33:1); so also were Samuel (1 Sam. 9:6), Elijah (1 Kings

17:18) and David (Neh. 12:24). Does the fact that Paul called young Timothy 'a man of God' mean that there was something extra-special about him? Yes and no. Although he was timid and he obviously felt inadequate for the work laid upon him, none the less Timothy was still called a man of God. He was a man of God because God had called him into his service. It is true to the Bible, and also to Christian experience, that if God calls anyone to work for him (however ordinary that person might be) then God also promises to equip him for the work required of him. In the New Testament we see that men of God were not just special, important men, who had been endowed with great dignity and holy powers. We find that they were just ordinary Christians, who were seeking to serve God to the very best of their abilities. Paul was later to write, 'All Scripture is God-breathed and is useful for teaching, rebuking, correcting and training in righteousness, so that the man of God may be thoroughly equipped for every good work' (2 Tim. 3:16).

Timothy, as a man of God, was to flee away from all the worldly attractions which could hinder him in his efforts to be a man of God. He was not merely to turn his back upon worldly ambitions; he was to run away from them. How unscriptural it is, then, to hear about so-called men of God who revel in the applause of men!

However, Timothy was not just required to flee from worldly success; on the positive side he was commanded to **'pursue righteousness, godliness, faith, love, endurance and gentleness'** (6:11). When we first believed in the Lord Jesus Christ for salvation, we were accounted righteous. This is what Christ did for all of his people when he shed his blood upon the cross of Calvary: he took away the filthy clothes of our own self-righteousness and clothed us with the precious robe of his righteousness. If we have been truly born again, then we are saved, washed from our sins and made righteous in the eyes of God. But this righteousness is not of our own doing; it is the righteousness of Christ which he credits to us when we first trust in him as our Saviour (see Rom. 4:18-24).

Even though the righteousness of Christ is a gift, given freely to all believers, that is not all that is required of God's people. Believers are exhorted to 'pursue righteousness'. In other words, we must always be seeking to live in ways which are right, and these are the ways of godliness (see 2:2).

Then Paul speaks of a trio of virtues which are often mentioned in Scripture — faith, love and endurance (i.e. patience).

Faith is 'the confidence which enables believers to trust God in everything'.[1]

Love is one of the fruits of the Spirit (Gal. 5:22). It is the basis of Christ's new commandment (John 13:34), but it is a love which is unrestricted. We should have a fervent love for God above everything else and we should extend a warm love to all of our fellow-believers, among whom we live, and with whom we worship and witness. We should also show genuine love to all of those around us who are lost and heading away from God. Our love should reach out to them as Christ's love did to us.

Endurance means remaining steadfast, whatever the trials and testings of our lives. Timothy must often have felt like giving up, yet Paul urged him to pursue faith, love and endurance. The apostle wrote to the young church at Thessalonica, 'We continually remember before our God and Father your work produced by faith, your labour prompted by love, and your endurance inspired by hope in our Lord Jesus Christ' (1 Thess. 1:3). All of God's people should work, labour and endure in that way. (The contrast is found in the letter to the church at Ephesus in Revelation 2, where the Lord commends the believers for their deeds, hard work and perseverance, but he makes no mention of faith or hope and rebukes them for having forsaken their first love.)

Finally, Paul says that Timothy should pursue *gentleness*. In this world it is so easy to get stirred up by all the things that are wrong around us. In spite of these things the man (or woman) of God should always seek to show a gentle spirit in all his dealings with each of his fellow men and women. Jesus was 'gentle and humble in heart' (Matt. 11:29); we, too, should try to copy our Master in this respect.

The way to holy living

To live a holy life and seek to display righteousness, godliness, faith, love, endurance and gentleness does not mean that we have to allow everyone to 'walk all over us'. We are indeed to fight, but not for our own rights: rather, we should fight for God's rights. We should **'fight the good fight of faith'** (6:12).

Life is a battle, but it is a battle against sin, Satan and this world. All three of these will try to gain our allegiance on every possible occasion. But we must fight the good fight of faith relentlessly. At the end of Paul's life he declared, 'I have fought the good fight' (2 Tim. 4:7). He meant that he had sought to uphold all the teachings of the Christian faith continually, despite all the opposition which was thrown up against him. We too must live in the same way, however much our enemies try to prevent us from doing so.

A second thing which Paul said that Timothy must do is to **'take hold of the eternal life to which [he had been] called'** (6:12). He already possessed eternal life; he was given that when he first trusted Christ as his Saviour and Lord. However, just as he had already been clothed in the robe of Christ's righteousness, so he still had to strive after these things. His constant need was to remind himself that although eternal life was a future reward (which he would obtain in heaven), it was nevertheless something which he already possessed in the present. He had been called to eternal life (this is God's gift to

186 *Passing on the truth*

every child of God), and he had made a good confession of his faith in Christ.

Paul now urged Timothy to look back to that time when he had first made a stand for the Lord, and to be encouraged. It is a good and noble thing to testify to our faith in Christ publicly. All of our friends can gather to witness our good confession, and they can encourage us in our declaration of faith in Christ. This is a comparatively easy thing for us to do in these days, but imagine what it must have cost the believers in those days when almost the whole world was opposed to the gospel of Christ.[2]

Paul continued to encourage Timothy by reminding him of the **'good confession'** which the Lord Jesus Christ had made before Pilate when he was on trial for his life (6:13). At that time the Lord stood firm and bore witness that he was Christ, the Saviour (Matt. 27:11; Mark 15:2; Luke 23:2-3; John 18:37).

Timothy had to bear all of this in mind. He was to keep **'this command'**. Paul surely meant that Timothy was to keep the injunctions contained in this letter because these are all based upon the commands of Christ. If we really love Christ, then we will keep his commandments (John 15:10,14), and we will seek to live our lives **'without spot or blame'** (6:14).

The incentive for holy living

Christ is coming again. The reminder of this fact will surely encourage us all to live in ways that are honouring to God. Believers must keep living holy, godly lives right up till the time of Christ's coming. No one knows when this will be (6:15 — see also Matt. 24:36; Mark 13:32; Acts 1:7). However, it will be the great and glorious event at the culmination of all history.

Peter spoke of the destruction of this old world order. He said, 'Since everything will be destroyed in this way, what kind of people ought you to be? You ought to live holy and godly lives as you look forward to the day of God and speed its coming' (2 Peter 3:11-12).[3]

When Paul mentioned Christ's first coming, he led into a doxology — that is, a song of praise to God (1:17). Now, as he alludes to Christ's second coming, the apostle bursts forth into another doxology (6:15-16), but this one is an expansion of the first. He affirms that God is **'the blessed and only Ruler'**. 'The kings and rulers of the earth may think they have power and authority, but God is sovereign over all (Ps. 2).'[4]

God the Father is also **'King of kings and Lord of lords'**. He is supreme. These titles are applied to the Lord Jesus Christ in Revelation 17:14 and 19:16. He is immortal.

Not only is God not subject to death, he is life and the giver of life. He **'lives in unapproachable light'**. Timothy, like all of us, had to live in the darkness of this world, with all its sin and greed, but God lives in unapproachable light. This is a symbol of purity and holiness. No one can approach God because he is so holy, and all human beings are so sinful. Moses was privileged to see some of God's glory (Exod. 33:18-23), and John says, 'No one has ever seen God' (John 1:18). It is only in Christ that mortal man can see some of the glory of God. He is revealed in Christ.

It is to God, the Father, Son and Holy Spirit, and to him alone, that all honour and might can be ascribed. As we consider this passage, how does it make us feel? Are we measuring up to the challenges of it? Have we turned our backs upon the world and all of its attractions (which will eventually fade away)? Are we seeking to live holy lives? And are we encouraged when we look back to the time when we first came to embrace Christ as our Lord and Saviour and confessed him publicly?

22.
True riches

Please read 1 Timothy 6:17-21

'If I were a rich man...' — so sang Tevja, the poor Jewish Russian farmer who was the main character in the musical *Fiddler on the Roof*. I suppose we all day-dream from time to time about what it would be like if we had an abundance of money at our disposal. Of course, we would give some of it for the relief of need. We would see that our elderly parents and our young children were all catered for, and we would buy ourselves some of those luxuries of life which we had never been able to afford before.

Surprisingly, perhaps, almost the last thing that Paul wrote in this first letter to Timothy is addressed to those who really are rich. In 6:9 he had spoken about those who wanted to get rich, but now, in verses 17-19, Paul tells Timothy to issue commands to those who actually were rich.

What rich people should do

Paul addresses **'those who are rich in this present world'**. The first thing that the apostle says is that they are **'not to be arrogant'**. If they have managed to accumulate a great deal of wealth in this life, then they should not boast about it. They should not behave as though they were more important than

others who are less well off. 'There is nothing in this world
which gives a man any right to look down on any other man,
least of all his possession of wealth.'[1] However, if there are any
in a congregation who have inherited a fortune, or who have
been successful in business, so that they are now extremely
well-off, they should not let that make them behave as though
they were better people than the other church members. They
have no warrant to be 'high and mighty'. Rather they should
be humble (which is the constant injunction of Scripture —
e.g. Eph. 4:2; Col. 3:12). If God has blessed them with riches,
then they should be full of gratitude and praise to him for all
his goodness to them.

These people are not to put their hope in wealth because it
'is so uncertain'. They could lose their money as easily as
they gained it. It can be spent before they know it (this is what
the prodigal son did in Luke 15), or it can lose its value
overnight by being placed in investments which fail.

Not only is wealth uncertain, in itself it is not satisfying. If
they want real enjoyment (and there is nothing wrong with
that!) Paul urges them to **'put their hope in God'**, because he
'richly provides us with everything for our enjoyment' (see
Acts 14:17). We should take pleasure in the blessings of life
now, because life will end one day (Eccl. 2:24; 3:12-15,22;
5:18-20; 9:7-10; 11:9-10). Pleasure, which is wholesome, is
not condemned in the Bible. It is the *love* of pleasure, for its
own sake, which is denounced — as is the love of money
(6:10).

Rich people are commanded to do certain things. This is the
second 'command' which Paul gives in the two verses
6:17,18. Timothy is to **'command'** rich people **'to do good'**
with their money. All kinds of people are exhorted to do good
in the Pastoral Epistles. Good deeds are required of all church
members (Titus 2:14; 3:8,14). Christian women are to do good

(1 Tim. 2:10; 5:10). Church leaders are to do good (Titus 2:7), and here rich people are urged to do good deeds. In fact, Paul makes a play on words: they are **'to be rich in good deeds'**. This idea of being rich is used several times in this section of the epistle.

The way in which these wealthy people are to do this is by being **'generous and willing to share'**. Jesus told a parable about a rich farmer who was not generous or willing to share his wealth with others. He said, 'I will tear down my barns and build bigger ones, and there I will store all my grain and my goods. And I'll say to myself, "You have plenty of good things laid up for many years. Take life easy; eat, drink and be merry"' (Luke 12:18-19). But God had other ideas. He said, 'You fool! This very night your life will be demanded from you. Then who will get what you have prepared for yourself?' (Luke 12:20).

Riches are given to us so that we can help others. He is a fool who thinks only of himself. This attitude is quite contrary to the whole teaching of God's Word. There is nothing wrong with money itself. What matters is what we do with it. Having money is a great privilege, so long as we remember that it is given to us so that we can share it with others.

However, although we may not be rich in monetary terms, we who know and love the Lord as our Saviour are spiritual millionaires. If we have Christ in our hearts, then we have all things; we are rich. In any case, many of those of us who live in a 'Western culture' are rich in material things in comparison with so many in the Third World.

Those who use money for the benefit of others will **'lay up treasure for themselves'**. Jesus spoke about this in the Sermon on the Mount. He said, 'Do not store up for yourselves treasures on earth, where moth and rust destroy, and where thieves break in and steal. But store up for yourselves treasures in heaven, where moth and rust do not destroy, and where thieves do not break in and steal. For where your treasure is, there your heart will be also' (Matt. 6:19-21). Those who are rich towards others are laying a good foundation for the coming age. They are doing the right thing, which is pleasing to God, and they will be rewarded, in heaven, for their good deeds. Those who follow God's commands, and live in his ways, are taking hold of **'the life that is truly life'** (see 6:12). They are entering into life to the full (John 10:10).

Does this mean that all those who perform a certain number of good works and share their wealth with other people will automatically go to heaven when they die? It does not mean that at all. Paul makes it abundantly clear elsewhere that no one gets to heaven by his own righteous deeds. He was to write to Titus, '[God] saved us, not because of righteous things we had done, but because of his mercy. He saved us through the washing of rebirth and renewal by the Holy Spirit' (Titus 3:5). What Paul is saying here is the same thing that Jesus referred to in Matthew 25:34-40, when he spoke about giving the hungry something to eat: the good works of the righteous were evidence that they were already members of God's kingdom.

Good deeds do not save us from the consequences of our sins. Salvation is entirely by grace, through faith in Christ; Christ has purchased redemption for us when he died upon the cross for our sins. However, when, by God's grace, we get to heaven, we who have served the Lord well will discover that we can stand upon a firm foundation. Our good works, and our observance of religious ceremonies, will not get us to heaven, but they will gain us a reward in glory. This is one of our motivations for living as Christians. Paul said, 'There is in store for me the crown of righteousness, which the Lord, the righteous Judge, will award to me on that day — and not only to me, but also to all who have longed for his appearing' (2 Tim. 4:8; see also Dan. 12:3; 2 Cor. 5:10; Rev. 20:12).

What Timothy should do

He was to **'guard what [had] been entrusted into [his] care'** (6:20). The word 'guard' here has something to do with looking after a deposit. Just as we put a certain amount of money in the bank for it to be looked after, so Paul had deposited something very precious with Timothy, and he gave strict instructions that it should be kept safe. Timothy was to take very great care of it. He was to guard it with his life and make sure that it did not get stolen, or be allowed to deteriorate in any way.

What is this treasure — these riches — which had been left with Timothy? It was the gospel message itself. But Timothy was not going to be left to guard this treasure without any help; Paul said that the Holy Spirit would stand by this young man and assist him in this vital task (2 Tim. 1:14). The glorious gospel had been entrusted to Paul (1:11), and the apostle had committed it to Timothy. It was Timothy's responsibility to guard this deposit, but at the same time he was to pass it on to others who would, in turn, continue to pass it on (2 Tim. 2:2).[2]

How was Timothy to guard this gospel? He was to do it by deliberately and continually turning away from **'godless chatter'**. There were so many who engaged in futile arguments; Paul had already warned Timothy about these people in 1:3-4. He had told him to command them to refrain from teaching error. Why did not Paul urge Timothy to engage in a debate with these people, and try to get them to see things from his point of view? He merely told him to **'turn away'** from these false teachers and their evil works. Paul said this because he knew that if his young friend stayed and argued with these false teachers then he would just be giving some kind of respectability to their godless chatter, and that was the last thing that Paul wanted. These men were only out for a fight, and they had debated all of the arguments over and over again.

If Timothy was to waste time in holding discussions with them
the outcome would probably be that they would make what he
was saying seem to be foolish.

People like this are around today in great numbers, and they
are very clever. However, instead of trying to confound their
arguments ourselves, we should get an experienced Christian
apologist to oppose them. One of the elders in our church is a
scientist, but he is often embarrassed when he reads articles
opposing Darwin's evolutionary theories which have been
written by Christians who have no scientific training. He says
that it is very easy for a scientist to dismiss these objections
because the writers of these pieces are not reasoning from a
scientific point of view. Our task, as simple believers in the
Lord Jesus Christ, is to 'preach the truth positively, and [then]
the myths will be shown to be false'.[3]

From whom is the gospel to be guarded? It is to be defended
against those who have **'opposing ideas of what is falsely
called knowledge'** (6:20). There were in Ephesus some of the
early Gnostics; these people considered that they had superior
knowledge of spiritual things. We must make sure that we turn
away from those whose understanding of the truth is based
upon anything other than the clear teaching of the Bible.
Whether these people assert that the Bible is corrupt, or
whether they claim to have some special 'words of knowledge' over and above the teaching of the Scriptures, we should
turn away from them. This means that we can only truly guard
the gospel by sticking closely to the Bible as the inerrant,
revealed Word of God to mankind.

Finally, Paul says that, in professing to have special knowledge of God's will, these people **'have wandered from the
faith'**. The apostle does not say that they have left the church.
He says that they have departed from the faith (he means the
true beliefs about God and salvation). These people who
engage in false teaching have wandered away from a sincere

faith and have 'turned to meaningless talk' (1:6). Some, 'eager for money, have wandered from the faith and pierced themselves with many griefs' (6:10). Likewise those who have 'opposing ideas of what is falsely called knowledge ... have wandered from the faith' (6:21). This means that we must take great care that we do not drift away from the doctrines of God. How can we ensure that we are firm in the truth? We can do so by sticking closely to the gospel of God's grace, and steering clear of 'theological' teaching which denies the sole and supreme authority of the Word of God over everything in the church.

Paul ends where he began this letter by saying, **'Grace be with you'** (6:21). Grace is 'God's favour in Christ towards the undeserving, transforming their hearts and lives and leading them to glory'.[4] This very brief benediction covers everything that is vital. The apostle ends each of these three Pastoral Epistles in the same kind of way. He tells Timothy that he craves these blessings for 'you' (and the word is plural). He is not just wishing this grace for 'bishop' Timothy. He in addressing the whole of the Christian community — in every age.

2 Timothy

23.
An old man remembers

Please read 2 Timothy 1:1-7

Memory is a wonderful thing. We store up in our brains an enormous amount of information, much more than could be held in the largest computer. Sometimes things happen to us which trigger off in our minds the recollection of some long-forgotten event, and we see it 'in our mind's eye' as plainly as if it were yesterday. There are many people in their nineties who cannot remember what they had for their last meal, but they can recall, in great detail, what happened to them when they were seven years old.

Paul was in prison

Paul was now an old man. He had written the first epistle to Timothy some years before, and he had also written to Titus; now he was writing what was to be his last letter, right at the end of his life.

Actually, Paul was probably only around sixty-six years of age when he wrote this second letter to Timothy, but he had endured a life which seems to have been full of persecution and misunderstanding (certainly since he had become a Christian). He had suffered beatings, stoning, shipwrecks and imprisonment, and his age was beginning to tell upon him. He had

written his short letter to Philemon about six years before this
one, but even in that letter he had described himself as 'an old
man' (Philem. 9).

However, Paul was not only showing his age because of all
the ill-treatment he had received; he was feeling old because
of the hard work in which he had been engaged for so long. He
had travelled very many miles to minister to the needs of God's
people and preach the gospel, and he often had to endure bitter
disappointments. His first letter to the church at Corinth shows
us some of the unchristian behaviour which was going on in
that church. Dealing with such matters must have drained him
of much spiritual energy.

In addition to all of that he had the care of all the church
resting on his shoulders. I find that to pastor just one small
church causes me many heart-aches and much stress, but Paul
had awesome loads placed upon him in his service for the
Lord. In 2 Corinthians 11:24-28 he details some of these
things: 'Five times I received from the Jews the forty lashes
minus one. Three times I was beaten with rods, once I was
stoned, three times I was shipwrecked, I spent a night and a day
in the open sea, I have been constantly on the move. I have
been in danger from rivers, in danger from bandits, in danger
from my own countrymen, in danger from Gentiles; in danger
in the city, in danger in the country, in danger at sea; and in
danger from false brothers. I have laboured and toiled and have
often gone without sleep; I have known hunger and thirst and
have often gone without food. I have been cold and naked.
Besides everything else, I face daily the pressure of my
concern for all the churches.'

But Paul was not only an old man, he was in prison again.
At the end of the book of Acts we see him under house-arrest.
At that time he was in his own rented house and he stayed there
for two whole years. Although he was imprisoned, he had a
certain amount of freedom. He could receive and welcome

guests, and he could, and did, preach the kingdom of God and teach about the Lord Jesus Christ. He did all of this with great boldness and no one tried to prevent him from doing so (Acts 28:31).

It was at this point that the Acts account ended and it seems that after a while Paul was released. He was able to travel around to many churches. He visited Crete (Titus 1:5), Ephesus (1 Tim 1:3-4) and Macedonia (1 Tim. 1:3).[1] It is possible that he also visited Spain (which had long been his intention) and some people believe that he even travelled as far as Britain.[2]

However, in the year A.D. 64 something happened which altered everything: the city of Rome was set alight. It was well known that Nero, the emperor, was behind this so that he could rebuild the city to his own design (tradition said that he fiddled while Rome burned). To deflect criticism away from himself he blamed the disaster upon the small, but growing, band of Christians who were then in the capital. Minority groups tend to be blamed when things go wrong in any community.

Paul was again arrested, but this time his circumstances were not nearly so pleasant. In 2 Timothy 1:8 he describes himself as '[Christ's] prisoner'. He did not regard himself as a prisoner of Rome; he knew that his sufferings were for the sake of Christ .[3] This time he was not put into his own hired house. He was imprisoned in such an out-of-the-way place that Onesiphorus, a Christian friend, had a great deal of difficulty in discovering where he was being held (1:17). He was in chains (1:16). In fact he says that he was 'chained like a criminal' (2:9). Tradition tells us that he was held in a deep dungeon.

This imprisonment caused him considerable distress. He was suffering (1:12; 2:9) and he was very lonely (4:9-13). It seems that the preliminary hearing of his case had already taken place (4:16-17) and, as he wrote this letter, he was awaiting the full trial, but this time he was not expecting to be acquitted. Death appeared to him to be inevitable (see 4:6-8).

However, instead of being down-hearted because of his old age and difficult circumstances, he turned his thoughts to his younger friend Timothy and wrote this second letter to him.

Paul looked back

He remembered that he was **'an apostle of Christ Jesus'** (1:1). Apostleship was not something which he had decided to take up. He was an apostle **'by the will of God'**. The Lord himself had called Paul to this great task. He had always sought to be an ambassador for the Lord, wherever he went and whatever he did.

To encourage himself, he reminded himself that his life's work was **'according to the promise of life that is in Christ Jesus'** (1:1). He was in his damp, dark, cold prison cell, anticipating the arrival of the executioner, but his thoughts went to 'the promise of life that is in Christ Jesus'. He knew that whatever happened to his physical body, his spiritual life was one which would go on for ever. A few years earlier he had written to the Philippians from another prison, 'For to me, to live is Christ and to die is gain' (Phil. 1:21).

As he thought, he recalled his dear young friend Timothy. He referred to him as **'my dear son'** (1:2; see also 1 Tim. 1:2). It seems that it was Paul who had led Timothy to faith in Christ (compare Acts 14:6-7 with 16:1) and because of this there was a special bond of attachment between the two of them.

He wished Timothy **'Grace, mercy and peace from God the Father and Christ Jesus our Lord'**. Most of Paul's letters start with 'grace' and 'peace', but both of these letters to Timothy place the word 'mercy' between these other bless-ings. God's 'mercy' is that which is completely undeserved (just like 'grace'), but 'mercy' has the special quality of something which is shown to those who are weak and helpless. The tax collector in one of Jesus' parables stood at a distance in the temple and beat his breast saying, 'God, have mercy on me, a sinner' (Luke 18:13). In 1 Timothy 1:13 Paul had told his friend that he had been 'a blasphemer and a persecutor and a violent man', yet, he said, 'I was shown mercy.'

So Paul thanked God for Timothy as he remembered him in his prayers (1:3). He had said the same kind of thing to the Philippians: 'I thank my God every time I remember you' (Phil. 1:3). We, too, should remember our friends and thank God for them. That is friendship indeed. Do we pray for our friends, and do we tell them we remember them in prayer? Paul brought back to his mind the last time he had bade farewell to Timothy. He recalled how Timothy had shed many tears at their parting. This may have been at Miletus when all of the Ephesian elders 'wept as they embraced [Paul] and kissed him' (Acts 20:37).

The apostle longed to shed tears again, only this time tears of joy, as he looked forward to seeing Timothy once again. In fact, he wanted to be **'filled with joy'** (1:4). This is one of the reasons why Paul wrote this second letter — he wanted Timothy to come to him (see 4:9,13,21). He remembered Timothy's upbringing. Something had triggered off in his mind the sincerity of Timothy's faith. This is why he says, **'I have been reminded...'** (1:5). Perhaps he had heard about another brave young Christian who was witnessing boldly to the Lord there in Rome. Whatever the case, something had reminded him of Timothy and of this young man's faith.

Timothy's faith was **'sincere'**. This means that it was wholesome. There was nothing unworthy mixed with it. It was not contaminated with the slightest doubt about God's love or power. His faith was also *devout*. It was the same kind of faith which had lived in his grandmother Lois and his mother

Eunice. This faith was firmly based in the Word of God. Every Jew was brought up on the Scriptures (the Old Testament), and it was presumably these two ladies who had taught Timothy the Scriptures from his infancy (3:15). But their faith had been given by the Holy Spirit, who enabled them to believe in the Lord Jesus Christ. The only faith which will take anyone to heaven is faith which *has Christ as its object*. In Acts 4:12 Peter said, 'Salvation is found in no one else, for there is no other name under heaven given to men by which we must be saved.' Jesus himself said something similar: 'I am the way and the truth and the life. No one comes to the Father except through me' (John 14:6). How important it is, then, to have a firm grasp of salvation by grace alone, and how vital it is to teach these things to our children — and other little ones!

Timothy's responsibilities

Although Paul was restricted, uncomfortable and lonely, he still remembered his duty to encourage Timothy in his work. This is why he reminds him to **'fan into flame the gift of God'**, which was in him (1:6). This does not mean that Timothy had grown listless in the work, or that he was weary of the responsibilities of the church at Ephesus. If that had been the case Paul would not have been so warm in his commendation in verse 5. But all fires die down unless they are regularly stoked up and have fresh fuel added to them. Timothy had been called to the Christian ministry (this was God's gift to him). The body of elders had laid hands upon him. This was to symbolize their unity and also God's blessing upon Timothy's future work (1 Tim. 4:14). It seems that Paul had been one of that number because he laid his own hands upon Timothy as well (1:6). Each of us tends to grow weary, and sometimes disillusioned, in our work for God. One antidote to this is for us to remember what God has done for us, just as Jesus urged the church at Sardis to 'Remember ... what you have received and heard' (Rev. 3:3).

Then Paul reminds Timothy of the gifts which God had imparted to him. He says, **'God did not give us a spirit of timidity'** (1:7). Timothy seems to have lacked confidence in his own abilities, but Paul had already said to him, 'Don't let anyone look down on you' (1 Tim. 4:12). He also told him to be strong despite his 'frequent illnesses' (1 Tim. 5:23). False humility is not a gift which God gives to his people; we should beware of everything which is designed to make us appear to be humble but is not sincere.

Instead of a spirit of timidity God has given us **'a spirit of power, of love and of self-control'** (1:7). These gifts were needed in the face of the thunderclouds of persecution which were already beginning to fill the sky. Timid Timothy needed 'aggressive energy in the face of difficulty, which overcomes the weakness of cowardice and enables one to work, to endure, to suffer, and to die if need be'.[4] This power is what God promises to give to humble believers. Paul said, 'For when I am weak, then I am strong' (2 Cor. 12:10).

Church leaders also need a great deal of love in their hearts. Their task is to encourage, warn and rebuke God's people, and they must to do this in love. They should always speak the truth, but they should do so in love (Eph. 4:15).

Finally, church leaders need to exercise the gift of self-discipline. They must not just do those things which give them pleasure. They should not neglect duties which cause them anxiety. They must face up to the task of leading the people of God in a self-disciplined way. They will do well to remember all the way the Lord has led them during the whole of their Christian pilgrimage.

24.
Suffering for the gospel

Please read 2 Timothy 1:8-12

I greatly admire those people who can soldier on despite many obstacles to their faith. Corrie Ten Boom was a lady of great faith. She and her family were arrested in Nazi-occupied Holland in 1944 and she suffered many indignities and deprivations, yet her trust in God never failed. Her faith was often sorely tested and she sometimes felt like giving it all up, but God upheld her to the end. Even when her dear sister Betsy died in the inhuman Ravensbruck Concentration Camp, Corrie's belief in God was not found wanting. She willingly suffered many indignities, as her Lord had done before her.

During the writing of this second letter to Timothy Paul was also undergoing a great many afflictions as he lay in his Roman prison. He was aware that he did not have long to live (4:7). He knew that almost all of his friends had deserted him (1:15), but perhaps his greatest distress was caused by his inability to meet with his Christian brothers and sisters for worship, encouragement and fellowship.

It seems that he suspected that some of the believers could have visited him if they had the will to do so. Perhaps they were afraid to go to the prison because they thought they might be arrested too. Maybe they were beginning to wonder whether Paul had been too bold in proclaiming the gospel, and they just did not want to get involved in his plight. All of these kinds of thoughts, and many more, probably flitted through his mind as he waited in his lonely prison.

Paul's agony of loneliness seems to sweep through this letter as he sits down and writes to Timothy urging him to leave Ephesus and come to see him during the final months of his life. We have no evidence as to whether Timothy ever made that journey to Paul's prison, or if he did, whether he arrived in time. What we do know is that this urgent letter has been preserved for nearly 2,000 years and it is found within the sacred Scriptures of God's Word.

Timothy must be bold

Paul pleaded with his younger friend not to be ashamed *to testify about the Lord*. By using the word **'testify'** Paul meant that he wanted Timothy to give witness to the Lord. In a court of law, a witness testifies to what he, or she, has seen or heard, but this testimony only counts as valid if the witness speaks about something of which he has a personal acquaintance. It is very salutary to realize that the Greek word for 'witness', transliterated into English, is 'martyr'.

Paul encouraged Timothy to be unashamed of giving a personal testimony concerning the Lord Jesus Christ. The apostle knew that Timothy was effective in testifying to the power, love and grace of the Lord, but even so he wanted his young friend to keep pressing on with it. Christians are not required only to give one testimony to Jesus (as they do when they are first converted). It is demanded of them that they be living witnesses of Jesus' life, atoning death and resurrection (see 2 Cor. 3:2-3).

We were not present during those events, as the disciples were, but if we know Christ living within us today then we can, and must, testify to the presence of God in our lives. Yet so often we are ashamed to speak for Jesus. This may be because we think that we are going to be laughed at if we confess Christ to our friends. We assume that we shall be ignored and treated as intellectual dead-weights, or we fear that no one will believe us and that people will imagine that we are deluded in some way.

However, Paul said, **'Do not be ashamed to testify about our Lord.'** No believer in the Lord Jesus Christ ought to be ashamed when he considers what the Lord has suffered for his people. Christ was not ashamed to declare the Word of God, to be arrested, to be ignominiously treated, to be laughed at, to be despised like a fool and to be ignored. Paul also suffered the same indignities. In the same way we should make sure that we do not fail our Lord when our faith in Christ is tested. Paul repeats the word 'ashamed' three times in this passage: **'Do not be ashamed to testify ... or ashamed of me... Yet I am not ashamed'** (1:8,12).

Secondly, Timothy was not to be ashamed *of the apostle*. Paul calls himself the Lord's prisoner (1:8). He often described himself in this way (e.g. Eph. 4:1). Paul was a Roman prisoner, yet he knew that his destiny was in the hands of someone much more powerful than mighty Cæsar. His life was, as it always had been, in the hands of the Lord God Almighty. He knew what Jesus had taught on this subject: 'Do not be afraid of those who kill the body but cannot kill the soul. Rather, be afraid of the One who can destroy both soul and body in hell. Are not two sparrows sold for a penny? Yet not one of them will fall to the ground apart from the will of your Father. And even the very hairs of your head are all numbered. So don't be afraid; you are worth more than many sparrows. Whoever acknowledges me before men, I will also acknowledge him before my Father in heaven. But whoever disowns me before men, I will disown him before my Father in heaven' (Matt. 10:28-33).

Because of this, Paul said, 'So do not be ashamed ... of me.' Timothy may have been timid, but, the apostle tells him, 'God did not give us a spirit of timidity, but [rather he gives us] a spirit of power, of love and of self-discipline' (1:7). God does not give his people power so that they can perform many miracles to draw attention to themselves; he gives them power so that they can testify about our Lord. Believers have nothing to be ashamed of when they bear a good witness to Christ; indeed, they are given a holy boldness to declare the wonders of God.

Thirdly, Paul urged Timothy not to be ashamed *of joining him in suffering for the gospel*. This is a challenge for us all. How much are we prepared to suffer for the sake of the gospel? In the past many godly people have been burnt at the stake rather than deny their Lord. Some have even been forced to look on as their own wives and children have gone through untold sufferings, just because they have refused to turn their backs on the Lord.

Yet what are we prepared to suffer for the sake of Christ? It makes us thoroughly ashamed of ourselves when we remember what feeble excuses we make for not meeting with God's people in worship. Some church members do not go to church because they have a slight headache, or they are feeling cross with the believers, or they would rather have a quiet evening in before the fire. Some never attend a Sunday evening service merely because they have not been in the habit of doing so. Would they have behaved like this if they had lived in Paul's day, when Christians had to 'stand up and be counted'?

Remember what the gospel is

The gospel is **'the power of God'**. Paul, writing to the Roman believers said, 'I am not ashamed of the gospel, because it is the power of God for the salvation of everyone who believes: first for the Jew, then for the Gentile. For in the gospel a righteousness from God is revealed, a righteousness that is by faith from first to last, just as it is written, "The righteous will live by faith"' (Rom. 1:16-17).

This gospel is powerful enough even to change stubborn people's hearts, their desires and their whole motivation for life. There is no greater power in the whole universe than the power of God. In creation God unleashed his power. He created the earth out of nothing. He caused great mountains to arise, and huge valleys to be formed. He created the vast heavens. 'For by him all things were created: things in heaven and on earth, visible and invisible, whether thrones or powers or rulers or authorities; all things were created by him and for him. He is before all things, and in him all things hold together' (Col. 1:16-17).

This same mighty power is brought to bear in the gospel. Paul prays that the Ephesians will know '[God's] incomparably great power for us who believe. That power is like the working of his mighty strength, which he exerted in Christ when he raised him from the dead and seated him at his right hand in the heavenly realms' (Eph. 1:19-20).

It is by this same power that we are **'saved'**. Salvation did not happen simply when we made a decision to follow Christ. Those who merely make a decision for Christ, or who hand their lives over to Christ, can just as easily change their minds when things start to go wrong.[1]

Paul had so much to say about this subject that his words trip over themselves and each new thought overlaps the previous one as he qualifies what he has said, or he adds to it. When we are saved we are **'called … to a holy life'**. Believers are obliged to live a holy life. That is one of the reasons why we have been saved. We have not been saved just so that we can have a good time, and enjoy the blessings of God's salvation. If that is the only reason we became Christians, then we are behaving very selfishly. We have been saved so that we can bring glory to God's name.

However, no one is saved just because he does good works. That is the way many people think that they can become Christians. They assume that God will look favourably upon them if they help other people. They attend church regularly. They are kind to their pastor and they live in an unselfish way. There is no mistaking the fact that every one of us should seek to live holy lives. But if someone is relying on such activities to gain an entrance into heaven, then he is seriously deluded.

Paul writes, **'God ... has saved us and called us to a holy life — not because of anything we have done but because of his own purpose and grace.'** The amazing thing is that **'This grace was given us in Christ Jesus before the beginning of time'** (1:9). God was not caught unawares by what was happening. He knows everything that has taken place, and that will take place, throughout the whole universe. In fact he knew you and me even before we were born (cf. Jer. 1:5). This is very difficult for us to take in but when we realize that God is almighty then we shall understand how he can do all of these great acts. He planned everything and he brought all things to fruition according to his purposes and grace (1:9). 'For he chose us in him before the creation of the world to be holy and blameless in his sight. In love he predestined us to be adopted as his sons through Jesus Christ, in accordance with his pleasure and will — to the praise of his glorious grace, which he has freely given us in the One he loves' (Eph. 1:4-6).

Then Paul added that the grace of God **'has now been revealed through the appearing of our Saviour, Christ Jesus, who has destroyed death and has brought life and immortality to light through the gospel'** (1:10). The Lord Jesus Christ has unveiled God's plan of salvation. He did this when he came to this earth, as a baby at Bethlehem, and by his death on the cross he has destroyed death (Paul means that he has taken away the power, 'the sting' of death — see 1 Cor. 15:55-57). The life that we received when we were born again is eternal life. That is not just life that goes on and on for ever. It is something far richer than the sceptic's view of heaven as a place where everyone is bored with twanging harps on clouds for thousands of years. What the Scriptures tell us about is life eternal, which is rich and full and lived in the presence of our Lord and Saviour (see 1 Peter 1:4).

Follow the example of Paul

Paul tells Timothy, **'Of this gospel** [no other] **I was appointed a herald and an apostle and a teacher'** (1:11). The same thoughts were expressed in 1 Timothy 2:7 (see also 4:2). As a *herald* Paul must announce and loudly proclaim that gospel, as John the Baptist had announced the coming of the kingdom of heaven (Matt. 3:1-2). As *an apostle* Paul had to say and do nothing except that which he had been commanded to say and do. We, too, must stick to this apostolic gospel which calls people to repentance and faith. Finally as *a teacher* Paul must carefully instruct the people in the things which have to do with salvation and the glory of God, and he must admonish those who were deviating from the Christian pathway.[2]

That is the very reason why Paul was suffering as he was. He was not ashamed to proclaim the gospel message, and to live by it. He cared not that people would misunderstand him, and persecute him. Despite the consequences, he was faithful to the work which God had called him to do. Now he had to suffer for his stand for Christ.

His physical and mental distress had not shaken his faith in his risen Lord and Saviour. He said, **'I know whom I have believed.'** He did not say, 'I know *about* him', or 'I know *who* *he is.*' He wrote, 'I know *him.*' He meant that he knew Christ personally. All who live in Britain know who the queen is. They probably know a great deal about her, but I doubt if many could say, 'I know her personally. I am a great friend of the queen.' However, we can know Christ in a personal way. We can know him by confessing our sins to him, turning away from them, believing in him and receiving him as our Saviour and Friend. Then, and only then, will we enter into the experience of becoming a true child of God.

That is the believer's view of salvation. But what Paul explains here is God's plan of salvation. He tells us that if we have been saved it is not because of anything which we have done. It is solely because of God's own purpose and grace. This grace, which no one can earn, was given to us in Christ Jesus before even the beginning of time. We are not saved because of anything which we decided to do; we are saved because God chose us in Christ before the creation of the world (Eph. 1:4).

When Christ appeared, the power of God was unleashed and he destroyed death and brought life and immortality to light through the good news of salvation. Those who have been saved not only were called by grace before time began, they are also called to live holy lives in the present. It is no wonder that Paul was so taken up with the grace of God that he was prepared to suffer any deprivation in order to preserve and pass on that gospel message.

Paul ends this section by saying, '**I ... am convinced that [Christ] is able to guard what I have entrusted to him for that day**' (1:12). What had Paul entrusted to God? He had entrusted his whole life and his salvation to the Lord. In 1 Timothy 6:20 Timothy was exhorted to guard what had been entrusted into his care — that is, the gospel. But here Paul speaks about something which he had entrusted to God. Paul knew that the judgement day was coming, when God will judge everyone. In view of that great day the apostle was reminding Timothy that his life, and Timothy's life, and the life of every believer down through the ages, is perfectly safe in the hands of God. When the wrath of God descends in divine judgement upon this world then every believer will be safe because he or she is 'hidden with Christ in God'. Paul told the Colossians, 'When Christ, who is your life, appears, then you also will appear with him in glory' (Col. 3:3,4).

25.
Loyalty to the gospel

Please read 2 Timothy 1:13-18

Loyalty is a commodity which is short supply. In past generations to fail to attend both the Sunday morning and evening (or, in the countryside, afternoon) services was something unheard of among church members. Today the second service is often poorly supported and the visit of friends or relatives is considered sufficient reason to stay away from church altogether.

But it is not only loyalty to church services which is poor in these days; loyalty to the Word of God is not as strong as it once was, even among those who call themselves evangelicals. For the past 150 years the teaching of the Bible has been under attack from those who are sceptical about its authenticity. Even those who still believe in God reject much of what is recorded in the Bible. They say that a great deal of it is merely the writings of men who, although they are inspired, are none the less giving their own ideas. These doubters of God's Word say that we have grown up since the days when our forefathers accepted every word in the Bible as God's truth. They cannot accept the supernatural elements in the miracles of Jesus, nor the inerrancy of the Scriptures in their entirety.

What a contrast there is between those who disbelieve God's Word and those who accept the teaching of Paul! God had raised Paul up to be an apostle who founded many

Christian communities, and established them in the teaching of Jesus Christ. Even though he was in prison when he wrote this letter, even though he was suffering great deprivations, even though he was lonely and somewhat depressed, the one thing that concerned him more than anything else was not his own situation, but the preservation of the truth of the gospel message.

Loyalty to sound teaching

Paul wanted Timothy to remember the teaching he had imparted to him on many occasions. Timothy had **'heard'** many things from the apostle: he had heard about Paul's sufferings; he had heard about the many other groups of believers all around the Mediterranean region; but, far more important than any of these things, Paul wanted Timothy to remember, above everything else, the message of the gospel.

This **'teaching'** concerned the Lord Jesus Christ. It declared that he is the Son of God, and that Christ has died to take away the guilt and power of sin. These things were all in accordance with the Scriptures. Everything that had happened to Jesus had been foretold in the Old Testament. Jesus was the long-promised deliverer of God's people.

The apostle had told the Corinthian Christians, 'I want to remind you of the gospel I preached to you, which you received and on which you have taken your stand. By this gospel you are saved, if you hold firmly to the word I preached to you. Otherwise, you have believed in vain. For what I received I passed on to you as of first importance: that Christ died for our sins according to the Scriptures, that he was buried, that he was raised on the third day according to the Scriptures, and that he appeared to Peter, and then to the Twelve. After that, he appeared to more than five hundred of the brothers at the same time, most of whom are still living, though some have fallen asleep. Then he appeared to James, then to all the apostles, and last of all he appeared to me also, as to one abnormally born' (1 Cor. 15:1-8).

The reason why Timothy was to keep this teaching was because it was **'sound'**. Paul meant that it was wholesome because it was teaching that would build up God's people in their Christian faith. There was nothing erroneous or unhelpful about it in any way (see Titus 1:9). The main task of any minister of the gospel is to keep to this sound teaching. The reason why Paul emphasized the need for Timothy to be faithful to the Word of God was because there were many in those days who were failing to keep to the pure teaching of the gospel message. Even at Ephesus there were some who were teaching false doctrines (see 1 Tim. 1:3-4), and Paul knew the danger of wrong teaching about Jesus: it would quickly spread like a bad infection (see 2:17).

In our day, we all need to make sure that we do not depart from sound teaching. We can do this by safeguarding the pattern which Paul and the other apostles have laid down and recorded for us in the Bible. This pattern was the main outline of the teaching about Jesus Christ and his dealings with his people.

In thinking about Paul's use of this word **'pattern'**, I am reminded of a sermon I heard in the mid-1970s at Westminster Chapel in London. John Appleby, a missionary who had then recently returned from India, was preaching on this verse at the evening session of the Annual Meetings of what was then called the Strict Baptist Mission. He said that this pattern of sound doctrine was rather like a child's colouring book which was meant to be filled in by the little one. The infant had an outline of an animal or tree, or whatever, to follow and, if he or she did it well, then the result would be a lovely picture. But if the child was too young, or too clumsy, to crayon carefully enough, and scribbled all over the edges of the outline, then the whole thing would be spoilt. The preacher said that, in the same way, we are required to stick to the pattern of the gospel, as we find it in the Scriptures. If we veer from the truth, even a little, then the teaching of Christ will be corrupted.

Unfortunately that is what many people, especially theologians, are doing today. They are saying that they cannot accept some of the teaching of the Bible, but at the same time they are adding details to the gospel message which were not in the original. In behaving like this they are 'going over the edges of the outline'. Paul would have called these people 'unsound', and so must we — even if they are very important in the professing church. Such people say, for instance, 'Well, we can't any longer believe in the need to humble ourselves and come to the foot of the cross to confess our sins. All that talk about blood and sacrifice is now outdated. We must find some other model of salvation.' They are spoiling the pattern of sound teaching. They are not keeping to the truth of the gospel any more than the false teachers of Paul's day.

However, the apostle does not leave this important subject there. To reinforce what he has said he turns to banking terminology as he tells Timothy to **'Guard the good deposit that was entrusted to you.'** Paul used this same term in his first epistle, when he said, 'Guard what has been entrusted to your care' (1 Tim. 6:20). In both passages he speaks about this same gospel message and uses the very strong word, 'guard'. That is what banks do with our money when we place it into their care. They lock it away safely and put a very strong guard upon it. What do bankers guard money from? They guard it against loss, destruction and change.[1] When we put our money into a bank we do not expect it to be lost. We assume that the bankers will make sure that it is not destroyed. We trust them to see to it that the value of what we have deposited does not decrease in any way. All this is very important to us because one day we may well want to draw it all out again, without losing any of it, or finding that it is worth less than when we deposited it with them (naturally we would not object if it had increased its market price!).

That was exactly how Timothy was to guard the gospel message. He was to care for it so that when he passed it on to other people nothing of the message would be lost and none of it would be destroyed or be altered in any way.

Timothy's task was the same as that which is entrusted to God's people today. It is our responsibility to see that what we preach and teach and pass on to others is the pure message of the gospel. It is to be the same message which those first followers of Jesus passed on to those whom they evangelized in the first century A.D. Of course, the way in which we present this message must be understandable and relevant to the needs of the people of today, but the essential truths of it must remain unsullied. We must keep to the pattern of sound doctrine. Paul is saying to all of us today, **'What you heard from [these epistles], keep as the pattern of sound teaching, with faith and love in Christ Jesus. Guard the good deposit that was entrusted to you — guard it with the help of the Holy Spirit who lives in us'** (1:13-14). He places great emphasis on the words 'keep' and 'guard'; these things require great effort and diligence on our part.

How are ordinary believers like us to undertake the enormous work of passing on this gospel message? We are to tell it with faith. We must believe that this gospel is God's word for our needy world, and we are to act as though we believe it to be the truth. Just as in Paul's day, so today we are to have nothing to with any multi-faith dialogue which has as its aim merging Christianity with other religions.

Also we are to tell this good news with much *love* in our hearts. God loved the world so much that he gave his only Son to save it (John 3:16), and because of the great love that there is in the heart of Jesus we too should demonstrate that love as we seek to urge men, women and children, to repent of sins and turn to the Lord Jesus Christ in faith.

We are also to pass on this message and keep it pure 'with the help of the Holy Spirit who lives in us'. When we first believed in the Lord Jesus Christ, we were given the Holy Spirit who has now taken up residence within us (see Rom. 8:9). It is he, with his tremendous power, who will give us the grace and the strength to keep and guard this gospel message from all impurities, and he will help us to pass it on to others.

The disloyalty of many

Immediately following on from this lofty theme Paul's thoughts turned to those who had let him down. He reminds Timothy of Phygelus and Hermogenes. These people lived in the area of Ephesus, and they were known to Timothy as well as Paul. We know nothing else about them, except that they were believers who had let Paul down in some way. He needed them, and others, to come and testify on his behalf at his trial, but these men failed to show up. Paul nowhere says that they were not true Christians; however, he tells us that they, and many others, have **'deserted me'**, and that in his great hour of need. We do not know why these people refused to journey to Rome to speak up on behalf of Paul. Perhaps they were not prepared to sacrifice the time it would have taken to travel all that way. It may be that they were not willing to spend their money on the fare. No doubt they would have been afraid that if they were identified with Paul they too might be arrested and imprisoned. All we know for certain is that they did not visit Paul, and this depressed him. To be let down by your friends, in your hour of great need, is a very bitter blow to withstand. But Paul would have gained comfort in remembering that his

Lord also suffered the same sense of loss when all of his disciples fled for fear of the Jews (Mark 14:50).

In writing these things, Paul was not telling Timothy something he did not know. The latter was aware that **'everyone in the province of Asia'** had deserted the apostle (1:15). Naturally Paul does not mean that all of the population had deserted him. He was referring to the believers. No doubt in his sadness he felt rather like Elijah, who said, 'I am the only one of the Lord's prophets left,' when in fact there were 7,000 in Israel who had not bowed the knee to Baal! (1 Kings 18:22; 19:10,14,18).

How things had deteriorated since the time when Paul had spent three whole years at Ephesus![2] At that time we read that the Ephesians 'were all seized with fear, and the name of the Lord Jesus was held in high honour' (Acts 19:17). So now we find Paul, with these things in his mind, writing to Timothy and saying, **'You know...'** about it. He probably meant, 'What are you doing about it?' However, despite his distress Paul ends on a high note.

The great loyalty of one man

Onesiphorus had come to Rome and had visited Paul in prison. It would seem that this brother was a member of the Ephesian church (see 4:19), and for some reason he had come to Rome (maybe he had business there). It is obvious that he was someone who was not easily put off because Paul tells us that he had sought diligently until he found the prison where the apostle was held. No doubt Onesiphorus put himself in great danger by even asking where Paul as imprisoned. Therefore, we must conclude that he was one who **'was not ashamed of [Paul's] chains'**. His visits to Paul had encouraged the apostle and **'refreshed'** him. He was of great benefit to Paul because

of the material things that he took with him, but even more
valuable was the fact that he sought out Paul and visited him;
the presence of Onesiphorus was a blessing to the apostle.
When people are close to death they find it a great comfort to
have their loved ones near them, and the fellowship of God's
people brings us all wonderful refreshment of spirit.

Onesiphorus had also helped Paul in many practical ways
while he was in Ephesus (1:18). It seems that by the time that
Paul wrote this letter, this servant of God had left Rome and
was on his way back to Ephesus. We can see this because Paul
says, **'When he was in Rome...'** (1:17). In thinking about the
great efforts that Onesiphorus had made in searching hard
until he found him, Paul's mind turned to the Day of Judgement and he prayed, **'May the Lord grant that he will find
mercy from the Lord on that day!'** The apostle makes a play
on the words 'found' and 'find'. Paul also prays for **'the
household of Onesiphorus'** and at the end of the letter, he
sends greetings to them (1:16; 4:19). Whatever a servant of the
Lord does for his Master, his whole family is involved. They
too are called upon to make sacrifices for the Lord, and they
too should be prayed for, and praised for their faithfulness.

26.
Perseverance in the gospel

Please read 2 Timothy 2:1-7

One of the characteristics of young men seems to be a tremendous enthusiasm for what they are doing. It does not matter whether it is collecting things, or pursuing a hobby — if something catches a young man's imagination he will dive head-first into it, exerting a great deal of energy as he works hour after hour at that project.

When my eldest son reached the age of eleven it seemed as though he could remember hardly anything which was required by his schoolteachers. He used to say, 'I just can't learn this stuff.' Yet one weekend he suddenly developed an enormous interest in football. This started on the Friday evening and by the time Monday morning had arrived he knew something about each of the major football clubs, and he could recite the names of all of the players in his favourite team. He could also go into great detail about the positions they played in, and what each person was particularly good at. For a while all we heard from Tim was information about football. However, within a few months the craze had died down, and before much longer we heard nothing more about the subject.

The Timothy of the Bible was a comparatively young man when Paul wrote this letter to him, and the apostle knew something about the changeable characteristics of youth. This may have been one of the reasons why Paul spent a great deal of time in encouraging Timothy to press on with the work of the gospel. As we saw earlier, in 1 Timothy 1:3 he wrote, 'Stay there in Ephesus.' He knew that the work of the church was hard, and the opposition of some people was becoming fierce, so he urged Timothy to stick at it.

Then in 1 Timothy 4:12 he wrote, 'Don't let anyone look down on you because you are young.' No doubt sometimes Timothy had difficulty in getting some of the older church members to accept his authority over them in the gospel, so Paul enjoined him to press on with the work and set an example in the way he lived his life.

Here, in 2 Timothy 1:7, Paul seems to suggest that this young servant of God was of a timid disposition, although this may well not have been the case — otherwise Paul would not have sent him to so many places which demanded a great deal of courage to face numerous difficulties and challenges. However, the apostle implored him to remember that God gives to his faithful servants a spirit of power, love and self-discipline.

Seeking to be strong

Paul speaks tenderly to Timothy and calls him **'my son'** (see also 1:2; 1 Tim. 1:2). He was Paul's son in a number of senses. He was not a blood relative of Timothy's but there were stronger ties than that of blood. Paul was Timothy's father in the sense that he had led him to trust in the Lord Jesus Christ as his Saviour. Following on from that he had nurtured him in the faith. He saw that Timothy had much inducement to grow up and develop in the ways of God. He also did everything he could to protect the younger man from evil influences. He showed him what to avoid as a Christian and pointed out the dangerous traps of the Evil One, and he tried to see that Timothy did not fall, or fail, in the Christian life.

This is why Paul writes to Timothy, **'Be strong in the grace that is in Christ Jesus'** (2:1). This grace had been given to him before the beginning of time (see 1:9), and Timothy could be strengthened in it by looking back to those people who had been examples of faithful living. Paul had written of the sincere faith of Lois and Eunice (1:5). He had reminded Timothy of his own convictions about the Lord's reliability (1:12), and he had spoken in glowing terms of the faithfulness of Onesiphorus (1:16-18). We can gain great strength and encouragement from seeing how other believers are strong in their zeal for the Lord, and we in turn should be those who seek to encourage others to live the life of faith.

Timothy was also to be strong when he remembered the teaching which Paul had given, **'the things you have heard me say'** (2:2). This young man must have often heard Paul preach. He had heard Paul's expositions of the Word of God many times. He had listened as the apostle had proved from the Scriptures that the Lord Jesus Christ is God's chosen deliverer from sin, and he had been strengthened in his faith as he had paid attention to Paul when he pleaded with men and women to leave their sinful ways and turn in faith to the Lord Jesus Christ for salvation.

Timothy had heard the apostle outline the main tenets of the Christian faith **'in the presence of many witnesses'** (2:2). Paul may have been referring to the occasion when Timothy was 'set apart' for the Christian ministry, or to some other event. The point is that many other people, as well as Timothy, had heard Paul explain God's plan for lost mankind. To keep him strong in the faith Timothy was to recall and reflect on these things.

Then Paul went on to point out one of Timothy's main tasks: **'The things you have heard me say ... entrust to reliable men who will also be qualified to teach others'** (2:2) The apostle knew that his own work was nearly finished.

At the end of this final letter he was to write, 'For I am already being poured out like a drink offering, and the time has come for my departure. I have fought the good fight, I have finished the race, I have kept the faith. Now there is in store for me the crown of righteousness, which the Lord, the righteous Judge, will award to me on that day — and not only to me, but also to all who have longed for his appearing' (2 Tim. 4:6-8).

Timothy was to be one of those who were to carry on the task of spreading the gospel and teaching people how to live in God's ways. So it was vital that the sound teaching of the Christian faith should be preserved. It was to be kept pure and secure (1:13,14). It must not be added to, or detracted from, in any way; the apostle's doctrine must be kept free from all contamination. No aspect of its truth was to be watered down. The simple gospel message must be safeguarded so that it could be passed on through each of the succeeding generations.

This same gospel has been kept intact right down until today. This has happened because people like Timothy have faithfully kept this message and they, in their turn, have entrusted it to other reliable men. Timothy was to be constantly on the watch for people who had the same kind of characteristics as Lois, Eunice, Paul and Onesiphorus, and he was to pass on to these people the pure message of the good news of salvation in Christ because they could be depended upon to pass it on to others, unsullied.

One of the main tasks of a faithful preacher of the Word is to keep a watch out for those who have the ability to also become teachers of the Word and to teach and train them to be able to pass this message on to others. Each time a man comes to Christ for salvation in the church of which I am the pastor I keep an eye on him to see if he might have a preaching or teaching gift and, if so, then I make sure that he has the opportunity to use and develop that gift. There should be no room for jealousy in the church of Jesus Christ. I was once a member of a church where if we told our minister that we benefited from the preaching of a certain visitor then we noticed that the pastor never invited that brother to come again; he did not want the congregation to think more highly of a visitor than they did of their own minister.

Modern man says that preaching has had its day and people cannot sit still and listen to a sermon which goes on for more then ten minutes or so. But God still calls men to preach the Word of God in all its fulness, so that the people might be built up in their faith. From time to time the Holy Spirit falls in exceptional power upon such preaching of the Bible.

Three models

Each of us finds help in learning from the aid of pictures of some sort. Jesus usually used stories to illustrate Bible truth and we also should seek to find ways of opening up God's truth. A sermon without illustrations (I do not necessarily mean stories or anecdotes) is like a house without windows — very dull. Pictures let in the light. We can grasp more easily what is being taught if we are pointed towards something which we already understand. All good instructors who wish to teach something new start off with what their pupils already know. Then, when this is understood, they take them on to the next step, from the known to the unknown.

It is for this kind of reason that Paul wrote to Timothy about a soldier, an athlete and a farmer. He had used these figures in 1 Corinthians 9:7-11,24-25 and here he again takes up the same pictures and employs them to reinforce his message that Timothy must work hard in passing the gospel message on to others. Timothy would have known a great deal about soldiers; they were everywhere, preserving the Roman peace. The Olympic, Isthmian and other games were also well known throughout the Greek-speaking world, and everyone knew who farmers were in those days because most food came from the land.

The soldier

One important thing about soldiers is that they endure hardship; I certainly did on occasions when I was in the army! However, soldiers go on leave sometimes, and once in a while they have a posting where they have an easy time. But Paul was writing here about a serving soldier. The Greek word he used emphasizes this; this soldier is on active duty.[1] In such circumstances a soldier cannot just turn around and say to his officer, 'I don't feel like fighting the enemy today.' A soldier is one who obeys orders, even if it means advancing towards certain death. Tertullian, writing about 150 years after Paul penned this letter wrote, 'No soldier comes to the war surrounded by luxuries, nor goes into action from a comfortable bedroom, but from a makeshift and narrow tent, where every kind of hardness and severity and unpleasantness is to be found.'[2]

The Christian too should be like a good soldier; he has a battle to fight for his Lord. This means that he should have his eyes firmly fixed on the goal of passing on the Christian message. He must not let anything stand in the way of his presenting the claims of Christ to a fallen world. He must be single-minded in his determination to press on with the gospel message. Nothing should occupy his attention more than his service for God. Just as a good soldier should not get involved in civilian affairs (because he has a battle to fight, and nothing must be allowed to distract him from this task), so a Christian should not become entangled with the affairs of this life. Any worldly pursuit which gets in the way of our service for God must be pushed to one side.

The Christian should have one aim in life: he should seek to please his commanding officer. In Hebrews 11:5 we read that Enoch was 'commended as one who pleased God'. To the Corinthians Paul writes, 'We make it our goal to please him' (2 Cor. 5:9). If our aim is to please our Master then we must be prepared to endure hardship as we tell others of the Lord and his wonderful salvation. We achieve that most effectively by being disentangled from worldly pleasures and amusements. As an encouragement Paul says, **'Endure hardship with us.'** We too should remind ourselves that we serve Christ along with others who have this same goal in their lives.

The athlete

In speaking of an athlete Paul singles out the fact that an athlete strives to win his race fairly. The apostle had often used this picture to speak about the Christian life. He told the Philippians that he pressed on towards the winning post. He forgot everything which was behind him, and he strained towards what was ahead. He did this so that he could 'win the prize' — that is, the enjoyment of Christ's presence now, and the glories of heaven in the future. In using this figure Paul is not saying that believers should seek to be selfish and push every other Christian into second, third, fourth or fifth place, as they strive to win the race. He means that we should all live our lives as though winning the applause of God is what matters to us, rather than the cheers of the crowd.

But our crown of victory will only be valid if we keep to the rules. An athlete who cheats is not worthy of the title he is awarded; when he is 'found out' he will be stripped of his crown. Rules are in place to be obeyed. In the Christian life, 'Unless a man performs special service in God's kingdom, observes the rules — for example, to preach and teach the truth, and do this in love; to exercise discipline in the same spirit ... he will not receive the wreath of righteousness.'³

The farmer

'The hard-working farmer should be the first to receive a share of the crops' (2:6). Again in this figure the emphasis is on faithful service. A soldier's life can be exciting — especially in the great victory parade which will take place at the end of the war. An athlete who wins a great race receives the adulation for the crowds as he does a lap of honour. But what exhilaration does a farmer receive? None. He has to be patient in his work, and wait for the harvest-time before he achieves any benefit from his hard work. It is the same with the Lord's servants. They are to spend their time faithfully and systematically ploughing the hard soil of men's hearts. They do this week by week as they sow the seed of the Word of God and as they tend the slightest evidence of spiritual life in the people. Then, at the appropriate time, they will reap a harvest of precious souls.⁴

A quiet contemplation

At the end of all this teaching Paul exhorts Timothy to reflect on what he has told him: **'Reflect on what I am saying, for the Lord will give you insight into all this'** (2:7). There come times when we all need to stop and consider what is happening in our lives; we need to look at ourselves in the mirror of the Bible. There will be much about our circumstances which we do not understand, but we must never despair or give up. The Lord will give us insight into everything that we need to know, if only we seek it.

In the meantime we should be strong in our determination to press on in the Christian life, seeking to tell others of the Lord Jesus Christ and his atoning death upon the cross for sinners. We must be prepared to put up with many discouragements and much pain as we seek to declare the Word of the Lord. We are required to press on in the things of God, keeping to his rules, concentrating upon him and leaving aside the entanglements of the world.

27.
The path to glory

Please read 2 Timothy 2:8-13

Many films which were made during the Second World War, and immediately following it, went into a great deal of graphic detail about the suffering and deprivation undergone by those who were caught up in the hostilities. Yet the people involved did not dwell on these sacrifices when victory finally arrived.

Paul had been writing to Timothy about the suffering which inevitably has to come before a believer receives the crown of glory. Throughout the opening section of this epistle the apostle has been hammering home this main point. He has drawn this lesson from the analogy of soldiers, athletes and farmers, and he now goes on to speak about the experience of the Lord Jesus Christ (2:8), the deprivations which Paul himself endured (2:9-10) and the troubles which befall many ordinary Christian people (2:11-13). His message is that eternal blessings come through pain, fruit through toil, life through death and glory through suffering.[1]

Suffering in the life of Christ

Paul exhorts us to **'Remember Jesus Christ'** (2:8). This is always a good principle, whatever condition we might be in. If we remembered the Lord on all occasions, we should not feel so sorry for ourselves when things begin to go wrong. If we remembered our Saviour more often we would not say unkind and unhelpful things. Neither would we think so many unworthy thoughts. If we remembered Jesus Christ more regularly we would not encourage improper desires to arise in our minds.

When we forget Jesus Christ, we are liable to end up in trouble. However, the Lord has promised to be with us to guide and protect us by his Spirit. How sad it is, then, that sincere Christians frequently forget him! When we dismiss him from our minds we are tempted to go astray. Living without a consciousness of the Lord Jesus Christ means living at a low spiritual level.

Paul exhorts us to remember Jesus Christ, **'raised from the dead'**. We need to recall that Jesus Christ lived on this earth as a man. He was born to a virgin and laid in a manger, because there was no room in the inn. He went about doing good, preaching about the kingdom of God and healing the sick. He was arrested and unjustly found guilty and hung upon a cross to die, like a common criminal.

The Lord Jesus Christ died a cursed death even though he was the spotless Son of God. He was the only man who ever lived on this earth who never sinned. He was 'holy, blameless, pure, set apart from sinners' (Heb. 7:26) and when he died, he offered himself as a sacrifice to take away the sin of his people. It is rightly said of him:

> There was no other good enough
> To pay the price of sin
> He only could unlock the gate
> Of heaven and let us in.[2]

However, we also need to remember that Jesus did not remain in the grave; he was raised from the dead. That is the glorious message of Easter. Christ has risen and he is now alive, and he will remain alive for ever.

Paul also exhorted Timothy to **'Remember Jesus Christ, raised from the dead, descended from David.'** In every other place in this letter Paul calls the Lord 'Christ Jesus', but in this verse he has reversed the order to 'Jesus Christ'. He no doubt puts the human name of the Lord first to emphasize that Jesus was also a man. He came from a royal line. He was a descendant of the great King David who had unified the nation of Israel and ruled as its king. Paul emphasized this because the long-awaited Messiah (the promised deliverer of his people) had to arise from David's line. Prophecy declared it to be so.

But not only did Jesus come from the human line of David, he is also divine. Paul said that the believers are to 'remember Jesus Christ, raised from the dead' because Christ's resurrection demonstrates the efficacy of his sacrifice on the cross. He not only died for our sins, he was raised from the dead and is now reigning on David's throne in glory.

At the season of Christmas we often read the portion from Isaiah 9:7 about Christ's kingdom:

> Of the increase of his government and peace
>   there will be no end.
> He will reign on David's throne
>   and over his kingdom,
> establishing and upholding it
>   with justice and righteousness
>   from that time on and for ever.

There are also other places where the same thought is expressed (e.g. 2 Sam.7:12-13,16; Jer. 33:15,20-22).

It is this same Son of David who is declared to be the Son of God. Paul writes to the Roman church about the gospel God had 'promised beforehand ... regarding his Son, who as to his human nature was a descendant of David, and who through the Spirit of holiness was declared with power to be the Son of God, by his resurrection from the dead: Jesus Christ our Lord' (Rom. 1:2-4).

It is these facts which make up the gospel message, what Paul here calls **'my gospel'**. He does not mean, of course, that he instituted the gospel, or made it up. He means that this message is that which he received directly from the Lord (see 1 Cor. 11:23). It is this same message which he entrusted to others, and he longs to see that these others, in turn, faithfully pass it on to yet others also (2:2).

Suffering in the life of Paul

It is because of what the Lord Jesus went through that Paul was content to suffer in prison. Paul was no masochist; he took no pleasure in his own sufferings. He would rather be anywhere else than in that dark, damp prison. Given the choice, he would much prefer to be standing, unfettered, in a crowded syna- gogue declaring to all who would listen the good news of salvation in Christ.

However, God had allowed him to be shut up in a cold, inhospitable Roman prison. This was so that believers in succeeding generations could benefit from the letters which he wrote from prison. If Paul had been granted his freedom he would have spent all of his time going from place to place preaching about deliverance from sin through faith in Christ; but because he spent two lengthy periods in prison the only way he could communicate his teaching to the churches was by setting it down on paper in the form of letters, and sending these to various groups and individuals. God willed that Paul should be imprisoned so that the teaching of Christ should be preserved in written form, and passed on down through the centuries right up to today. In more recent times, it was because John Bunyan was shut in prison for many years that he had time to write *The Pilgrim's Progress*.

Despite his imprisonment Paul said that God's Word was not chained. Paul was restricted, but God's Word was liberated. It was sent far and wide throughout the world by means of letters. The message spread to all the churches and it has been preserved so that today it has reached almost every country in the world.

For this reason Paul was prepared to put up with any pain. Just as a soldier undergoes hardship for the sake of victory, so Paul endured suffering for the benefit of the elect. He explains who **'the elect'** are in verse 10. They are all those who have already obtained, or who will at some time in the future **'obtain the salvation that is in Christ Jesus'** (2:10). The elect are God's chosen ones. As we speak to people about the Lord we do not know who will respond to the gospel message, but the Lord does know because he has chosen each one of them before the creation of the world (Eph. 1:4). A few verses further on Paul writes, 'The Lord knows those who are his' (2:19).

Some years ago many of those who are now reading these words would not have envisaged, in their wildest dreams, that they would become believers in the Lord Jesus Christ. However, he has called them to follow him, just as he called his first disciples long ago. They responded to his call and now they follow him. Even those who find this doctrine of election difficult to understand would never deny that the work of salvation is God's alone. By his Spirit he convicts people of sin, grants them the desire to forsake their ungodly ways and gives them the ability and power to respond in faith to his gospel call. These people can look back to the time when they were saved and say, 'I am one of those elect people of whom Paul writes.'

Suffering in the life of believers today

For a fourth time in these Pastoral Epistles, Paul uses the phrase, **'Here is a trustworthy saying'** (see also 1 Tim. 1:15; 3:1;4:9; Titus 3:8).

This is followed by what some scholars say is part of an early Christian hymn:

> **If we died with him,**
> **we will also live with him;**
> **if we endure,**
> **we will also reign with him.**
> **If we disown him,**
> **he will also disown us;**
> **if we are faithless,**
> **he will remain faithful,**
> **for he cannot disown himself.**

It has as its theme suffering which leads to glory. It is in four parts, and each starts with the word 'if'. 'In the first two lines the if-clause describes the attitude and action which proceeds from loyalty to Christ... In the last two lines the if-clause describes the attitude and action which proceeds from disloyalty.'[3]

The first line (or couplet in the NIV and other versions such as the NKJV) speaks of our having *died with Christ*. This means that when he died on the cross we died with him. We died in the sense that we have been identified with Christ through his crucifixion. We have died to worldly comfort, ease, advantage and honour. Once, when I was driving Dr Martyn Lloyd-Jones to some television studios where I was going to interview him, I asked him what it was like having a daughter who had a title. He replied, 'I gave up all ambition for that sort of thing when I left medicine and went into the ministry.' He explained that as Lord Horder's assistant he would have been almost certain to have inherited his job and his title!

If we have to choose between the applause of the world and life with Christ, then the spiritual believer will choose Christ and, as a result, he will die to self. If we have been identified with the suffering Saviour we now enjoy the life of the risen Christ. In other words, as his children we shall never die but live eternally with him in glory (see Gal. 2:20).

The second line tells us that if we *endure hardship* with Christ then we shall also reign with him in glory. In Christ we are of royal blood because we are now joined to him through repentance and faith; we are now members of his royal family. In Christ we have been made a kingdom and priests to serve God, our Father (Rev. 1:6). After the sufferings comes the reward of glory and honour.

Following these glorious truths there is a warning. The third line reminds us what will happen *if we disown Christ*. Jesus himself told us what he will do in that case. He said, 'Whoever disowns me before men, I will disown him before my Father in heaven' (Matt. 10:33). If we really took the Scriptures seriously we would tremble every time we read the Lord's words in this passage. Imagine how awful it would be on the Day of Judgement to hear the Lord saying, 'Depart from me, you who are cursed' (Matt. 25:41; see also Matt. 7:23). Will Peter hear these words one day? After all, he denied that he knew the Lord; three times he said it. No. Peter will not have these words spoken to him, because in his great mercy Jesus heard Peter's bitter cries of repentance (Luke 22:62) and forgave him.[4]

Finally, we receive a surprise in the last line. We would have expected to read, 'If we are faithless, he will also be faithless,' but he does not continue in that vein. Instead he declares, 'If we are faithless [and how often we are!], he will remain faithful.' Nothing can stop the Lord being faithful to his word. It is one of those things which he cannot do; he cannot disown himself. This is one of the most wonderful things about the Lord. He is always true to himself, and he never lets anyone down. However badly a believer may treat his God, the Lord never stoops to our level of ingratitude. When he says, 'Whoever comes to me I will never drive away' (John 6:37) he means it, and he welcomes sinners who approach him in repentance and faith.

Paul ends this section here because he wants Timothy to remember that he has died to self; his own desires have been nailed to the cross (Col. 2:14), and he must gladly endure suffering for the sake of Christ. Timothy must not shirk his duty, despite any ridicule which may be hurled at him. He must be faithful to the Lord who has called him by his grace.

And what Timothy was required to do by Christ's law of love — so are each one of God's people.

28.
The work of a minister
of the gospel

Please read 2 Timothy 2:14-19

Have you ever thought what it is like to pastor a church? When I told my father that God had called me to the Christian ministry he said, 'I never thought a son of mine would have a one-day-a-week job.' I know that he was joking, and he realized that there was more to the task than just turning up on Sunday mornings and evenings and taking the services, but I doubt if he had any idea of all of the different pressures that come to bear upon a minister of the gospel. Martin Luther once said, 'Prayer, study and suffering make a pastor.'[1]

The Christian minister has the responsibility to preach the Word of God in all its fulness. The pastor stands at the front of the church each week as a man who is answerable — not just to the other elders and deacons, but to God. On the Day of Judgement the Lord will question him and say, 'Did you carry out all of your obligations diligently? Were you faithful to the Bible? Were you true to the charge laid upon you to "Preach the Word; be prepared in season and out of season," whether you felt like it or not, and to "correct, rebuke and encourage — with great patience and careful instruction"?' (4:2).

Those who are pastors know that preaching the Word of God week by week, to the same congregation, is an awesome task. That is why Paul compares a minister to a craftsman. If a workman wants to sell his wares, the purchaser will want to know about the quality of his work. If you were going to buy a handmade chair from a craftsman you would examine it before you handed over your money. You would look at it closely. You would feel it and run your fingers over the joints to see that each one fitted snugly. You would touch the chair carefully to see that there were no rough edges on it, and that the polishing had been done to perfection. Above all, you would sit on it to make sure that it bore your weight without falling apart under you.

It is the same with a minister of the gospel. His work is carefully tested, by people (to see whether they can understand what he is saying) and by the Lord God Almighty (to make sure that the gospel of salvation is being faithfully proclaimed).

Build up the church

One important purpose of all Christian preaching and teaching is to edify the people. Everything that is done in the church should be aimed at building up the congregation in their faith, and if they have no faith, then the preacher and teacher must point his hearers to the Lord Jesus Christ as the only Saviour from sin. He should urge them to believe on the Lord and seek his forgiveness for their sins and make them his children.

A sermon is not just a little diversion which is placed in between the pieces of music. It is not a pleasant little talk which is designed to make people feel better inside. Its purpose is not merely to give people information about the religion called Christianity.

The function of a sermon is to nurture the people in the truth of God. That means that it should instruct them in the teaching of the Bible. It should encourage them to follow closely the

Lord Jesus Christ, and it should show everyone the way in which they can live more Christlike lives. All preachers need to be reminded constantly that these are the aims of good preaching.

A sermon is not meant to be an oration which gives the speaker the opportunity to show off his knowledge. No minister should spend his time just arguing about words (2:14). He should not take 'an unhealthy interest in controversies and quarrels about words that result in envy, strife, malicious talk, evil suspicions and constant friction between men of corrupt mind' (1 Tim. 6:4-5). This does not mean, of course, that he shies away from the task of confronting error; Jesus was often very controversial, but he never took an unhealthy interest in the hobby of fault-finding. Paul felt so strongly about this that he wrote, in verse 14, **'Keep reminding them... Warn them before God against quarrelling about words.'**

Some Christian people seem to take great delight in writing to Christian newspapers and magazines to complain about what another brother or sister has said or written. Indeed certain Christian groups are noted for their pedantic 'nit-picking' on doctrine and church practices. This is not what a good Christian minister of the Word should spend his time doing. Paul's verdict on these kinds of exercises is that they are **'of no value'**.

The danger of this kind of behaviour is that 'quarrelling about words' is not only of 'no value', but, far worse, it **'ruins those who listen'**. The Greek word which is translated 'ruin' is *'katastrophe'*, from which we get our English word 'catastrophe'. We should make sure that our work for the Lord does not end up like that. We should beware lest our Christian activity ruins others. Instead we should desire to use the Word of God correctly so that God's people will be built up in the way in which God wants them to go.[2]

Seek to please God

The great temptation which comes to pastors so often is that
they want to please men — especially those who pay them.
They do all in their power to make sure that they do not offend
the officers of the church. If a pastor does not preach well, or
fails to tell the people what they want to hear, then if his
congregation is unspiritual, he is in danger of being dismissed.

However, in the end, it is not to men that preachers are
answerable, but to God, and Paul says that God's servants
must always **'do [their] best'** to please him. This phrase is also
used in 4:9 and 4:21. Ministers are required to work hard, to
pray diligently and to study and minister the Word of God. The
idea of effort, striving and hard work runs all the way through
these letters to Timothy. In 3:17 the preacher is described as a
man of God who is to be 'thoroughly equipped for every good
work', and in 4:5 the task of an evangelist is described as work.

Many years ago a great servant of God was asked by some
students, 'What is the secret of your success in the ministry?'
It seems that they were expecting him to say something like,
'I get up at 1 a.m. every morning and then spend five hours in
prayer.' This would then have been regarded by them as
something far beyond their attainment and, therefore, a matter
which they could ignore. However, the old minister replied
with two simple words: 'Hard work'. At this the student
ministers left him and got on with their coffee break.[3]

Preachers should try to present themselves to God as those
who are approved (2:15). God is the one who will test their
work, and they need to pass his test. In fact they should do their
work with the aim of presenting it to God. Just as the Old
Testament believers offered their sacrifices of animals, or
meal, to God, so ministers should present their work to God for
his approval.

Preachers should be workmen who have nothing to be ashamed about. If they are taking their responsibilities seriously and spiritually they will know that they have worked hard at their task. They will have put much time, energy, thought and prayer into the preparation of their services, and they will have done much background reading. In short, they will want to please God. They will want to pass the test. Their aim is to be those who are not ashamed of their offering. They do not only desire to be able to say, 'Well, I've done my best.' They want to be those who have laboured hard to bring glory to God and his blessings to his people (see Phil. 1:20), and the way in which they do this is by **'correctly [handling] the word of truth'** (2:15).

The same idea is found in Proverbs 3:6 and 11:5, where we read of making a straight path or way. The expression used means 'cutting a straight road through a forest or difficult country so that the traveller may go directly to his destination'.[4] A preacher should work hard to give an accurate explanation of the meaning of the passage, and he should make that meaning clear and plain to his hearers by ramming home the truth of it with relevant and practical illustrations.

Highlight wrong teaching

In his work the pastor should **'avoid godless chatter'**. Indeed on the Day of Judgement all men will have to give an account for 'every careless word they have spoken' (Matt. 12:36). There were those in Ephesus who engaged in hair-splitting and 'fictitious genealogical histories' (1 Tim. 1:4). It seems that they took the teaching of Paul and 'interpreted' it in the light of their own foolish speculations,[5] but this kind of thing is deceitful.

The Christian pastor must do all in his power to silence anything which tries to twist the clear teaching of God's Word. Those who seek to make Scripture mean something other than its plain meaning are leading people away from God. Many modern heresies have arisen through the teaching of people like Barbara Teiring (who has developed ideas from the Essenes) and Bishop John Spong (who advocates homosexual marriages). These, and many others, have their basis in the ancient heresies and errors of the early church. Many new ideas also seem to have come about through those who research for a Ph. D degree in Theology. Because students are required to produce original thinking, this kind of research has proved to be a breeding-ground for false doctrines which arise from outside of the Scriptures. It is the gospel preacher's task to denounce all of these things which are contrary to the Word of God; he thus shows that he is a faithful **'workman who does not need to be ashamed'**.

In the time of Paul and Timothy it was necessary to speak out against the teaching of people like Hymenaeus and Philetus. Hymenaeus had already been excommunicated for at least a year (see 1 Tim. 1:20). Now this man reappears and brings with him his friend Philetus; he is still causing trouble in the church. Paul's verdict on these men is that they must be silenced. They should be given no opportunity to teach error among the people of God because their teaching was **'like gangrene'**. I always think of the fighting in the trenches of the First World War when I hear that word. So many young soldiers were wounded and left unattended in the mud for many hours, or even days, and by the time they eventually reached the field-hospitals gangrene had set in. This infection not only damaged their wounded limbs, it would also spread to affect the remaining healthy tissues of their bodies. The only remedy in such cases was to amputate the affected hand or foot before the terrible disease could spread any further around the body.

This is the exact reason why false teachers and wrong teaching must be dealt with immediately before the error spreads and causes a great deal of trouble. Erroneous teaching causes some people to become **'more and more ungodly'** (2:16) and it even destroys the faith of some (2:18). This wrong teaching came in various forms but we only have one example given here, and that is a very subtle one. It must have started with a grain of truth, as error usually does. The Lord Jesus Christ certainly rose from the dead and, in Christ, all believers have also risen with him in a spiritual sense. But these false teachers were teaching that this spiritual resurrection is all we should expect. They were denying the truth that one day each of God's people will rise from our graves to reign with Christ in glory (see John 5:28). Paul taught this same truth very clearly in 1 Corinthians 15. Philippians 3:21 says that Christ 'will transform our lowly bodies so that they will be like his glorious body'.

Because false teachers are still with us, we should be very quick to eradicate any wrong teaching, and certainly never give them the opportunity to preach and teach in any church for which we have responsibility. Even high church dignitaries must be shunned if they teach error. God's Word must be upheld at all costs.

Encourage God's people

None of the things which go wrong in our service for God should cause us to be discouraged. We may get the impression that the church is falling apart around us and that no one else is supporting us in the work. Sometimes the devil seems to be having it all his own way and, almost everywhere we go, wrong teaching is gaining ground. When we feel like that we should take courage because, as Paul says, **'Nevertheless** [despite all of these disappointments], **God's solid foundation stands firm, sealed with this inscription: "The Lord knows those who are his"'** (2:19).

The foundation which God has already laid for his church is none other than the Lord Jesus Christ (1 Cor. 3:11). He is absolutely stable and will never fail anyone. Individual churches may 'go off the rails' sometimes but God's church is secure because it is built on the rock which is Christ Jesus, and it has the seal of God's ownership upon it, just as a sack of corn was often marked with the owner's seal while it was awaiting his collection at the market-place. This is God's seal: 'The Lord knows those who are his.' He knows which individuals are his own people because he sent his Son to die on the cross for them.

God 'chose [each one of his people] in him before the creation of the world' (Eph. 1:4). There was certainly nothing good in any one of us to make the Lord set his choice upon us; in fact we were, and are, sinners in thought, word and deed, but he has set his love upon us. Ephesus 1:4 goes on to say, 'He chose us … to be holy and blameless in his sight.' This is the same teaching with which Paul continues here: **'Everyone who confesses the name of the Lord must turn away from wickedness'** (2:19).

There are two sides to being a Christian. There are things to believe — 'The Lord knows us and died for us' — and there are things to obey — we must 'turn away from wickedness'. When we were first converted we came to believe in the Lord Jesus Christ as our Saviour and we also turned away from our sins. These two aspects of salvation continue with us throughout the whole of our Christian lives; repentance and faith must be exercised daily by each of us who profess faith in Christ.

This teaching is illustrated in the Old Testament in Numbers 16. There we read about a rebellion instigated by Korah and some of his companions. Just like Hymenaeus and Philetus, Korah and his friends rebelled against the Word of God. Because of their disobedience the ground opened up and swallowed them. When the authority of God was challenged Moses said to Korah and the others, 'In the morning the Lord will show who belongs to him and who is holy' (Num.16:5). Then, just before the judgement of God fell, he said to the rest of the Israelites, 'Move back from the tents of these wicked men! Do not touch anything belonging to them, or you will be swept away' (Num. 16:26).

The same warning held good for those false teachers at Ephesus; unless they repented, they too would be utterly destroyed. The people of God would then be aware that the Lord knows those who belong to him; these should, therefore, turn away from all wickedness.

This is the work of the Christian minister: through the preaching of the gospel he affirms those who belong to the Lord. These are the ones who repent of their sin and turn to Christ in faith. The preacher also must exhort those who are true believers to make it their constant endeavour to turn away from all wickedness. Repentance is not something which we do once only, when we first become Christians. It is something which we should spend a lifetime doing. We should always be seeking to be more holy, and more Christlike. If we profess to belong to God, and to be his servants, then we should make every effort to live a life which is fully consecrated to the Lord and his work.

29.
The character of a minister

Please read 2 Timothy 2:20-26

'He leads such a holy life,' said the person sitting opposite me at a wedding reception. We were talking about a certain minister of the gospel who was known to both of us.

My neighbour went on to say that this particular pastor spends many hours in prayer and working in his study. 'In fact,' he continued, 'he is nearly always shut up in his room and few people see him during the day, except some elderly folk whom he visits from time to time.' This pastor is so taken up with his pursuit of holiness and the study of the Word of God that he appears to have cut himself off from most of the people in his congregation. His sermons are full of the teaching of the Bible. They are long and saturated with very profound thoughts — so much so that many of his hearers do not understand what he is talking about.

Is this the way in which Paul wanted Timothy to behave? I think not. The apostle certainly wanted Timothy to be holy, but he also wanted him to be active among the people. In the previous verses Paul had been comparing the church of Jesus Christ to a great building which had been erected on a very solid base. This foundation will never let the church, or any of its members, down. Not only that, this church has two inscriptions high up in its stonework. They read: 'The Lord knows those who are his,' and 'Everyone who confesses the name of the Lord must turn away from wickedness' (2:19).

From thinking about the outside of the building, Paul then turns his attention to the inside of the house, and especially to the instruments (or utensils) which are used in the kitchen and the dining room.

Ready for the Master's use

Paul divides these containers into two kinds: some are made of precious metals like gold and silver. Obviously these are the special bowls and goblets which are used at the master's table. They are kept strictly for the use of the owner of this large house and his important guests. Because they are expensive, they must be handled with care. After the meal, when they are finished with, it is important that these are washed up and put away safely before anything else.

These vessels are those which are used **'for noble purposes'**. However, there are the other containers. These are all made of wood and clay (or earthenware). They are never used on the master's table. They are objects like buckets and bowls into which the left-over scraps are put and the dirty washing-up water is poured. These are described as those which are for **'ignoble'** purposes. When these are cracked or chipped (as they easily will be) they are taken to the rubbish dump and thrown away.

We can tell that Paul is depicting a large house because in smaller homes of ordinary people there would be no silver or gold cups and plates — only cheap receptacles. He is using this picture of a large house for the sake of his illustration and because he is comparing it to the professing church which, even in those early days, covered a very wide geographical area. Of course, he is not demeaning poor homes and implying there is something intrinsically shameful about vessels made of cheaper materials; he is only pointing out a contrast.

So what was Paul referring to when he wrote about these articles, which are for noble and for ignoble purposes? He was speaking about preachers and teachers. The objects which were used for noble purposes are like the true servants of God — people like Paul and Timothy who preach God's Word faithfully instead of distorting it for their own ends. Paul's message is that all true servants of God must cleanse, or, in other words, dissociate themselves from the erroneous teachers and all their works.

Paul then writes about three marks of a noble Christian character. He is referring to ministers of the gospel, elders and others who preach and teach God's Word.

Firstly, those who stay away from false teaching (cleanse themselves from it) will be made **'holy'**. They will want to be free from the contamination of the world. They will turn away from wickedness (2:19) and will be wholly given over to seeking to be pure in thought, word and deed. They will obey the injunction of God which says, 'Be holy, because I am holy' (1 Peter 1:15). They will want to free their thoughts, their speech and their actions from anything which is unrighteous. In other words, they will want to be like Jesus Christ.

Secondly, those who cleanse themselves from false teaching will be **'useful to the Master'**, the Lord Jesus Christ. Those who serve God will want to become slaves of Christ; their desire will be to obey him in all things. This is how they will show that they love him: they will obey his commandments. He told his disciples, 'If you love me, you will obey what I command' (John 14:15). The wish of every true servant of Christ is to be useful to the Lord. Whatever personal cost or inconvenience he might have to go through, God's will is what will come uppermost in his mind.

Thirdly, those who cleanse themselves from false teaching will be **'prepared to do any good work'**. The Boy Scouts' motto is 'Be prepared' — and presumably that means, 'Be prepared to do anything which is wholesome.' Likewise the servant of God should always be prepared to do any good work.

Some people think that they are saved because of their own good works. But we know that is not the case because it is the blood of Christ alone, which he shed upon the cross, which cleanses us from our sins. The servants of God (whether they are preachers or those who do tasks in the background) must be constantly performing deeds of kindness. Paul tells us that 'We are God's workmanship, created in Christ Jesus to do good works, which God prepared in advance for us to do' (Eph. 2:10).

Pure in thoughts and actions

If a servant of God is to be useful to God then he must turn aside from those things which would hold him back from holiness. He must **'flee the evil desires of youth'** (2:22; see also 1 Tim. 6:11). Not everything that young people want is evil, but they do have strong desires which are sometimes quite contrary to God's Word.

Timothy was comparatively young, probably in his mid-to-late thirties. Paul would certainly have known about the urges that young people have.

First, Paul means that they have powerful sexual drives which must be channelled into right avenues. He was aware that there was much immorality around in Corinth, so he counsels that 'Each man should have his own wife' (1 Cor. 7:2). He continues, 'It is better to marry than to burn with passion' (1 Cor. 7:9). Our modern day is every bit as bad as ancient Corinth. Christian young people must make sure that they flee away from immoral behaviour.

Secondly, young people have natural desires for power. They crave to be 'number one'. They want to dominate in the crowd and they despise authority (see 2 Peter 2:10). However, these strong desires must be subdued by the young believer.

Thirdly, young people crave after more and more possessions. They want the 'glory' of being able to show off their latest acquisitions to their friends. As I write, hi-tech computer games are a great status symbol. The fashion industry has capitalized on this craving for possessions. They know that it is the young, unmarried men and women who often have money burning a hole in their pockets, and so they aim their advertisements at them. But young Christians must make sure that they get things into perspective instead of thinking only of themselves.

If anyone wants to be useful to God then he or she must turn away from all the evil desires of youth. The rest of us, too, need to remember that it is not only the young in years who have these desires; older Christians too, must turn aside from unhealthy, lustful passions.

At this point (2:22), Paul turns from the negative to the positive in his teaching. He says not only that a servant of God should flee from the evil desires of youth, but that he should **'pursue righteousness, faith, love and peace'**. He should run away from all evil urges and run towards good desires. He should seek after those good things with all his might. He should seek *righteousness*. He should endeavour to see that the desires of his heart and mind are in harmony with God's law.[1] He should also pursue *faith*. This means that he should have great confidence in God and trust everything into his care and control. He should also desire *love*. This does not mean the sloppy, sentimental kind of love that the music industry deals in. This love is the love which God generates in the hearts of his obedient people. It is a deep personal affection which reaches out to every brother and sister in Christ, and even to the enemies of believers in Christ. Finally, the child of God should want *peace* above everything else. This is that deep-down security which comes to all those who are in a right relationship with God. It is the 'peace of God, which transcends all understanding', which guards the hearts and minds of all those who are in Christ Jesus (Phil. 4:7)

The believer should engage in the pursuit of all of these virtues, and should delight to do so in company with **'those who call on the Lord out of a pure heart'** (2:22). These are the kind of people he or she should mix, or go around, with. It is the company we keep that so often stamps out the pattern for our behaviour. The young people who get caught up in the wrong crowd are often those who spend their time hanging around street corners with nothing special to do.

So often younger people want to mix with those who love arguments; in churches we sometimes find that those in their early twenties, who have newly graduated from university, behave as though they think that the purpose of church Bible studies is to give them the opportunity to air their knowledge and sharpen their intellectual wits.

This is exactly what the Greeks and the Hebrews enjoyed doing. 'They were greatly given to controversies of various kinds; and many of the questions discussed pertained to points which could not be settled, or which, if settled, were of no importance.'[2] Paul had already said that quarrelling about words is of 'no value' (2:14). It is no wonder, then, that the apostle calls these arguments **'foolish and stupid'**. In the end these 'discussions' only lead to quarrels, and quarrels are futile. They produce more heat than light. The apostle reminds Timothy that he already knows about these dangers: **'You know they produce quarrels'** (2:23). This is another warning for us not to get involved in controversies about words. Rather, we should be pursuing righteousness, faith, love and peace.

Always gentle

Despite the fact that a minister has much to put up with, he should always be gentle. He ought to be **'kind to everyone'** (2:24). Sometimes a pastor will know that certain members of the congregation are saying horrible things about him, and he may even be aware that some are trying their best to have him dismissed from his post. Paul told Timothy that when a minister knows of such things he must handle the matter gently. Also when he realizes that some of the congregation are achieving greater success than he is able to do, he must **'not'** be **'resentful'** of their achievements. Hendriksen translates this phrase by saying that the Lord's servant must be 'patient under injuries'.[3]

When a pastor is hurt, he must not retaliate; he must leave everything in the Lord's hands. He must always act in a gentle manner. Naturally he will not like it when people oppose him, but he must always behave towards others in a Christlike way — however badly they treat him.

A servant of God must **'gently instruct'** those who oppose him (2:25). He must be **'able to teach'** (2:24). No one who is continually 'flying off the handle' teaches anyone anything. Those with quick tempers must learn to control them. Paul had already said that elders must be able to teach (1 Tim. 3:2). This means that they must have a thorough knowledge of the truths of the gospel. They must so love these truths that they have a strong desire to pass them on to others. They should be so enthusiastic about this task that they will spend a great deal of time learning how to do this successfully.

A servant of God must be gentle in the way he gives his instruction because his desire is that those who are wrong will be led to repent of their errors rather than simply be punished for them. **'Repentance'** is God's gift. Sinners cannot just decide that they will leave their old ways. God has to be at work in their hearts, leading them into his ways. Also those who truly repent will turn away from their wrong ways and turn towards **'a knowledge of the truth'**. True Christians have not just turned over a new leaf. They are those who have turned their backs upon their old paths, and turned to God. They have faith in him because of what the Lord Jesus Christ did on the cross of Calvary.

God's servants preach the gospel in such a way that people will **'come to their senses'** (2:26). Jesus teaches about this in the parable of the prodigal son, There was a time when that young man came to his senses (Luke 15:17). He realized what a sad condition he was in. He knew that his life was heading nowhere, and so he stopped in his tracks and did something about it. He came to his senses when he thought about his father and his home. When people start to think of the grace of God and the joy of heaven, then they will want to turn away from the snares of the devil and reach out for God.

But the devil is very subtle. His evil work is to trap people, and the ones whom he especially wants to ensnare are the servants of God — those who have a leadership role within a church (1 Tim. 3:7). Satan loves to see God's servants disgraced. He delights when he is able to lure a pastor into wickedness. He uses all kinds of methods to do this, including the evil desires of youth. How many Christian leaders have fallen into sin (sometimes very public sin) because of the lust of pride and sex, because of the love of money and power, or because they wanted to show off their vast stores of knowledge?[4] The Evil One wants to prevent Christian people from doing God's will, because he wants them to do his will.

How can we be vessels who are useful to the Lord? We can serve God best by being what he wants us to be. He desires that we should be clean and ready and eager to serve him. He wants us to run away from everything which is evil and not to be sidetracked into foolish speculation. We are to be kind and gentle as we carry out our work for the Lord, and to help to rescue others from the clutches of the devil. We can only do any of these things as we trust in the Lord with all our heart, mind and soul.

30.
Beware of counterfeits

Please read 2 Timothy 3:1-9

Why do people go to church? Some like to go because they can spend an enjoyable hour in the company of nice people; they discover that they feel a lovely warm glow spreading all over their bodies. Others like to have a good sing and be made to feel really happy; while others like to have their intellects stimulated so that they can go home and have a great argument with their friends over some point of doctrine or church practice.

These, and many others, are the sorts of reasons people often give for going to church. They want to be ministered to. They want to be made to feel content. They want to have their needs met, and they hope to leave, at the end of the service, with a sense of satisfaction and well-being.

Yet when Paul wrote this part of his letter to Timothy it was not his intention to impart such a cosy feeling to his young friend. The apostle warns Timothy to be on his guard against false teachers, as he does all the way through this letter. He has constantly been exhorting the young pastor to be careful of those who were trying to wreak havoc among the people of God.

Today God's servants need to be wide awake because among the professing church of Jesus Christ there are those who are not displaying true marks of grace. There are those, even in important positions in certain churches, who are teaching and preaching things which are contrary to the gospel of salvation.

The character of these people

It is clear from these things that we are living in **'the last days'** today. In the upper room on the Day of Pentecost, Peter and the other apostles were suddenly filled with the Holy Spirit (Acts 2:4) and, as a consequence, they rushed out to the crowds at Jerusalem and with great boldness preached to each section of the crowd, using the language spoken by each of the nations represented. At the beginning of his sermon Peter quoted from the prophet Joel. He said, 'In the last days, God says, I will pour out my Spirit on all people' (Acts 2:17). These 'last days' were those which began with the first coming of Jesus. They continue today, and they will go on right until the end of this age. The writer to the Hebrews makes it clear that the last days are not just those which will immediately precede Christ's return in glory. He says, 'In the past God spoke to our forefathers through the prophets at many times and in various ways, but in these last days he has spoken to us by his Son' (Heb. 1:1-2).

Paul goes on to inform Timothy, not only that he was living in the last days, but that there will be **'terrible times'** in these days. What is more, these 'grievous seasons' will vary in intensity. Ever since the time of the early church there have been, and there will continue to be, specific periods when life becomes extremely difficult for God's people.

John Stott tells us that in Classical Greek the word translated 'terrible' was used both of dangerous wild animals and of the raging sea.[1] Imagine what this phrase must have meant to the early believers as persecution was just beginning to get under way in the church. There would have been terrible times in the arena when defenceless believers were left to the mercy of hungry lions (simply for the entertainment of the Roman crowd). Or consider what it must have been like to have been caught out in the Aegean Sea in one of those frail sailing vessels, when winter descended with the whole force of its destructive power in the winds and waves (see Acts 27).

Timothy and the believers at Ephesus may have already been experiencing the onslaughts of their oppressors, but Paul did not say, 'Never mind! That's all over now.' Instead he warned them that things would go 'from bad to worse' (3:13). Being a Christian in those days was no easy thing. 'In fact,' Paul told Timothy, 'everyone who wants to live a godly life in Christ Jesus will be persecuted' (3:12). This is a very positive statement. There is nothing vague about it at all. Clearly it was no easy thing to be follower of Christ then, any more than it is always effortless today. But if we find things hard now, how will we fare in the coming days when our faith in Christ will be tested more and more severely? Are we ready for that to happen? Will we bear up under the trial?

Paul then lists the characteristics of these people who claim to be believers in the Lord Jesus Christ, but are not. There are at least eighteen different distinctive things which he says about them. He uses very clear words and phrases which we can easily understand as he catalogues the awful events which are to come.

Each of these matters is centred around the love of self. This is the exact spirit which pervades the lives of people in this age in which we live. These false Christians were **'lovers of themselves, lovers of money ... not lovers of the good'** (in God or in other people) and **'lovers of pleasure rather than lovers of God'** (3:2-3).

Ephesus was a wealthy port. There were many very rich people living there in those days. The ruins of the city which have been unearthed, and which can be visited today, show what a wealthy place it was. Obviously the love of money, power and possessions had a great influence upon those who claimed to be members of the church, but who were, in fact, unbelievers.

A few verses earlier Paul has been telling Timothy that the servant of God must be clean, holy and useful to the Lord (2:21). Now he contrasts this with the kind of attitude that the people of the world were then displaying. He says that those who claimed to be members of the church (but were not) were **'boastful, proud, abusive...'**. Each of these properties was an indication of the selfishness that existed in the hearts of these false believers.

Then he spoke about their attitude to their parents. One of the awful things about the world today is the way in which children treat their parents. It was the same in Paul's day. Young people were **'disobedient to their parents'**. They were **'ungrateful'** for all that their mothers and fathers had done for them, and the sacrifices which they had made on their behalf. They were not prepared to submit to the leadership which God had placed over them when he put them into families. And they had forgotten the fifth commandment: 'Honour your father and your mother, so that you may live long in the land the Lord your God is giving you' (Exod. 20:12).

Next Paul writes about their attitude to God's natural laws. He said that they were **'without love'**, and what they called love was misdirected. Furthermore they were not prepared to forgive one another for the things they had inflicted on each other. They allowed themselves to be under the control of the devil; and they devoted themselves to saying **'slanderous'** things against one another. They failed to exercise normal **'self-control'**, such as God requires and society at large demands of its citizens. They knew little about gentleness; instead in their dealings with one another they were **'brutal'**, just like wild beasts. And they did not see 'goodness, truth and beauty' anywhere around them; rather they hated everything which was good and wholesome.

Paul continues this list of evil by pointing out that these false Christians were just like Judas. They betrayed Christ (who never did any wrong to anyone). They were **'treacherous'** (like icy roads in the winter-time); **'rash'** (they never took the trouble to think ahead before they acted); and **'conceited'** (there appeared to be nothing that they did not know!).

Finally, these people were hypocrites. They made out that they were lovers of God, while, in effect, they were lovers of pleasure. That is all they wanted out of their religion — to have a good time. We certainly find many people like that today. They only go to church to get something out of it for themselves. These people feel cheated if they do not get a blessing from the service. If they do not come away from church feeling important, then they start to look for another church which will enhance their self-esteem.

The people of today are no better than those of whom Paul was writing to Timothy. They are lovers of pleasure rather than lovers of God. They have a form of godliness, but they deny its power. They are more interested in their own prestige than in the power of the gospel.

The craftiness of their actions

People who are active in churches but are not real Christians are very subtle. They have to be because the whole of their life is a lie and they are trying to deceive the elect of God. They are enemies of the gospel. They are apostates, who have turned aside, away from the faith (see Gal. 1:6), and they are seeking to drag many others down with them.

Because they wish to do the maximum possible damage, they set to work on the weakest people in the church. They attack **'weak-willed women'** (3:6). Paul does not say that all women are weak-willed, nor does he imply that all men are strong. In the society of those days women were not allowed 'to see anything, to hear anything, or to ask any questions'. They were never allowed to appear alone on the streets, even on a shopping expedition, and they were never permitted to go to a public meeting. But the coming of Christ emancipated women, and they took a much more prominent role in the church than they ever did in Greek or Roman communities.[2]

However, there were some women who could not cope with the extra responsibilities placed upon them. Some ladies are particularly liable to be taken advantage of because women tend to be more caring, more understanding and more sensitive to the needs of other people. Certainly, there were women in Ephesus who were weak-willed, and it was mainly they who were taken in by false teachers. Today some men, who are undoubtedly Christians, are so weak and ineffectual that they too could be described as 'weak-willed [old] women'.

The teachers of error wormed their way into the homes of those who were vulnerable. We can imagine their smarmy talk as they slithered their way into the houses of these weak women. They were up to no good, but these silly women either did not realize it, or they did not care. Perhaps they were so bored with life that they were pleased to talk to anyone who would stop and spend time with them.

The aim of these preachers of error was to **'gain control'** over these weak-willed women. The leaders of certain sects of today have, to a remarkable extent, gained control over the lives of their followers and many of them have ended their lives in disaster.[3]

These women, whom the false teachers influenced so effectively, were already **'loaded down with sins'**. Paul meant that when they committed one sin, then they quickly and easily fell into another, and another, until these were piled up one upon the other. The weight of these sins was so heavy, and they had borne them for so long, that because of the pleasure they received from them, they were prepared to put up with the heaviness of their iniquity. In any case, these women were so **'swayed by ... evil desires'** that they had even forgotten what was right and what was wrong. Gratifying self was at the very top of their agendas.

The false teachers not only led these women astray, they blinded them with a show of knowledge. They started teaching them about God and man and what they said seemed to make sense. Yet all the while these false teachers were preaching doctrines which were contrary to the Word of God. Because of the skill of these apostates, the women were led away from the truth as it is in Jesus.

'Jannes and Jambres' were the names which Jewish tradition had given to the two leaders of Pharaoh's magicians of whom we read in Exodus chapters 7-9. They **'opposed Moses'** and counterfeited almost every miracle he did. On the face of it they appeared to be displaying the power of God. Yet in fact they were just imitating the works of Moses. Likewise, the apostates of Timothy's day were merely imitating true religion: they had **'a form of godliness but [denied] its power'**. They had depraved minds, and only God could straighten them out.

The destiny of their souls

Paul does not say to Timothy, 'Get alongside these people and try to bring them to see the error of their ways.' He had said that about true believers who had opposed the teaching of Timothy. He urged his young friend to gently instruct the latter 'in the hope that God will grant them repentance [and lead] them to a knowledge of the truth' (2:25). But these apostates had to be handled quite differently. They were crafty people who were the enemies of the truth. There was only one thing that could be done with those who were set so rigidly in their opposition to the Lord Jesus Christ, and that was to **'have nothing to do with them'** (3:5).

This seems to be very harsh treatment, but the command is here in Scripture and it makes sense. It will do us no good to say, 'I'm strong enough to resist the evil efforts of people who distort the truth of God.' Let us not be so foolish. If they persistently reject our Lord and his Word, then they will reject us and our efforts to win them over. All we can do is to leave them to the mercy of God and pray that he will bring them to repentance. If that happens then will be the time for us to speak to them and do our best to help them back into the paths of God's Word.

God has already done something about these people. Paul tells us that **'as far as the faith** [the whole body of Christian belief] **is concerned,'** these men **'are rejected'** (3:8). How awful for anyone to reject Christ's offer of mercy, but how much more solemn it is for God to reject a soul!

These people are still active in their opposition to God and his Word. The verdict of the Scriptures upon them is that **'They will not get very far.'** However, in one sense, they had already gone too far.[4] Their foolishness has already been displayed to those who have the illumination of the Holy Spirit and one day their stupidity will be on show for the whole world to see.

What should we do about false teachers in our day? We should never allow them to perpetuate their ideas in our hearing. However brilliant their preaching is, we must never allow any of them to minister in any place where we have responsibility. Those who wish to pick and choose which parts of the Bible are divinely inspired and which are not should never be allowed to teach in any place where we have any influence.

We live in difficult days, but let us not live only for ourselves and the easy way of life. Let us live for God. The truth of God's Word and the sound teaching of it are what really matters. Let the teaching of the Bible control our minds and all of our actions.

31.
Pressing onward

Please read 2 Timothy 3:10-17

At the time of writing this, the oldest member of the church of which I am the pastor is ninety-one years old. She is totally blind and, because she is unable to move around very much, she lives almost the whole of her time in her room in the home where she is cared for. Apart from occasional visitors, her only companions are her radios, each of which is tuned to one of her two favourite radio stations. When I visit her and ask her how she is, she usually looks up, smiles and says, 'Pressing on.' She lives a very lonely existence because her few relatives live several hundred miles away from her, but she trusts in the Lord every moment of each day as she tries to bide her time patiently until he calls her to himself.

Timothy was only a comparatively young man, but Paul wrote to him encouraging him to live his life pressing on. He urges him to move forward in his Christian life and his pastoral responsibilities, saying, 'Continue in what you have learned and have become convinced of' (3:14).

Looking backwards

There was much to discourage Timothy. All around him were evil men. They lived only for what they could get out of life for themselves, and they were also bent on leading others astray from the paths of godliness.

This young servant of God must have often been cast down because of the activities of these wicked teachers of error. He must have felt at times like running away from his responsibilities in the church, yet on at least two occasions Paul appealed to him 'stay there' (1 Tim. 1:3) and carry on with the good work of preaching and teaching the gospel.

Timothy had often suffered in his work, but Paul encouraged him not to allow that to dishearten him. One of the ways in which he could seek inspiration was to look back on his life and see how the Lord had led him thus far. We can learn a great deal by remembering some of the things which have happened to us in the past. We can compare our situation today with what it was some ten or twenty years ago. We shall find that we can trace God's hand at work in our lives as we remember how he has brought us through many times of trial and testing. We can say, with the psalmist, 'A righteous man may have many troubles, but the Lord delivers him from them all' (Ps. 34:19).

Paul does something here which we must be very wary of doing: he draws attention to himself. When some people do this we learn, to our grief, that their only topic of conversation is themselves. They can talk about nothing else but what they have done, where they have been, whom they have met and what they are planning to do in the future. We shy away from such people because they are bores! But Paul only refers to himself in order to encourage Timothy. He says, **'You ... know all about my teaching.'** Of course Timothy knew about it because he had often listened eagerly to Paul as he had expounded the Word of God and explained God's plan and purpose for mankind. Paul lists nine things here which particularly belonged to him. Each once is preceded by the word 'my'. The teaching of God's Word is important for Christian living. Anyone who tries to live as a Christian and ignores the doctrines of the Bible is going to be a very poor Christian.

Out of this Bible teaching sprang many of Paul's qualities. His **'way of life'** was dictated by what he believed. His **'purpose'** for living was determined by the teaching of the Bible, and because of this his life displayed four great features. He had **'faith'** — this means that he clung on to God. He possessed **'patience'** — he lived his life for God's glory, so he had patience with all those many people who tried to make his existence difficult. He glowed with **'love'** — he had love for God and for other people (unlike the false teachers who were only lovers of themselves, of money and of pleasure, see 2:2,4). He demonstrated that he possessed **'endurance'** — he had God's grace which enabled him to display a positive attitude to the effects upon him which the pressures of life brought. And because he had all of these qualities, he could cope with all kinds of **'persecutions'** and **'sufferings'**.

Then Paul reminds Timothy of the things which he himself had had to endure while he was on his first missionary journey in Galatia. This was the region where Timothy was born. It may well have been that Timothy had personally witnessed many of the things that Paul had to go through at that time. It was at about this time that Timothy came to know the Lord Jesus Christ as his Saviour. Maybe he had been challenged by Paul's trust in God, despite his sufferings. At that time, as a very young man, he may have thought something like this: 'What is it that enables this man to still love people when they reject the message which he brings?' Perhaps it was because of the firm trust which Paul had in God that Timothy was led to seek the Lord, confess his sins and come to the foot of Christ's cross crying out to be cleansed and made a new man in Christ.

We can learn about some of the things which had happened to Paul by reading Acts chapters 13-14. At Pisidian Antioch the leading citizens had chased the apostle out of the city (Acts 13:50). At Iconium he had barely escaped a stoning (Acts 14:5), and at Lystra he actually was stoned, dragged out of town and then left for dead (Acts 14:19).

Paul reminds Timothy of the age-old fact that God does care for his own. He says, **'Yet** [despite all the afflictions I went through] **the Lord rescued me from all of them'** (3:11). Following this statement he states two indisputable facts.

The first is that **'Everyone who wants to live a godly life in Christ Jesus will be persecuted'** (3:12). Jesus had said the same kind of thing to his disciples in Matthew 10:22: 'All men will hate you because of me.' Paul himself had told the believers, 'We must go through many hardships to enter the kingdom of God' (Acts 14:22), and Peter wrote in his first epistle that Christians should not 'be surprised at the painful trial [they were] suffering' (1 Peter 4:12).

The second fact which Paul states is that **'Evil men and impostors will go from bad to worse, deceiving and being deceived'** (3:13). These false teachers were nothing but frauds (they were like those magicians who impersonated the miracles of Moses, see 3:8). They professed to be making progress while, in fact, they were going from bad to worse.

When evil people propound false teaching they do not even realize how wicked they are. They are so sunk in sin that they not only deceive other people, but they fool themselves as well; they are not aware of the awful state they are in. T. S. Eliot spoke of this age in which we live as one which disowns the church and 'advances progressively backwards'.[1]

Continuing in God's ways

Paul then turns from speaking about himself to Timothy and what is required of him. The apostle says, **'But as for you'**, just as he had previously said, 'You ... know all about my teaching ...' (3:10) and, earlier still, 'You then, my son, be strong in the grace that is in Christ Jesus' (2:1). It is as though Paul was saying, 'Don't let these false teachers get you down.

They are causing you much hassle, and many sleepless nights, but never mind about them. What you need to think about is what you should be doing.' This is how Paul says that Timothy should occupy himself: **'Continue in what you have learned and have become convinced of'** (3:14). Good teaching is something to hang on to. Timothy had been taught the truth about God, man and salvation from sin. Whatever happened, he was to persist in adhering to these truths.

We know that Timothy had been taught by worthy people. He knew, intimately, those who had instructed him in the tenets of the Christian faith. He respected them and he valued their teaching. He knew that these were honest people who had a tremendous regard for the Word of God. How different things are in our day! So many of those who are teaching theology in schools and colleges in these days regard the Bible merely as a manmade, and humanly inspired, book. Because so many of the tutors and lecturers in theological (and even Bible colleges) do not regard the Bible as the inerrant Word of God, their students are getting the message that it is not the voice of God they hear when they read the Scriptures. However, Timothy's teachers believed wholeheartedly that the Scriptures are holy and are the Word that is able to make people wise for salvation, when they have faith in Christ Jesus.

It was the apostle Paul who had taught Timothy, and the young man had no doubt been an attentive pupil. This is why Paul could write, 'You ... know all about my teaching' (3:10). Paul claimed to be a herald, an apostle and a teacher (1:11). What a teacher for anyone to have!

But Timothy not only learned from Paul; before that he had been taught by his mother and his grandmother. These two ladies are highly commended by Paul. In 1:5 Paul had written about the sincere faith which lived in Lois and Eunice. In Jewish homes the earliest teaching was always done by the mother, or the grandmother. She would have been responsible for all of the education of the children when they were small. After a while the instruction of a boy would have been taken over by the father and then, perhaps, the rabbi would have instructed him more fully.

How important it is, therefore, for us to train up our children in the ways of God! (Prov. 22:6). What they learn in infancy remains with them for the rest of their lives. To bring up children to know and love the Bible and its teaching is the greatest of blessings. The Bible is not usually taught in schools today as it used to be, and Sunday School teachers only have limited time available to them to teach the children. This means that every Christian family should set aside some period of time each day when the mother and father can sit down with their children and read the Bible and talk about its meaning.

Going onward with the Word of God

Paul reminds Timothy of what he already knew. He says, **'All Scripture is God-breathed.'** Until the last century most people who called themselves Christians also knew that the Bible owes it origin and its contents to the breath of God. Few people had any doubts that the human authors of the Scriptures were powerfully guided and directed by the Holy Spirit. But it is a matter of serious concern that, today, many who are preaching Sunday by Sunday deny that the Bible is God-breathed even though they claim to have a reverence for it. For them the Word of God is only inspired in the way that Shakespeare was inspired when he wrote his poems and plays, or Beethoven was inspired when he wrote uplifting music. They will not accept what Bishop Handley Moule wrote, 'The breath of God was in each "scripture," as man's breath is in his words, making them to be the vehicle of his thoughts.'[2]

Because it is the very Word of God, the Bible is of great *usefulness* to God's people. It is vital that the Word of God should form the basis of all of our teaching. Every doctrine which we hold must come directly from the Bible. Everything that we know about God the Father, God the Son and God the Holy Spirit comes straight out of the pages of this sacred book.

The Bible details sins which must be condemned. It is when we prayerfully read God's Word that we are convicted of our wrong actions, and the thoughts and attitudes which are dishonouring to the Lord. God makes it absolutely plain what is contrary to his will. This is why the Ten Commandments are so important and why they are put in the negative: 'You shall not...' The Bible *rebukes* us for our misbehaviour, and it also helps us to counteract wrong teaching when we hear it.

But we are not just left standing there, feeling condemned because of our wrong-doing; the Scriptures give us *correction*. Those who have wandered and strayed from God's paths are guided back by the Word of God. So many people are far off from God, and when the gospel message is faithfully preached then they hear the word of rebuke (they are convicted of their sins and brought to repentance); but they are not left there as condemned sinners, trembling because a Christless eternity awaits them. The Scriptures move them onwards. Repentant sinners are given a word of correction. And God's Word leads them back to himself. He says, 'Come to me, all you who are weary and burdened, and I will give you rest' (Matt. 11:28). Sinners respond by trusting in the death of the Lord Jesus Christ to wash them clean from their sins, so that when they are forgiven they are wonderfully saved, for ever.

Finally we are told that the Bible is **'useful for ... training in righteousness'**. Every Christian needs to be discipled. We should all be followers (and learners) of Christ. So the teacher must train his pupils in righteousness; they must be taught the need to live in righteous ways.

Every man (and woman) of God is required to go forward. We are commanded to be engaged in good works; and what better work is there than to teach others the ways of the Lord? It is a through knowledge of, and obedience to, the Scriptures, that enables any of us to lead others into the truth.

It is the Bible which thoroughly equips us for our work as God's people. In these days when so many are teaching false doctrines, we need to be using the Bible to bring benefit to others, we must be bold in declaring its truth and we ought to be demonstrating that the teaching of the Bible is affecting the way we live. In these days when many are living without any real aim or purpose, we need to show much faith, patience, love and endurance as we suffer pain and persecution for the sake of Christ. Each of God's people should be servants of God who are workmen (and women) who need not be ashamed because we are correctly handling, and teaching, the Word of God.

32.
Proclaim the Word!

Please read 2 Timothy 4:1-5

'You should come with me to listen to our minister preach. He has all of us in stitches throughout the sermon; he tells a joke practically every other sentence. It's really entertaining to go to our church.' Sometimes we hear people say things like that, but no one could describe the apostle Paul's ministry as entertaining. But is that the reason people go to church — to be made to feel comfortable and to be amused? No, or at least it should not be! We should go to church to meet with God and other believers so that we will encourage others in their Christian lives and be helped ourselves. We also go to hear God speaking to us, personally.

A solemn command

Paul gives Timothy a very serious charge, and he does so **'in the presence of God and of Christ Jesus'**. They are witnesses of what Paul is telling Timothy, and they gladly listen as Paul explains to the young pastor what God's will is. If we were to be given specific instructions while we were in the presence of Her Majesty the Queen and Her Majesty the Queen Mother, we would take very careful notice of what we were told to do. We would not easily forget it and, because it had their blessing, we would do everything in our power to see that we carried out the responsibilities which had been placed upon us.

The seriousness of the charge to Timothy was further reinforced by the fact that Christ Jesus is the one who will, in God's appointed time, **'judge the living and the dead'** (see Acts 10:42). Many people sneer at the thought of divine judgement. They say, 'I don't want to go to a church where you hear all that hell-fire and brimstone preaching.' But what does God say about judgement? 'He has set a day when he will judge the world with justice by the man he has appointed' (Acts 17:31). The Lord Jesus Christ is going to judge the world, and to do so justly. No one will be punished if he has done nothing wrong, but no one will escape from being punished if has committed evil, or omitted to do something which he ought to have done. On the judgement day everything will be done fairly, and no one allowed to be absent on that day. Elsewhere Paul says, 'We must all appear before the judgement seat of Christ, that each one may receive what is due to him for the things done while in the body, whether good or bad' (2 Cor. 5:10).

Then Paul tells us that Jesus, who gives witness to this charge, is going to appear and establish his kingdom. Everyone is going to be judged at the time when Christ will appear again. When Jesus came the first time, as a little baby at Bethlehem, only a few people were made aware of his arrival — Joseph and Mary, perhaps the innkeeper, certainly some shepherds and, later on, some wise men. However, when Christ comes in judgement it will be a very public event. John records:

> Look, he is coming with the clouds,
>   and every eye will see him,
> even those who pierced him;
>   and all peoples of the earth will mourn because of him.
>   So shall it be! Amen
>   (Rev. 1:7).

Not everyone will enter God's heavenly kingdom; only those **'who have longed for his appearing'** will be subjects of that realm (4:8). Only those who have had their sins washed away in the precious blood of Christ will be qualified to reign with him in his heavenly kingdom (see Rev. 1:5-6); and the charge which is given to all of God's people, especially those who have been called into the ministry of the Word, is simply this: **'Preach the Word'** (4:2).

By 'the Word' Paul means the good news of salvation in Christ. That is the meaning of the word 'gospel'. Earlier the apostle had written to the Corinthian believers, 'When I preach the gospel, I cannot boast, for I am compelled to preach. Woe to me if I do not preach the gospel! ... I am simply discharging the trust committed to me' (1 Cor. 9:16-17). The word which is translated 'preach' means in this verse, 'to herald' or 'to proclaim'. Warren Wiersbe tells us, 'In Paul's day, a ruler had a special herald who made announcements to the people. He was commissioned by the ruler to make his announcements in a loud, clear voice so everyone could hear. He was not an ambassador with the privilege of negotiating; he was a messenger with a proclamation to be heard and heeded.'[1] Those of us who are called to preach the gospel must make sure that we do just that. Naturally we will do everything in our power to urge people to take notice of God's words, but it must be the Word of God which we proclaim, not the words of men, or our own words.

Then Paul gave Timothy five imperatives; these must be obeyed. First of all, he must **'be prepared in season and out of season'** (4:2). This means that he must always be ready to preach the Word of God. He does not have to wait for the time of the formal gathering of God's people before he can expound the Bible. He has to be prepared to speak God's Word whatever the time and wherever the place — even on his day off — and he is compelled to preach whether he feels like it or not.

Secondly, his preaching is required to include an element of *correction*. No one has truly preached the gospel unless he has tried to make his hearers see their own sinfulness. Before people can become real Christians they must be brought to see themselves as God sees them — that is as poor, worthless sinners, whose behaviour and thought-life only deserve the punishment of hell. A man called Alcibiades used to say to Socrates, the ancient Greek philosopher, 'Socrates, I hate you, because every time I meet you, you make me see what I am.'[2]

This sums up the first task of a preacher: it is not to make people happy; it is to show them themselves as God sees them. People have to realize that the Bible is a mirror. As Sherwood Eliot Wirt said, 'I am not an authority on the Bible; the Bible is an authority on me.'[3] One of the main tasks of a preacher is to point out that 'All have sinned and [fallen] short of the glory of God' (Rom. 3:23). He is to emphasize that 'There is no one righteous, not even one' (Rom. 3:10). This means that even the best-living person is a sinner. Most people do not like to hear that kind of thing, but the preacher's task is to bring the members of his congregation to a point where they are deeply convicted of the awfulness of their sin, and to realize that their iniquity separates them from God.

Thirdly, his preaching must include *rebuking*. Not only does a sinner have to be convinced of his sin, he has to be admonished because of it. He has to be made thoroughly ashamed of his wrong deeds, his bad thoughts and his evil desires. But this is not why people come to church. They want to be made comfortable, not told that they are sinners. However, until a person comes face to face with himself and sees himself as he really is, he will never want to seek God's salvation.

Fourthly, the preacher must *encourage*. He must encourage all those who are under conviction of sin to repent of it (turn their backs upon it) and to turn to Christ, believing that when he died upon that cruel cross, he took upon himself their own personal punishment. The Bible is full of encouraging words like those in Isaiah 55:7:

> Let the wicked forsake his way
>> and the evil man his thoughts.
> Let him turn to the Lord, and he will have mercy on him,
>> and to our God, for he will freely pardon.

The preacher is going to aim to achieve this great work by preaching **'with great patience'**. He will not seek another ministry because the numbers of people listening to him have not dramatically increased in the first year of his pastorate. Not everyone will respond straight away. William Carey, the first modern British missionary, laboured for many years before he saw any of the Indian people becoming Christians, yet he continued faithfully in the work to which God had called him. No preacher should quickly become exasperated. We deal with people who are all different from each other, and we must be gentle and patient with them.

Also the faithful preacher of the Word must *carefully instruct* his congregation. Often the cause of people making a mess of something is because they have not been given clear and precise instructions. A good teacher is someone who tells his pupils what he wants them to do, one step at a time. He breaks down the task into small pieces which follow on from one another in a logical manner. Likewise the preacher of the gospel should give **'careful instruction'**, as Paul did to the elders at Ephesus. He said, 'I have not hesitated to proclaim to you the whole will of God' (Acts 20:27). In the synagogue at Ephesus he had spent three months 'arguing persuasively about the kingdom of God' (Acts 19:8). Following on from that he explained the Word of God in daily discussions in a hired hall. This was not done in a rush (although Paul was a very busy man); these meetings continued for about two years. Paul had already outlined to Timothy the need to be patient and give careful instructions in 2:24-25.

A reason for the command

Paul warns Timothy about a time which is coming **'when men will not put up with sound doctrine'**. This was the reason why Timothy had to be very diligent in his task of preaching the Word. If people are not grounded in the truth of God's Word, there is a danger that they will be deceived by the teachers of false doctrine. That is why we, today, must be careful what we teach children in our Sunday Schools and Bible Classes, as well as what we teach the young people and adults in the Sunday services and mid-week meetings. We must make every effort to make sure that we are teaching the pure Word of God — the Bible. We should check every reference when we quote from the Bible, lest we are misquoting and, therefore, in danger of building false doctrines. We must not speculate about matters which the Scriptures do not make clear, and we must stick to the 'old paths' (Jer. 6:16, AV) lest false teachers (or even good Christian men) lead us astray from the pure Word of truth.

For us the time has already arrived when people want something other than the Word of God. They have become dissatisfied with preaching; instead they want entertainment. John MacArthur says that one American church, 'to perk up attendance at Sunday evening services ... staged a wrestling match, featuring church employees'. They had special training in 'pulling hair, kicking shins and tossing bodies around without doing any real harm'. Dr MacArthur comments, 'No harm to the staff members, perhaps, but what is the effect of such an exhibition on the church's message? Is not the gospel itself clouded and badly caricatured by such tomfoolery?'[4] Later he comments, 'The church has no business marketing its ministry as an alternative to secular amusements (1 Thess. 2:2-6). That corrupts and cheapens the church's real mission... We are Christ's ambassadors (2 Cor. 5:20), knowing the terror of the Lord (2 Cor. 5:11), motivated by the love of Christ (2 Cor. 5:14), utterly made new by him (2 Cor. 5:17), we implore sinners to be reconciled to God (2 Cor. 5:20).'[5]

We live in an age when people say they need something which stimulates their desires. 'We are free', they say and, because of that, they do not want to be under the shackles of Christ (which is how they see being a Christian). They do not want to have what they believe are unnecessary restrictions placed upon them. We see evidence of this in the cry for unlimited Sunday trading and unrestricted violence and pornography on television, regardless of the effect this kind of thing has on those who watch it, and especially on the young and vulnerable in society.

It was the same in Paul's day. He spoke about those who wanted **'to suit their own desires'**. Today in many churches the standard demanded is that of the world. It does not seem to matter what God says in his Word; it is what is acceptable in society which appears to govern the thinking of some Christian people. Women have had a 'raw deal' in the community (that is undoubtedly true); does that mean that they should be ordained as ministers of the gospel, regardless of what God says in 1 Timothy 2:12? Likewise some teach that those of a homosexual tendency should be accorded a role in the church, as homosexuals, regardless of what Paul says in Romans 1. Let us resolve to make sure that our desires, our longings and our aspirations are ones which are commended in the Word of God, and not those demanded by the mores of society.

Paul used a picturesque figure of people who had **'itching ears'**. If your ear itches, then you will want to scratch it. He says that those whose ears itch for worldly pleasure will find that their itch can be eased by worldly amusements. The effect of this is that they will only flock to hear preachers who tell them what they want to hear. **'They will turn their ears away from the truth and turn aside to myths'** (4:4). The apostle means that these people will reject the Bible, because it makes them feel uncomfortable, and they will drink in the interesting stories of those whose only goal is to get a good payment for their story-telling (see 1 Tim. 1:4; Amos 8:11).

Timothy's response to the command

Paul then highlights what he wanted Timothy to do: **'But you, keep your head in all situations'** (4:5). Many of the believers at Ephesus were becoming drunk with the thrilling stories which were being told by the false teachers. Timothy must have been tempted to think, 'Why is it that a fairly small congregation is listening to my teaching, in comparison with the large numbers who are gathering around the false teachers?' But Paul said, 'Never mind, you just keep your head, whatever happens.' To remain calm in such a situation is a sign of maturity, as Rudyard Kipling wrote in his famous poem 'If':

> If you can keep your head when all about you
> Are losing theirs and blaming it on you...
> You'll be a man, my son![6]

'In contrast with those who are intoxicated by error, Timothy is required to retain that clarity of mind and sound judgement which will enable him to persevere in his God-given calling without faltering.'[7]

Paul ends this section by saying, **'Endure hardship, do the work of an evangelist, discharge all the duties of your**

ministry.' What a great deal to expect of any one person! Yet that is the task of a servant of God. He must endure hardship. He is to be a good solider (2:3), and he must do the work of an evangelist. One of his main responsibilities is to urge men, women and children to seek Christ, and to warn them of the dreadful consequences of rejecting God's offer of salvation. While this is true of every believer, for all are servants of God, it is especially demanded of those who are called to the gospel ministry.

Finally, Timothy is to **'discharge all of the duties of [his] ministry'**. What a great many activities that includes, but the highest and most important is to preach the Word! A young preacher once complained to C. H. Spurgeon, the famous London preacher of the last century, that he did not have as big a church as he deserved. 'How many do you preach to?' Spurgeon asked. 'Oh, about 100,' the man replied. Solemnly Spurgeon said, 'That will be enough to give account for on the Day of Judgement.'[8]

33.
Dying well

Please read 2 Timothy 4:6-8

John Wesley had to endure many criticisms. He was frowned upon because he spoke God's message in the open air. He upset the religious authorities because he preached outside of his own parish, and he annoyed the well-to-do people because he insisted that heaven was only for those who knew the Lord Jesus Christ as their own personal Saviour.

Throughout his life he had to suffer a great deal and the 'societies' which he founded were often despised. Yet he took much comfort from the way in which God had blessed the work of preaching the gospel, and one of his gladdest boasts was: 'Our people die well.'[1] He meant by this that whenever any of the early Methodists died they left this life in peace and departed with serenity because they knew, for certain, that they were going into the immediate presence of their Lord.

Paul was writing to Timothy about his own impending death. It seems that he had been tried before an unjust judge, found guilty and sentenced to death. As he drew towards the end of this final letter, he thought about what was happening to him, and he looked back over the previous thirty years of his service for God and contemplated the glories of heaven that awaited him.

Paul's situation

He says, **'I am already being poured out like a drink offering'** (4:6). Timothy would have known about the drink offerings which are detailed in the Old Testament book of Numbers (see Num. 15). When an animal was sacrificed certain procedures had to be followed. It was a solemn time of worship and everything had, therefore, to be done according to the law. When the final act of the offering was about to take place a mixture of oil and wine was poured out at the base of the altar of sacrifice.

As Paul wrote these final words in his letter, he visualized what would happen at the moment of his death. Not only did he feel that he was like a drink offering which was about to be spilled out, he said that he was '*already* being poured out'. His life was at an end, even though he could not yet hear the sharp rap of the executioner's footsteps coming down the cold, hard stairs. To Paul it seemed as though his head was already resting on the block waiting for the axe to fall upon his neck.

However, he was not frightened; he was prepared to leave this life. He wrote to Timothy, not because he wanted Timothy to feel sorry for him, but to warn his young friend to be ready to shoulder greater responsibilities. The apostle had said, 'You, Timothy, keep your head, be prepared, work well for the Lord' (see 4:5), 'because I am shortly going to lose my head!' John Stott comments: 'As Joshua had followed Moses, and Solomon David, and Elisha Elijah, so now Timothy must follow Paul.'[2]

Then Paul used another figure: not only was his life being poured out like a drink offering, but the time had come for his departure. The apostle must often have thought about his death. After all, he had been in many dangerous places. He gave a great catalogue of them in 2 Corinthians 11:23-28. Years before, as he wrote to the Philippian church, he had felt ready to die: 'Even if I am being poured out like a drink offering on the sacrifice and service coming from your faith, I am glad and rejoice with all of you' (Phil. 2:17).

We, too, many pass through many difficulties. We may often undergo great temptations and testings. We may come very close to death, but we must remember that our final moments on this earth do not lie in the hands of men; they are firmly in the control of God. He is the one who has each of our futures in his hands.

The time had come for Paul to leave this life. He called it his **'departure'**. This is a word used in various ways in the Greek language, such as for taking down a tent, or loosing an animal from its tether, or making a sailing ship ready to leave port. This is exactly what was happening to Paul at the time he wrote these words. The anchors of his life were being weighed. The sails of his bark were being hoisted and he was all set to leave the port where he had resided for the past sixty years or so. However, for him that was not the end of everything. He was ready to set sail for a new, and infinitely better, shore — heaven itself. The question we have to ask ourselves as we study these words is: 'Am I ready, if the Lord should call me now, to leave this earthly life?' We do not know the exact time when we shall die (even if we have a terminal disease), but we should be ready, like Paul, to leave at a moment's notice.

Paul looks back on his past life

The apostle says, **'I have fought the good fight.'** He probably had in his mind the contests which took place at the Isthmian or Olympic games. The word which is translated 'fought' is the Greek word *'agon'*, from which we get our word 'agony'. Paul was telling Timothy that the work of a Christian preacher was like taking part in a wrestling match.

Paul did not say that he had won the good fight. He only declared that he had been a contestant in the fight against evil (that is why it is called the 'good' fight). Life is a constant battle. There are many who will oppose the work of the gospel, yet we must agonize over them. We must seek to win them for the Lord.

Secondly, the apostle says, **'I have finished the race.'** Again he was not boasting. He did not say, 'I have won.' He was only concerned to complete the course. Those who run in a race, and who have not the stamina or the determination to complete the course and drop out before the end, will receive no commendation; these will not be given the certificate which says that they have gone all the whole way around the track. Paul was not boasting about his own achievement. In the original language these clauses are phrased like this: 'The grand fight I have fought; the race I have finished.' It was the fight and the race which mattered, not Paul's achievements in them.

In Acts 20:24 Paul explained what he meant more fully. This incident took place some years before Paul wrote to Timothy. His ship had docked at Miletus, and from there he sent for the elders of the church at Ephesus inviting them to come to him. When they arrived he gave them this parting message: 'I consider my life worth nothing to me, if only I may finish the race and complete the task the Lord Jesus has given me — the task of testifying to the gospel of God's grace' (Acts 20:24). So by saying, 'I have finished the race,' he was informing Timothy that he had put his every effort into the work of proclaiming to all the gospel of salvation. He had boldly declared that the only hope for anyone is to put their trust in the Lord Jesus and come to the foot of his cross to confess their sin and unworthiness.

Thirdly Paul writes, **'I have kept the faith.'** He now drops every metaphor and states the facts with great clarity: 'I have kept the faith.' He has constantly been urging Timothy to preserve the true doctrine of Christ (see 1 Tim. 6:20). He himself had not swerved aside from the teaching of the apostles. He had been faithful to the trust placed upon him. He had preached the Word, the truth of the Bible, and he had done his best to make sure that the teaching about the Lord Jesus Christ had been passed on to others.

Having done all of that, he was now ready to meet his Maker. He had carried out the work given to him by the Lord. He had been faithful to the Christian message, and he had kept right on to the very end of the road.

He looked forward to the glories of heaven

Paul had suffered a great deal during his life, but now he could take his rest. Although we all need our times of sleep at night, the sabbath day's rest and an occasional period of holiday, we must be aware that we are never off duty as Christians. It is only when we hear the final summons to leave this life that we can fully enter into our rest.

But Paul did not talk about rest as he wrote these words. He spoke of receiving a reward; this is a **'crown of righteousness'**. This has been stored away for Paul (as though it had Paul's name on it!). It had been kept in a safe place so that no enemy could deprive him of it. It was the same 'victor's crown' which he had written of in chapter 2:5. This reward was *a crown* of righteousness. It was not a wreath of laurel leaves (such as an Olympic winner received). The rewards of man's achievements eventually wither and die (even if they are made of gold) but God's reward lasts for ever. Peter tells us that it is 'an inheritance that can never perish, spoil or fade — kept in heaven for you' (1 Peter 1:4).

It is also a crown of *righteousness*. It is righteous because *it is the free gift of God*. Paul said earlier in this epistle that God has saved us 'not because of anything that we have done but because of his own purpose and grace' (1:9). We do not go to heaven because of our own good works; we gain eternal life through Christ's death on the cross.

Secondly, this crown is righteous because *Christ has earned it for us.* Paul had written to Titus, 'He saved us, not because of righteous things we had done, but because of his mercy. He saved us through the washing of rebirth and renewal by the Holy Spirit, whom he poured out on us generously through Jesus Christ our Saviour' (Titus 3:5-6).

This crown belongs to all those who are true believers in the Lord Jesus Christ. Paul said that **'The Lord, the righteous Judge, will award [it] to me.'** Occasionally in the Greek games there were umpires who judged unfairly. They had perhaps been bribed to declare a particular person the winner. However, no such judgement will be made in connection with us when we die. The reason is that it is the Lord Jesus Christ who will give the crown of righteousness. He will give it to those who have been faithful to him and his Word. In chapter 4:1 we saw that he does all things fairly; he is the righteous Judge.

This crown will be given on **'that day'**. 'That day' is the day of the Lord's return; the day of his appearing. On that day he will come to judge the living and the dead. However, unlike the winner of an Olympic race, Paul will not be the only recipient of this crown. It will be given to **'all who have longed for his appearing'**, or 'who love his appearing'.

We have to face the fact that our end will come one day. Are we looking forward to that day? This is one of the marks of those who truly love the Lord. They are longing for him to come again. The believer does not fear that time. He loves to look forward to it because 'Perfect love drives out fear' (1 John 4:18).

34.
Lonely but not alone

Please read 2 Timothy 4:9-22

None of us knows for certain how our days on earth will end. People die in all kinds of ways and in various circumstances. I suppose we all like to think that our own end will be calm and peaceful, and that we shall just drift out of this life and into eternity while we are asleep in our own beds.

Paul was fairly sure how his life would end. He expected that he would shortly be taken out of his prison, led to a place outside of the city, told to kneel down and then would have his head cut off. However, he was ready for that last great event. He was prepared to stand before his Maker and give an account of his life. He was contented because he knew that after his death he would face one who would judge him fairly and righteously.

He was alone — almost

Because of Paul's imminent death, he longed to have his dear young friend Timothy come to join him. He writes with great urgency, **'Do your best to come to me quickly.'** He wanted Timothy to break down every barrier which might delay his departure from Ephesus.

It is the same with us. When we hear that someone we love is lying seriously ill in hospital we drop everything and go to him or her as quickly as we can. We cancel every engagement, however important it may be, and we rush to the side of our loved one.

Paul had started this letter by saying that he longed to see Timothy (1:4), yet that was not the main reason he wrote it. We have seen, over and over again, that his chief concern was that Timothy (and many others) would preserve the gospel intact and spread it far and wide. But Paul was human too. He only had a little while to live and the presence of his young friend would fill him with joy during the closing period of his life (1:4). We do not know whether Timothy made it in time; that has not been recorded for us.

Paul's call had a great poignancy about it because practically everyone else had left him. The saddest departure of all was that of Demas. He had started well in the Christian life. In Colossians 4:14 we see that Demas was with Paul and sent his greetings to the believers at Colosse. In the letter to Philemon (verse 24) he is described as a 'fellow-worker' with the apostle. However, now Paul says of him, **'Demas ... has deserted me and has gone to Thessalonica'** (4:10). We do not know why he went to Thessalonica. Perhaps it was his home town, or maybe he had friends there.

We do not know why Demas left Paul; the apostle's only comment was that **'Demas ... loved this world.'** The world of suffering for the sake of Christ was obviously too much for him. He preferred the world of ease and pleasure. John tells us about the dangers of loving the world: 'Do not love the world or anything in the world. If anyone loves the world, the love of the Father is not in him. For everything in the world — the cravings of sinful man, the lust of his eyes and the boasting of what he has and does — comes not from the Father but from the world' (1 John 2:15-16).[1]

To apply this in today's terms, R.C. Lucas described an imaginary scenario in which Demas had been offered an

excellent job on a religious television programme in Thessalonica. He was very successful at this because he followed the
producer's instructions. He had been told that it was important
to keep up the ratings, so he was to say nothing which would
upset any viewer. Demas had to be grateful that so many
people tuned into the programme each week. So that his
popularity would not falter he had to be careful that he did not
speak against the Jewish religion (many Jews were devotees
of the programme) nor refer to those 'awful letters' which Paul
had sent to the church at Thessalonica. As a result of his
success Demas's wife was able to afford a brand-new kitchen;
and he enjoyed many of the good things of this life which had
been beyond his reach while he stayed with Paul.[2]

The question for believers to ask themselves today is: 'Do
I find it more pleasant to be with my non-Christian friends, or
to be among the people of God?' If we say, 'Christians are
boring people,' then we shall want to spend more time at the
pub, club, or disco. If we have that kind of craving for
amusement, then we are in danger of leaving the people of
God, because we love this world too much. We shall certainly
not be like those whom Paul wrote about in 4:8; we shall not
be longing for Christ on the great day of his appearing, nor
shall we be those who love his appearing. Instead we shall be
among those love the world and everything that goes with
earthly excitement.

Next we read that **'Crescens has gone to Galatia'** (or
maybe Gaul — i.e. France). We know nothing else about this
brother, but it seems that he had left Rome on the Lord's
business. There is certainly no note of censure here. He was
known to Timothy and known also to the Lord. These are the
things which matter above all things.

'Titus' had gone **'to Dalmatia'**. It seems that his work at
Crete had come to an end, and now the Lord had other tasks for
him to perform. This shows us that God's workers should

never retire from gospel work. Dalmatia is in part of what was formerly called Yugoslavia and, as I write, there is great turmoil in that land and a great need for the true message of Christ to be propounded there.

Finally, Paul had specifically **'sent Tychicus to Ephesus'** (4:12). Tychicus came from the Roman province of Asia, where Ephesus was situated (Acts 20:4), and several times we read of him acting as Paul's messenger to the churches (see Eph. 6:21; Col. 4:7-9). How committed to the gospel message he must have been, for Paul to entrust such a task to him! Earlier Paul had spoken of sending Tychicus to Crete to relieve Titus, so that the latter could go to see Paul (Titus 3:12). Now it seems that he has been sent by Paul to Ephesus to take over responsibility for the church there so that Timothy can travel to see the apostle.

However, Paul did have some human company: Luke was there. He writes, **'Only Luke is with me'** (4:11). Luke, the beloved physician, had spent a great deal of his time with the apostle, and we can be sure that much of the information for Luke's account of the Gospel and the Acts of the Apostles came from Paul.

Paul not only longed to have Timothy come and join him, he also asked Timothy to **'Get Mark and bring him with you'** (4:11). Many years earlier Paul had 'fallen out' with Mark while on his first missionary journey. The reason appears to have been because Mark could not stand the pace (Acts 13:5,13; 15:37-38). But by the time of Paul's first Roman imprisonment 'Mark is back in the apostle's circle of close associates' (see Col. 4:10).[3] Paul says of him, **'He is helpful to me in my ministry.'** Although had had once been a failure in Christian service, Mark was called back into the work of the Lord. There are many of us who have experienced this same grace of God. He calls failures back into his service, when they truly repent and are determined to suffer hardship for the sake of gospel. What higher calling can any Christian have than to be useful in the work of the gospel?

Paul desired some material comforts also (4:13). He was not so super-spiritual that he neglected his physical needs. He was not one of those saints who are 'so heavenly-minded that they are no earthly use'. Paul wanted the cloak he had left at Troas in the care of Carpus. We know nothing else about this man Carpus, any more than we know much about many gracious Christian men and women. However, we do know that the Lord has very many humble servants who are faithful in their service — even if it is only looking after some of the personal possessions of a preacher!

We do not know why Paul left his cloak at Troas. Perhaps he had to depart from there in a hurry. Certainly it would have been far too hot for him to wear it in the summertime. This cloak was probably a heavy piece of cloth with no arms, just a circular hole for his head to go through. It would have been designed to hang down and keep out a great deal of the cold. In his dark, damp prison cell Paul could have done with the comfort such a garment could provide.

Paul also wanted his books. These are described as **'scrolls'**. They would have been made of papyrus — the ordinary writing-paper of the day. But not only did Paul want his books, he **'especially'** desired **'the parchments'**. These were much more expensive and durable because they were made from stretched animal skins. We do not know what these books contained but we do know that Paul wanted to study. Even though his life was nearly at an end, he still wanted his mind to be kept alert. How sad it is that so many of the Lord's people today do not make time for the reading and studying of good, wholesome literature!

It may well be that these books were copies of the Old Testament which had been translated into the Greek language (known as the Septuagint). Among them there may also have been some accounts of the life and work of the Lord Jesus Christ. I wonder if these books were ever sent to Paul, and if they were, who inherited them after the apostle's death? Was it from these documents that Luke received much of the information which he used when he was writing his two Bible books of his Gospel and the book of the Acts?

Paul was attacked

Paul continues, **'Alexander the metalworker did me a great deal of harm'** (4:14). He is not referring to physical harm. He was not so worried about his own welfare; he was concerned about the good name of Christ. Alexander had strongly opposed the message of the gospel (4:15).

We do not know where Alexander lived. There is no reason to suppose that he was the same person who is spoken about in 1 Timothy 1:20, but he was certainly so active in his opposition to the gospel that Timothy was likely to come across him somewhere in his travels. This is why Paul wanted him to be warned, and to be on his guard against this enemy of Christ. It is from the attacks of people like Alexander that Timothy is to guard the gospel (1 Tim. 6:20). However, Paul was not bitter. He left such matters in the hands of the Lord, knowing that he would repay (see Rom. 2:6; 12:19).

Today we should be as active in our concern to guard against those who desire to bring the message of Christ into disrepute. Some of the people who do this call themselves evangelical Christians; indeed they may truly be born-again believers, nevertheless, by their actions and teaching, they are bringing the gospel into disrepute. We should be careful in our dealings with any Christian worker whom we suspect of having wrong motives.

Paul was attacked because of the absence of friends at his preliminary trial; the devil would have taunted him over this.

He said, **'At my first defence, no one came to my support, but everyone deserted me'** (4:16). It was at this trial that the judge had made it plain that there was no doubt about Paul's guilt and, in due course, he would be executed.

It was the Roman practice for a defendant to be allowed to bring someone into court to speak on his behalf. However, no one was prepared to do that for the apostle; he stood alone. Everyone was either too scared, or they did not know enough about Paul to answer the charges against him. We have no idea why Luke was unable, or unwilling, to speak on Paul's behalf.

We should take care that we do not indulge in idle speculation in biblical writings, but we cannot help wondering who spoke for the prosecution? Could it have been Alexander the metalworker? Was it at that time that he had strongly opposed Paul? Did he say that the apostle was the chief leader in Rome of this group who denied the deity of Cæsar, and were cannibals (because they were known to eat their own God in secret ceremonies before dawn)?[4] We do not know the answers to these questions, or exactly what the charges were which had been brought against Paul. We only know that he was found guilty and he was likely to be beheaded very soon.

Again Paul did not condemn his friends for turning their backs upon him in his hour of great need. When he remembered how he had treated Christ and his people before he had become a Christian, he gladly suffered for his Lord, as Jesus had suffered at the hands of men. Several times in this short letter he had written to Timothy about the need to suffer for Christ. He had urged him to 'Join with me in suffering' (in 1:8) and elsewhere to 'Endure hardship with us' (2:3). On both of these occasions Paul used a single Greek verb. Paul is so gracious that he comments, **'May it not be held against them.'** Although, quite naturally he felt let down, he showed a great understanding of the pressures that ordinary Christian believers were burdened with at that time. He probably remembered the words of the Lord: 'Love your enemies and pray for those who persecute you' (Matt. 5:44). Certainly he was present when Stephen was stoned to death, and he no doubt heard the martyr's final prayer: 'Lord, do not hold this sin against them' (Acts 7:60).

Paul was strengthened

As he was standing in the dock, proclaiming his innocence, he tells us that **'The Lord stood at my side.'** None of his human friends came to support him, but the Lord was with him. Years earlier Paul had been arrested in Jerusalem and suddenly at night the Lord 'stood near him and said, "Take courage! As you have testified about me in Jerusalem, so you must testify in Rome"' (Acts 23:11). The same Lord says to each one of us in our circumstances, 'Never will I leave you; never will I forsake you' (Heb. 13:5). If we, like Paul, put our trust in Christ, we shall also have the same assurance of the Lord's presence in all our difficulties, and in our joys.

Not only was the Lord with Paul, the Lord strengthened him. He enabled him to witness a good confession before his accusers. Paul tells Timothy that, there in court, the Lord strengthened him so that through him **'the message might be fully proclaimed and all the Gentiles might hear it'**. So it would appear that Paul preached the gospel right there in court, while he was charged with a crime worthy of the death penalty. We do not know who the judge was, but it could have been the Emperor Nero himself who sat in judgement against this leader of the Christian people in Rome.

Although the outcome was that the prisoner was found guilty, Paul goes on, **'And I was delivered from the lion's mouth.'** When he spoke of 'the lion' was he referring to Nero or, as Peter did in 1 Peter 5:8, to the devil? Whatever he meant, the outcome was that he knew that he had been delivered from all of his enemies by the Lord (see Ps. 22:20-21). No Roman citizen could be thrown to the lions in the arena, so Paul obviously meant more than that. There was a sense in which he had been granted freedom, though not freedom from his bonds. He had been given freedom to speak the message of salvation before his accusers. He also knew that he had been delivered from the snares of his enemies because, whatever they did to his body, he was secure in the arms of his Lord.

He goes even further when he writes with great confidence, **'The Lord will rescue me from every evil attack and will bring me safely to his heavenly kingdom. To him be glory for ever and ever. Amen'** (4:18). That was an end to it. The Lord had won the battle, and the apostle would shortly be face to face with his Saviour. He would no longer be attacked by his foes or by temptation to sin. 'Amen' — so be it.

His parting blessing

The apostle ends his letter by sending his greetings to his many friends in other places. **'Priscilla and Aquila'** had spent much time with Paul. This husband and wife team are mentioned six times in the Scriptures, and on four of the six occasions Priscilla, the wife, is mentioned before her husband (Acts 18:18,26; Rom.16:3; 2 Tim. 4:19). Hiebert comments, 'Their friendship has lastingly endeared them to Paul and he thinks first of them.'[5]

Then he greets **'the household of Onesiphorus'**. These believers are mentioned in 1:16-18. We do not know who **'Erastus'** was, but he may have been the companion of Timothy who was sent to Macedonia in Acts 19:22. **'Troph- imus'** was a great helper in the work of gospel. He is men- tioned in Acts 20:4 and 21:29 but he had been **'left sick in Miletus'** by Paul. We see, then, that even the great apostle, who had been given the gift of healing on occasions, could not exercise it whenever he chose. It is sometimes God's will that a person should be left in his sickness. God is sovereign and he knows what is best for his saints. This fact highlights the folly of those who conduct vast campaigns where the advertisements proclaim, 'Come and see healing take place!' This is not only unscriptural, it is very damaging to the Christian faith. We cannot tell how many people are turned off from hearing the gospel because they have been shattered when their loved one was in fact not healed even though the 'evangelist' had put his hands upon him and declared him 'healed'.

Paul not only sends his greetings to those far away from him, he also remembers those who were nearby in Rome. The Scriptures tell us nothing else about **'Eubulus ... Pudens, Linus, Claudia and all the brothers'**. Nevertheless we know that the Lord has many unknown followers and each one is important to him. Paul names seventeen people in this portion of his letter. He held each one as precious, and when he prayed for them he was not vague, but named them all as he called God's blessings down upon them.

Finally, right at the very end of the letter, Paul slips in another little plea to Timothy: **'Do your best to get here before winter'** (4:21). During the winter storms no ships plied the Mediterranean (see Acts 27). This is why Paul wanted Timothy to leave before the final autumn ship departed from Ephesus. He was cold and lonely. It was nearly winter in his soul, and he desired the cheering presence of his dearest friend on earth.[6]

So he ends with a special message addressed to Timothy: **'The Lord be with your spirit'** (4:22). That was much more important than anything else. To everyone else who, in future years, would read this letter the apostle writes, **'Grace be with you.'** The 'you' here is plural, as in each of these Pastoral Epistles. This farewell greeting is the apostle's signature mark to show that it is authentic (see 2 Thess. 3:17). He wishes each of us the grace of the Lord Jesus Christ — his saving and keeping grace. Although the message is addressed specifically to Timothy, in his time, it is also for all of God's people in every age. It is especially addressed to this servant of God, Timothy, but its teaching applies to all servants of God (pastors/teachers first of all, then to all who name the name of Christ).

How vital is the message of this letter for God's people today! Each one of us should do everything within our power to preserve the gospel which has been entrusted to us. We should make sure that it is not undermined by those who wish to imply that it is not the inerrant Word of God; nor should we allow others to add to this Word by saying, 'Thus says the Lord, I am saying unto you...' as if the Bible were not sufficient for us today.

However, we do not preserve the gospel by hiding it away in a bank vault to make sure that it does not get tarnished. We should preserve it by passing it on to everyone we can, on every possible occasion — even if, like Paul, we have to suffer for doing so.

Notes

Introduction
1. William Hendriksen, *Commentary on I and II Thessalonians and I and II Timothy and Titus,* Banner of Truth Trust,1983, pp.4-44.
2. Geoffrey Wilson, *The Pastoral Epistles,* Banner of Truth Trust, pp.11-14.
3. Donald Guthrie, *The Pastoral Epistles,* Tyndale Press, pp.11-53.

Chapter 1 — Meet Paul and Timothy
1. William Barclay, *The Letters to Timothy, Titus and Philemon,* Saint Andrew Press, 1956, p.20.
2. As above, p.21.
3. Hendriksen, *Commentary on ... I and II Timothy and Titus,* p.54.
4. Ajith Fernando, *Leadership Lifestyle,* Tyndale House Publishers (USA), 1985, p.16.
5. Robert H. Mounce, *Pass it on, A Bible Commentary for Laymen on 1 and 2 Timothy,* Regal Books, California, USA,1979, p.10.
6. Quoted by Donald Guthrie, *The Pastoral Epistles,* The Tyndale Press, 1957, p.56.

Chapter 2 — The antidote to false teaching
1. Warren Wiersbe, *Be Faithful,* Scripture Press, p.18.

Chapter 3 — Obey the Ten Commandments
1. Hendriksen, *Commentary on ... I and II Timothy and Titus,* p.64.
2. Wilson, *The Pastoral Epistles,* pp.24-5.
3. Hendriksen, *Commentary on ... I and II Timothy and Titus,* p.69.
4. Wilson, *The Pastoral Epistles,* p.26.

5. Hendriksen, *Commentary on ... I and II Timothy and Titus,* p.70.
6. Wiersbe, *Be Faithful,* p.20.
7. As above, p.21.

Chapter 4 — Give a good testimony
1. From the hymn by J. McGranahan, No. 371 in the *Redemption Hymnal.*
2. From the hymn by John Newton, No. 50 in *Hymns of Faith.*
3. Wilson, *The Pastoral Epistles,* p.29.
4. See Hendriksen, *Commentary on ... I and II Timothy and Titus,* p.75.
5. As above.

Chapter 5 — Honour God
1. R. C. H. Lenski, quoted by Wilson, *The Pastoral Epistles,* p.31.
2. From hymn No.120 in Gadsby's hymnbook.
3. Michael Bentley, *Saving a Fallen World,* Evangelical Press, 1992, p.70.
4. Fernando, *Leadership Lifestyle,* p.34.
5. Hendriksen, *Commentary on ... I and II Timothy and Titus,* p.83.
6. Matthew Henry, *Commentary on the Whole Bible,* ed. Leslie Church, Marshall, Morgan & Scott, 1960, p.686.

Chapter 6 — Avoid shipwreck
1. Fernando, *Leadership Lifestyle,* p.43.
2. David Coleman in an unpublished essay.
3. Quoted by Wilson, *The Pastoral Epistles,* p.35.

Chapter 7 — Be prayerful
1. From 'Why, where and when should Christians meet?' in *Evangelicals Now* for February 1993.
2. Quoted in John Blanchard, *Gathered Gold,* Evangelical Press, p.288.
3. Mounce, *Pass it on,* p.26.
4. From the hymn, 'Come, my soul, thy suit prepare', No. 454 in *Hymns of Faith.*
5. Albert Barnes, *Notes on the epistles of Paul to the Thessalonians, to Timothy, to Titus and to Philemon,* William Tegg and Co., London, 1846, p.162.
6. Hendriksen, *Commentary on ... I and II Timothy and Titus,* p.95.

Chapter 8 — God's go-between
1. Wilson, *The Pastoral Epistles,* p.39.
2. As above.
3. See Hendriksen, *Commentary on ... I and II Timothy and Titus,* p.98.
4. As above.
5. Wiersbe, *Be Faithful,* p.34.

Chapter 9 — Men and women in church
1. Wiersbe, *Be Faithful,* p.35.
2. Barnes, *Notes,* p.168.
3. Wiersbe, *Be Faithful,* p.36.
4. Hendriksen, *Commentary on ... I and II Timothy and Titus,* p.105.
5. *NIV Study Bible,* p.1801.
6. See, for example, Michael Bentley, *Living for Christ in a Pagan World,* Evangelical Press, pp.111-13.

Chapter 10 — The role of women
1. John Calvin, *Sermons on Timothy and Titus,* Banner of Truth facsimile edition, 1983, p.231.
2. As above.
3. Wiersbe, *Be Faithful,* p.37.
4. Kent, *The Pastoral Epistles,* Moody Press, 1986, pp.107-8.
5. Calvin, *Sermons on Timothy and Titus,* p.224.

Chapter 11 — The role of elders
1. Barclay, *The Letters to Timothy...,* p.81.
2. Hendriksen, *Commentary on ... I and II Timothy and Titus,* pp. 121-2.
3. Barclay, *The Letters to Timothy...,* p.94.; See also Bentley, *Living for Christ in a Pagan World,* pp.147-8.
4. Wiersbe, *Be Faithful,* p.47.
5. As above.
6. Clifford Pond in a lecture at Borough Green Baptist Church in August 1963 on 1 Corinthians 13.
7. Wiersbe, *Be Faithful,* p.46.
8. Hendriksen, *Commentary on ... I and II Timothy and Titus,* p.127.

Chapter 12 — The role of deacons
1. Barclay, *The Letters to Timothy...,* p.98.

2. Charles R. Erdman, quoted by Wilson, *The Pastoral Epistles,* p.53.
3. See Hendriksen, *Commentary on ... I and II Timothy and Titus,* pp.133-4.
4. Kent, *The Pastoral Epistles,* p.137.
5. Barclay, *The Letters to Timothy...,* p.100.

Chapter 13 — Upholding the truth
1. Wiersbe, *Be Faithful,* p.53.
2. See Barclay, *The Letters to Timothy...,* p.102.
3. The Great Theatre at Ephesus is still standing and is a great tourist attraction. It may well be the only building still in existence which is mentioned in the Bible.
4. Hendriksen, *Commentary on ... I and II Timothy and Titus,* p.137.

Chapter 14 — Combating false teaching
1. Hendriksen, *Commentary on ... I and II Timothy and Titus,* p.149.
2. As above, p.150.
3. As above, p.151.

Chapter 15 — Silencing criticism
1. Fernando, *Leadership Lifestyle,* p.102.
2. Hendriksen, *Commentary on ... I and II Timothy and Titus,* p.158.
3. Kent, *The Pastoral Epistles,* p.157.
4. Said to me in a personal conversation during 1971 or 1972 by Rev. R. G. Martin, who was then pastor of Gurney Road Baptist Church in Stratford, London.
5. John Blanchard, *Whatever Happened to Hell?* Evangelical Press, 1993, p.218.
6. Calvin, *Sermons on Timothy and Titus,* pp.442-4.

Chapter 16 — Caring for the family
1. Fernando, *Leadership Lifestyle,* p.122.
2. Bentley, *Living for Christ in a Pagan World,* p.164.
3. Barclay, *The Letters to Timothy...,* p.121.
4. Hendriksen, *Commentary on ... I and II Timothy and Titus,* p.167.

Chapter 18 — The care of elders
1. From Acts 16:10-17 we can see that Luke travelled with Paul on some of his missionary journeys. Luke, the author of Acts, had been

speaking about Paul and his companions (16:6). Several times he says 'they' (e.g. in 16:7, 'they came ...'). Then in verse 10 he says, 'After Paul had seen the vision, we got ready...' Luke had evidently joined Paul and his companions at that point.
2. Wiersbe, *Be Faithful,* p.82.
3. See Hendriksen, *Commentary on ... I and II Timothy and Titus,* pp.184-5.

Chapter 19 — The responsibility of slaves
1. Hendriksen, *Commentary on ... I and II Timothy and Titus,* pp.191-2.
2. Barclay, *The Letters to Timothy...,* p.141.

Chapter 20 — The lure of money
1. This story was told in an address at the Evangelical Ministry Assembly at Westminster Central Hall, London, on 22 June 1993.
2. Kent, *The Pastoral Epistles,* p.186.
3. Hendriksen, *Commentary on ... I and II Timothy and Titus,* p.197.
4. As above, p.198.
5. Henry, *Commentary...,* p.690.

Chapter 21 — Holy living
1. Kent, *The Pastoral Epistles,* p.192.
2. See Hendriksen, *Commentary on ... I and II Timothy and Titus,* p.204.
3. See my comments in *Living for Christ in a Pagan World,* pp.240-42.
4. Wiersbe, *Be Faithful,* p.94.

Chapter 22 — True riches
1. Barclay, *The Letters to Timothy...,* p.159.
2. Wiersbe, *Be Faithful,* p.95.
3. Kent, *The Pastoral Epistles,* p.202.
4. Hendriksen, *Commentary on ... I and II Timothy and Titus,* p.213.

Chapter 23 — An old man remembers
1. John Stott, *The Message of 2 Timothy,* IVP, 1973, p.17.
2. Guy H. King, *To my Son,* Marshall, Morgan & Scott, 1944, p.7.
3. R. C. Lucas elaborates on this in a lecture on the second letter to Timothy at the Evangelical Ministry Assembly held at Westminster

Central Hall, London, on 29 June 1995 (Proclamation Trust Tape EMA95/103).
4. D. Edmond Hiebert, *Second Timothy,* Moody Press, Chicago, 1958, p.36.

Chapter 24 — Suffering for the gospel
1. See John F. MacArthur, Jr, *Faith Works,* Word Publishing, 1993, pp.196-9.
2. Hendriksen, *Commentary on ... I and II Timothy and Titus,* p.234.

Chapter 25 — Loyalty to the gospel
1. Kent, *The Pastoral Epistles,* p.255.
2. As above, pp.33-6.

Chapter 26 — Perseverance in the gospel
1. H. C. G. Moule, *The Second Epistle to Timothy,* The Religious Tract Society, London, 1906, p.76.
2. Quoted in Stott, *The Message of 2 Timothy,* p.53.
3. Hendriksen, *Commentary on ... I and II Timothy and Titus,* p.249.
4. Moule, *Second Epistle to Timothy,* pp.77-8.

Chapter 27 — The path to glory
1. Stott, *The Message of 2 Timothy,* p.65.
2. From the hymn, 'There is a Green Hill far away' by Mrs C. F. Alexander.
3. Hendriksen, *Commentary on ... I and II Timothy and Titus,* pp.255-6.
4. See, for example, Bentley, *Saving a Fallen World,* p.297.

Chapter 28 — The work of a minister of the gospel
1. Wiersbe, *Be Faithful,* p.151.
2. As above, p.149.
3. Told by R. C. Lucas in a series of lectures on 2 Timothy delivered at the Sydney Missionary and Bible College, Australia, in May 1995, available from the Proclamation Trust Tape Ministry.
4. Wilson, *The Pastoral Epistles,* p.144.
5. See Hendriksen, *Commentary on ... I and II Timothy and Titus,* pp.263-4.

Chapter 29 — The character of a minister
1. Hendriksen, *Commentary on ... I and II Timothy and Titus,* p.274.
2. Barnes, *Notes,* p.284.
3. Hendriksen, *Commentary on ... I and II Timothy and Titus,* p.274.
4. Kent, *The Pastoral Epistles,* p.270.

Chapter 30 — Beware of counterfeits
1. Stott, *The Message of 2 Timothy,* p.83.
2. Barclay, *The Letters to Timothy...,* p.220.
3. E.g. David Coresh, who deceived a large group of people, claiming that he was the Son of God. Their headquarters at Waco in Texas was beseiged by the USA Drug Enforcement Agency and stormed by American forces. Almost all of the members of the sect died in the ensuing fire.
4. Mounce, *Pass it on,* p.139.

Chapter 31 — Pressing onward
1. From 'Choruses from "The Rock"' in *The Complete Poems and Plays of T. S. Eliot,* Faber and Faber, 1969, p.161.
2. Moule, *Second Epistle to Timothy,* p.123.

Chapter 32 — Proclaim the Word!
1. Wiersbe, *Be Faithful,* p.170.
2. Barclay, *The Letters to Timothy...,* p.235.
3. Quoted in *Impact* for December 1993 and January 1994, the magazine of the Fishers' Fellowship.
4. John F. MacArthur, Jr, *Ashamed of the gospel — When the Church becomes like the World,* Crossway Books, 1993, p.69.
5. As above, p.71.
6. Found in numerous collections of poems including, *A choice of Kipling's verse made by T. S. Eliot,* Faber and Faber, 1941, p.273.
7. Wilson, *The Pastoral Epistles,* p.162.
8. Wiersbe, *Be Faithful,* p.172.

Chapter 33 — Dying well
1. Quoted by John Blanchard, *More Gathered Gold,* Evangelical Press, p.73.
2. Stott, *The Message of 2 Timothy,* p.113.

Chapter 34 — Lonely but not alone

1. Worldliness in the late 1990s is not so much refraining from attending dances or going to the cinema; it is much more subtle than that, as David Wells pointed out in his lecture, 'The Worldliness of Modernity', at the Evangelical Ministry Assembly at the Westminster Central Hall, London, in June 1995. Audio tapes available from the Proclamation Trust.

2. This illustration was given in lectures at the Sydney Bible and Missionary Conference in May 1995; audio tapes are available from the Proclamation Trust.

3. Mounce, *Pass it on,* p.155.

4. This refers to their twisting of the true meaning of the communion service where the believers obeyed the words of the Lord when he said, 'This is my body... This is my blood... Eat and drink of it.' See also Stott, *The Message of 2 Timothy,* p.123.

5. Hiebert, *Second Timothy,* p.123.

6. There is a delightful meditation on this theme in Charles R. Swindoll, *Come before winter and ... share my hope,* Scripture Press, 1988.